Managing and Motivating Contact Center Employees

Managing and Motivating Contact Center Employees

Tools and Techniques for Inspiring Outstanding Performance from Your Frontline Staff

Malcolm Carlaw • Peggy Carlaw •
Vasudha K. Deming • Kurt Friedmann

McGraw-Hill

New York   Chicago   San Francisco   Lisbon   London
Madrid   Mexico City   Milan   New Delhi   San Juan
Seoul   Singapore   Sydney   Toronto

The **McGraw-Hill** Companies

3 4 5 6 7 8 9   BKM BKM   0 9 8 7 6 5

ISBN 0-07-138888-5

Library of Congress Cataloging-in-Publication Data

Managing and motivating contact center employees : tools and techniques
for inspiring outstanding performance from your frontline staff / by
Peggy Carlaw . . . [et al.].
    p. cm.
Includes index.
    ISBN 0-07-138888-5 (Hardcover : alk. paper)
  1. Call centers—Personnel management. 2. Customer services—Management.
3. Employee motivation. I. Carlaw, Peggy.
    HE8788 .M35 2002
    658.8'12—dc21
                                                          2002152473

To our clients and customers, who have shown us time and again just how much of a difference good management can make.

Contents

Acknowledgments

We would like to acknowledge and thank the inexhaustible Josh Davis for his excellent research assistance and his many helpful ideas. We'd also like to thank our editor, Richard Narramore, for inspiring this book and for believing, as we do, in the power of positive management.

Introduction

It's estimated that in the United States alone there are some 75,000 contact centers staffed with more than 3 million agents handling more than 11 billion contacts (via phone or e-mail) a year. Managing and motivating these 3 million agents (many of them low-paid) is a tremendous challenge. As a contact center manager or supervisor, you have a profound, far-reaching influence. The work that your agents do, and the work that you do to manage and support them, makes a difference in the lives of hundreds or even thousands of people day in and day out. So, how do you ensure that the quality of those contacts will be satisfactory, or, better yet, outstanding? This book was written to give you detailed advice for coaching your contact center agents to deliver outstanding service. Stay tuned!

HOW THIS BOOK WILL HELP YOU

Managing and Motivating Contact Center Employees is for managers and frontline supervisors. Its purpose is to address the "people side" of contact center management and to give you a wealth of information, tools, and techniques for leading your frontline staff to extraordinary performance.

The first section of the book looks at ways you can boost motivation and performance by paying close attention to the atmosphere in which your agents work. The second section takes you through five key functions of the management role. The third and final section is devoted to helping you embody the skills and practices that characterize truly successful managers.

The book is a combination of theory and practice. In each chapter you'll find sound advice for managing and motivating your staff, and you'll also be given tools that you can use immediately in your day-to-day managerial functions. Our objective in putting together this book was to give contact center managers not just knowledge that could eventually be turned into expertise, but rather an abundance of information and resources that directly deliver that expertise. Following are just a few examples of these tools:

- An employee satisfaction survey
- A sample contact center job analysis for use in hiring
- Ten effective stress-relief activities
- Three skill models for giving feedback to agents
- Sample monitoring forms
- Six reproducible forms for use in training
- Ten team-building activities
- Twelve ideas for rewards and contests

In the appendix you'll find additional reproducible forms that you can turn into job aids. We suggest you read the book cover to cover the first time and then use it as necessary in your day-to-day duties as a manager.

WE KNOW IT'S NOT EASY

After more than 20 years of working with a diverse variety of contact centers and watching the industry evolve, we feel confident in saying that yours is not an easy job. In those 20 years, the labor pool has changed considerably, the technology has been radically transformed, a different work ethic has emerged, and the demands on managers have increased exponentially.

Frontline managers in today's contact centers are up against some considerable challenges. No doubt some, if not all, of the following will be familiar to you:

- Slim profits
- Not enough time to do everything the way it should be done
- Stiff competition for qualified employees
- Too little money to accomplish objectives
- Difficult or unmotivated agents
- Little understanding and support from upper management

The good news is that there *are* contact centers that are excelling at management and prospering in the marketplace. And yours can be one of them. Success in this field is largely about a manager's ability to communicate with agents, to meet their needs, and to inspire them to perform at their best. This book is designed to help you do just that.

A TALE OF TWO CONTACT CENTERS

Without meaning to, we recently stumbled onto an interesting case study in the making—a sort of "twins study" for the contact center industry. For us, and for the hundreds of agents arbitrarily designated to the two contact centers involved, the situation drove home the point that all other things being equal, a manager is often the make-or-break factor in the success of a team or a project.

Here's what happened: approximately 150 agents were hired for a four-month outbound customer service program. The project took place in two locations. Agents from the two centers were identically trained, as were their supervisors. The two managers (one for each location) and all supervisors were given the same tools, resources, and objectives. Call flow into each of the two centers was roughly equal, and the same base of customers was calling the two centers.

As soon as the project got under way, however, one center flourished and the other flailed. As the weeks went on, the pattern continued. Center A was able to handle all calls, maintain high customer satisfaction scores, and meet the other objectives of the program. What's more, the agents and supervisors seemed to genuinely enjoy what they were doing. Center B, on the other hand, had lower service levels and lower customer satisfaction scores. The agents and supervisors continually butted heads and the agents seemed to resent the "intrusion" of customers into their reading or socializing time.

What made the difference? We believe it was the approach taken by the two managers. All other conditions were more or less identical, but when it came to leading the project, two very different styles emerged.

At Contact Center A:

- The manager attended parts of the agent training and the supervisor training.
- Once the project was under way, the manager called regular meetings with the supervisors to calibrate the results of their call monitoring and to share information between supervisors.
- The manager used the appropriate feedback models (the same ones the supervisors learned during the training) to coach supervisors and agents.
- Supervisors listened to calls on every agent every day and gave feedback immediately after calls.
- The manager stayed involved and rallied the team toward success.

At Center B:

- The manager did not attend any of the agent training or the supervisor training.
- Once the project was under way, there were no call calibration meetings between the supervisors. The only meetings they had were emergency meetings to discuss how to deal with the numerous problems that were emerging on the project.
- The manager occasionally yelled at agents and very rarely praised them. The manager did not use appropriate feedback models.
- About half of the supervisors spent more time hanging out with one another than they did working with their teams.
- When they did monitor calls, many of the supervisors stayed at their own workstations and did not give feedback to agents.
- The manager stayed in the office and, it seemed, counted the days until the project would end.

Good management—or the lack thereof—makes all the difference.

IN THEIR OWN WORDS

One mistake common among contact center managers is that they assume they know what's important to their employees, what they like and dislike, what they need and don't need, and so on. In some cases this may be true, but we have found that managers are often wrong about what their agents want and how to motivate them. Throughout this book, one of the things we'll continually encourage you to do is to communicate with your agents and to get their input about what helps them enjoy their job and stay motivated. Management is as much about learning as it is about teaching. And the best way to learn what works for your agents (and what doesn't) is to ask them!

Following are some comments from contact center agents who were asked to say a few words about managers—past or present—who made a positive and lasting impression on them. You might be surprised to learn just what skills and characteristics inspired these agents to do their best work.

Agent 1

*The individual who demonstrated to me what an effective manager should be was an individual who **set clear expectations for me**. Her strong communication skills and attention to detail allowed for her to communicate these expectations as well as provide me with valuable feedback. She **understood the value of empowering me and respected my opinions**. This made me feel like a valued member of the team and encouraged me to take ownership of my own successes (as well as areas of opportunity) and always "think outside the box" to come up with creative solutions.—Debbie W.*

Agent 2

*The manager I respect the most is a woman who **leads by example**. She never gave me the answer to any challenge I was faced with. Instead, she helped me to find a solution. I admired her professionalism. She **never micromanaged**. She told me that she trusted me to make decisions, and even though she knew the answers to questions other people would ask, she referred them to me by saying, "This is Natalie's responsibility; she's your best resource." This only encouraged me to increase my own knowledge. I am now in management and I find myself leading with the same direction she provided me so that the employees I work with every day can experience the same satisfaction of knowing they are trusted.—Natalie C.*

Agent 3

*My most recent manager taught me all of the necessary skills to complete my job accurately by **staying late if needed to get the job done, putting her work down to help out if the need was there and even making sure our side was heard at each and every managers' meeting**. My manager was also a very caring and understanding individual who would always go the extra mile to make sure you understood any task at hand. She always had something nice to say about everybody, even if it was followed by a suggestion for improvement.—Tracy F.*

Agent 4

*She **shared her knowledge freely** knowing that that would make the company a better place. She also allowed us to make our own decisions. If we made a mistake, she talked to us about how to correct it in the future but she never ridiculed us for it. And **she listened**. I mean really listened. To ideas, gripes, thoughts, whatever. That makes a difference.—Ruth B.*

Agent 5
*My manager **believed in my talents** and gave me the freedom to use my own best judgment. She **showed me the power of eye contact and smiles** when speaking to coworkers and customers.—Maria V.*

Agent 6
*My manager **shows confidence in my abilities**. I am empowered to take charge of the call and drive for a resolution to all customer issues. He **created a sense of "team"** and the team motivated me to grow and to serve our customers more effectively. My manager is my mentor; I see in him what I want and need to become.—Nathan B.*

Agent 7
*She was the type of manager who would **jump right in to help** fix a problem and would stay until the job was done. I always felt like a valued member of the team by her based on **the way she presented her feedback**. She was the type of manager who **celebrated** your success with you and wanted to see her employees grow within the company.— Christine P.*

Agent 8
*The manager that had the most positive and lasting impression on me was a manager that **valued lifelong learning** and created an atmosphere to use critical thinking skills. The manager **created an open and honest team environment** and I was encouraged to try new and innovative approaches to resolve customer problems and to introduce new systems. I did not fear that I would be penalized for trying something new, even if the idea did not work as I thought.—Wanet T.*

WHY WE WROTE THIS BOOK

As you can see from these testimonials, and as you no doubt have experienced for yourself, a good manager influences productivity and lifts the morale of the workforce. Good managers help employees to develop into wiser, more productive, more mature human beings both at work and outside it.

Being a good manager takes work and discipline. It takes knowledge, determination, persistence and the occasional sacrifice. And it takes the courage to realize your own flaws and weaknesses and to work on them—the same courage you require of your agents in order for them to get better at the work they do.

There's really no way to get around the fact that if you want successful and lasting results, you may have to change the way you do your job. For some managers and some departments this means a little minor tweaking here and there; for others it means a revolution.

But take heart: you don't have to start from scratch to become a great manager or supervisor. You just have to start where you are and make small, incremental changes. That's how all great ends are achieved. The satisfaction you'll get from seeing how your center and your agents thrive under good and caring management will inspire you to keep at it.

"Do not avoid
But transform
The things that need
Transformation."
—Sri Chinmoy

Managing and Motivating Contact Center Employees

1 HOW TO MOTIVATE CONTACT CENTER AGENTS

Five Ways to Boost Morale and Performance

CHAPTER I

Managing the Mood in Your Contact Center

How to Lift Morale

THE DIFFERENCE BETWEEN MORALE AND MOTIVATION

In contact centers where morale is high, employees approach their work with energy, enthusiasm, and willingness. They *want* to come to work, or at least are enthusiastic about work once they get there. On the other hand, when morale is low in a contact center, employees can become bored, discouraged, and lethargic.

Motivation, on the other hand, refers to employees' drive to get the job done. Highly motivated employees tend to be high producers, but that doesn't necessarily mean their morale is high. In fact, contact center employees are often motivated by "negative incentives" such as a fear of losing their job, an excessive need for rewards, or an overly competitive need to outperform a colleague. Although these tendencies often result in an employee getting a lot of work done—and can even result in highly creative or innovative output—they diminish the overall health and morale of the team or the organization.

Two Good Ideas

One client has created a chief morale officer who monitors the pulse of the reps on the contact floor. When morale gets low, the morale officer distributes balloons or motivational stories or highlights a rep's inspirational behavior. As a consequence the contact center enjoys low turnover and a productive working environment. Another company regularly surveys its employees to get their opinions on the current "temperature" of the team and solicits ways to help increase morale.

Although morale and motivation are different things, they tend to work together in a continuous cycle. When morale is high, it's common to see that a high percentage of the employees are naturally more motivated to work hard. When morale gets low—and employees become less self-motivated—managers often resort to unpleasant, heavy-handed motivational tactics (such as nagging, threatening, making more rules, micromanaging, etc.), which in turn lower morale even further.

> "The whippings will continue until morale improves."
>
> —Anonymous

Understanding morale and motivation is vital to creating a high-performance center. Not surprisingly, we've found that the best results come when a center has both high morale and high motivation. There are two things we want to point out about raising morale:

1. It's not all fun and games.
2. Occasionally, you need fun and games.

Figure 1-1 shows what we mean. We've seen all four of these zones in contact centers and we've seen agents move between them with almost alarming agility. The ideal, of course, is to get your agents into the Efficiency Zone and keep them there. Throughout the rest of this chapter, when we refer to morale we mean this magical combination of morale and motivation that only exists in the Efficiency Zone.

Here's What We Know:

- The manager sets the tone for the entire department.
- Morale is contagious.
- Different things motivate different people.
- Environmental conditions affect morale.
- Motivations change.
- There's no magic formula or 100 percent guaranteed approach to creating high morale.
- Maintaining high morale is as much about caring as it is about caution.
- When employees' needs are met, they tend to be willing to do what you ask—and more.
- Increasing morale makes good business sense.

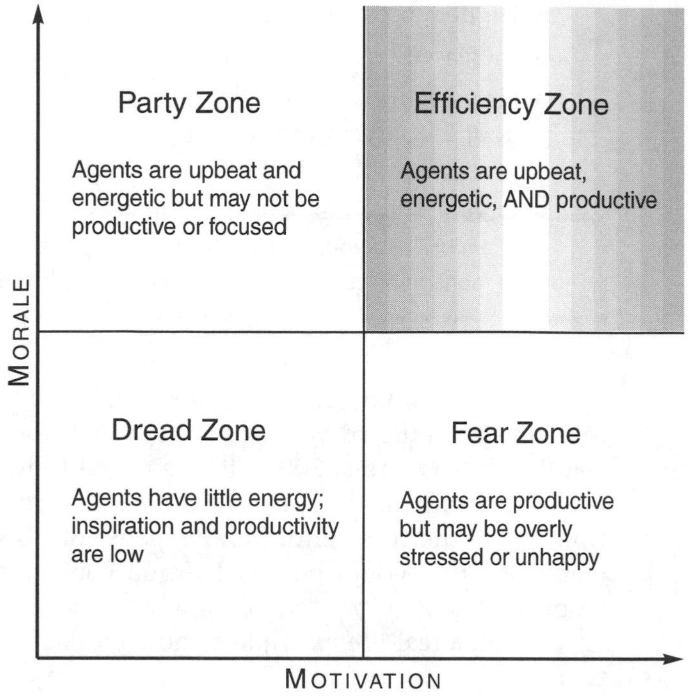

Party Zone

Agents are upbeat and
energetic but may not be
productive or focused

Efficiency Zone

Agents are upbeat,
energetic, AND productive

MORALE

Dread Zone

Agents have little energy;
inspiration and productivity
are low

Fear Zone

Agents are productive
but may be overly
stressed or unhappy

MOTIVATION

FIGURE 1-1   The four zones of contact center employees.

WHY IS MORALE SO IMPORTANT?

It's not impossible to have high productivity and decent bottom-line
results in an environment where morale is low, but it is unlikely. As
you'll see throughout this book, our approach is that you should care
about how your employees feel, if for no other reason than because it's
the right thing to do. But if you're not yet a convert to that way of
thinking and that style of management, we've got some other good
reasons for you to care about morale.

High morale in a contact center environment can lead to:

- Increased job satisfaction
- Lower turnover rates
- Higher productivity
- Reduced absenteeism
- Higher ownership of customer concerns
- Less job-related stress
- Increased identification with the company's mission

- Higher customer satisfaction
- Increased customer loyalty
- Strong "ambassadorship" (for example, through referrals) from your employees to their family, friends, and acquaintances

> The morale of your center will be conveyed to customers through the words, actions, and attitude of your frontline employees.

It's good for you, it's good for them, it's good for the bottom line. In a survey conducted by David H. Maister, the author of *Practice What You Preach* (Free Press, 2001), it was found that happy divisions outperformed unhappy ones by as much as 42 percent. What's more, just think of all the time, effort, and expense of hiring and training new employees that could be saved if you could just keep your current employees happy!

Here's a real-life example of how morale carries over to the bottom line:

A credit card firm had three contact centers in different parts of the country. Morale was generally high in two of the centers, but not in the third. This may or may not be attributable to the fact that in the third center the manager had held his position for more than 15 years, was close to retirement, and always acted from a "don't rock the boat" mentality. Many of the agents in that center also had a long tenure (6 to 10 years versus 1 to 2 years for the other two centers) and couldn't see why they should do anything differently than the way it had always been done.

The company initiated a large campaign to turn the account reps into salespeople by having them "sell" balance transfers (i.e., transfer your debt from other credit cards to this one and get a low interest rate for six months) to customers. The two centers where morale was high outperformed the third one by some 34 percent.

You Know It When You See It

High morale doesn't necessarily mean an absence of tensions, disagreements, or challenges. These are—and probably should be—present in any dynamic working environment. And it doesn't necessarily mean a complaint-free workplace. As we've all experienced at one time or another, complaints are often good ideas having a bad day.

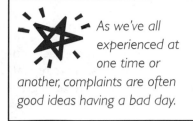

As we've all experienced at one time or another, complaints are often good ideas having a bad day.

However, when morale is high, the team invests its time and energy in finding solutions rather than creating problems. Employees show respect for one another even if they disagree. Despite the inevitable challenges of working life, in a high-morale environment employees take pride in what they do and as a result give their best effort. They go the extra mile for the team or for the customer. They look forward to coming to work and they attempt to make the workplace an enjoyable environment for themselves and others.

COMMON CAUSES OF LOW MORALE

Sometimes morale goes down temporarily and then naturally recovers. For example, after a major organizational change (such as layoffs or a downturn in sales), the resulting sadness and uncertainty can lead to a period of low morale. Once the remaining employees get their bearings, however, morale will often improve on its own.

But then there's the chronically low-morale workplace. Contact centers often find their way into this category. Whether a center handles sales, service, support, or all three, the job has some built-in difficulties that can adversely affect morale:

- Repetitious tasks
- Pressure to get through calls, e-mails, or chat sessions quickly
- Demanding or dissatisfied customers
- Agents' feeling of being tied to their workstation
- Fear or uncertainty

In some contact centers these challenges are compounded by additional factors such as:

- Little or no job security
- Lack of buy-in to the department or corporate mission
- Feeling of not being appreciated and/or valued by the organization
- Poorly designed working environment
- Sense of working a job rather than following a career path
- Lack of training

- Not having the necessary information to do the job
- Faulty or wrong equipment

One of the most disappointing things we've seen in contact centers (and, making it even more disappointing, we've seen it repeatedly) is the case of the employee who is eager and willing to do a great job but is prohibited from doing so by mismanagement or wildly dysfunctional organizational policy.

> *One of the most disappointing things we've seen in contact centers (and, making it even more disappointing, we've seen it repeatedly) is the case of the employee who is eager and willing to do a great job but is prohibited from doing so by mismanagement or wildly dysfunctional organizational policy.*

TIP!

Pass along good news.

Develop a way to share news about good things that have happened to employees at work or outside of it. A continuous flow of good news will contribute to morale and will help to build a strong sense of community in the center. Here are a few options for passing the news along:

- Ask employees to report news to you so that you can send daily or weekly good news e-mails to your team.
- Create a bulletin board area where good news announcements are posted.
- Reserve a few minutes for good news to be shared at your regular staff meeting.

According to an article by Kenneth Kovach in *Employment Relations Today*,* when employees were asked in 1946, 1981, and 1995 what they valued most about their jobs, the top three things they reported were:

1. Interesting work
2. Full appreciation for the work they had done
3. A feeling of being in on things

If it's been that way for more than 50 years, there's a good chance it will stay that way in the future.

*"Employee Motivation: Addressing a Crucial Factor in Your Organization's Performance," vol. 22, no. 2, Spring 1995.

HOW TO MEASURE MORALE

There are two ways to assess the morale of your contact center team. The first is to observe the team members and the second is to ask them. Both practices are important and should be carried out on an ongoing basis. But there is an important difference between the two: your own subjective impressions will give you only half the story, while asking for input from your agents will give you valuable insight that you might not otherwise acquire (assuming, of course, that morale is sufficiently high to make agents feel comfortable telling the truth).

All around you are signs of your department's current morale and omens of its future health. Your ability to intelligently read these indicators can only be sharpened by long-term experience as a concerned, reflective manager. For example, when the sales numbers are strong it often follows that morale is high. But it's also possible that the sales numbers are high because the agents were recently warned that they would lose their jobs if they didn't put up some higher numbers, in which case morale might actually be very low. (Again we see that morale and motivation often work independently of one another.)

When making your own assessment of your team's morale, note whether or not your agents:

All around you are signs of your department's current morale and omens of its future health.

- Smile and laugh
- Strive to complete initiatives
- Think creatively and expansively
- Clearly enjoy what they're doing
- Are more interested in their work than in distractions from it
- Do their work well
- Socialize with one another (go to lunch together, pop into their neighbor's cubicle, etc.)
- Interact informally with their manager and supervisors

Those are some signs of high morale. Conversely, low morale is often indicated by the following employee behaviors:

- Being overly quiet or withdrawn
- Not socializing with coworkers
- Coming in late and/or going home early
- High turnover

- Lackluster performance
- Being easily distracted from their work

> "'So many managers believe that you can't measure morale,' say Jack Stack, CEO of Springfield ReManufacturing Corp. 'That notion is not only wrong but dangerous. What gets measured gets done. If you don't measure morale, you wind up taking it for granted.'"
> —Jack Stack, "Measuring Morale," *Inc. Magazine*, January 1, 1997.

In addition to honing your own perception skills, you might want to gather information from your agents through a survey designed to measure their satisfaction with the job, the organization, management, and so on.

Employee Surveys

There are a number of organizations that publish and score employee surveys and that can help you interpret and respond to the results. If you don't feel ready for that or don't have the budget, you might want to conduct an informal survey in which your agents complete a self-assessment of morale and job satisfaction.

A survey can be helpful in a number of ways:

- It asks for agents' self-assessment—something you can't get from your own observations.
- By asking reps to complete the survey, you'll let them know that management is paying attention to issues of morale.
- It lets agents feel that they're being heard and it tells them that their opinions are valuable to the organization.
- Just knowing that the organization is interested in what they have to say often helps employees to feel valued.
- It provides documented feedback that can be tracked against similar surveys in the future.

Here's an example of how a satisfaction survey initiated a solution to an ongoing problem at one center:

A utility company in downtown Los Angeles conducted a satisfaction survey to see what the company could do to make the job better for its agents. A high percentage of agents lived in outlying areas, had long commutes, and were often late to work. As a result of the survey, the agents came up with the idea of team job sharing. The team was responsible for having 80 percent of its members there on time with the rest coming in within the next hour. (Due to the variance in call volume, this was a workable solution for the center.) This allowed for flexibility in the team. If one person had a car problem or a sick child, for example, he or she could find another team member to cover for him or her. Attendance issues dropped.

The survey we use has not been scientifically designed or normed, but you might find it a helpful way to get some valuable feedback from your employees. Of course the survey should not be used as a substitute for actually talking to your reps on a regular basis to find out how they're feeling about their work and their workplace, but it can help you to gauge the morale of your team.

Keep in mind that the survey results will inform you of general patterns or trends—it shouldn't be relied upon for any scientific or legal data. Think of it as something akin to sitting around in a group and asking people to raise their hands in response to your questions. You'll get spontaneous, direct feedback about how your agents are feeling about a particular issue on a particular day at a particular time.

A reproducible copy of this survey can be found in the appendix.

EMPLOYEE SATISFACTION SURVEY

Please answer each question by circling the response that best describes how you feel about each aspect of your job.

1. I have the tools, support, and resources I need to do my job well.	1	2	3	4	5	6	7
2. Management values my contributions to the organization.	1	2	3	4	5	6	7
3. I enjoy my work.							
4. I feel a sense of camaraderie with the others in my work group.	1	2	3	4	5	6	7
5. I am rewarded when I do well.	1	2	3	4	5	6	7
6. I am taught in a helpful and constructive way how I can improve at my job.	1	2	3	4	5	6	7
7. My manager and/or supervisor treats me with respect.	1	2	3	4	5	6	7

8. What would you change in order to improve the workplace and/or your job?

_____

_____

_____

_____

_____

9. In what ways do you hope to grow and learn in this job?

_____

_____

_____

_____

_____

_____

Creating Your Own Survey

You may want to try your hand at coming up with an informal survey that's customized to your unique work environment or to a particular area of concern. Another option is to create a few mini-surveys, each of which relates to a specific aspect of the agents' work life. For example, you might create one survey that assesses how agents feel about their day-to-day work activities, another that focuses on their feelings about the management and organization as a whole, and yet another that asks agents what incentives motivate them to perform well on the job. All three of these assessments will give you helpful feedback about the morale of your department.

If you want to create your own informal survey, our first suggestion is that you check with your legal department to find out if there are any constraints about the types of questions included on the survey. Following are a few additional guidelines for creating the survey:

- Phrase the statements positively.
  - _I feel valued_ rather than _I feel underappreciated_
  - _I have the necessary resources to do my job_ rather than _I do not have the necessary resources to do my job_
- Use a sliding scale with no exact middle.
  - _1   2   3_ yields an overabundance of "2" ratings.
  - _1   2   3   4_ forces respondents to lean either to the left or to the right of the exact middle.

- Include some questions that ask for free-form comments. You'll get feedback that's much more telling than a rating of 1, 2, or 3.

- Keep the survey short (fewer than 15 questions, including some that are free-form). Employees will be more apt to give the survey the time and thoughtfulness required if it's relatively short.

- Create questions that are simple, straightforward, and easy to interpret.

  - For example, if you were to ask, "How likely is it that you will be working for the organization two years from now?" you might get answers that really tell you nothing about an employee's feeling of loyalty (maybe the employee knows that his or her spouse is going to be transferred to another city soon). A more direct question would be, "This organization deserves my loyalty."

- Don't include questions about any subjects you're not willing to address. Whenever you ask people what needs to be changed, it's important that you be ready, willing, and able to make the changes (or at least to explain why the changes aren't feasible).

- Avoid asking agents to put their names on the survey. You'll get more honest feedback by keeping it anonymous.

What to Do with the Results

Asking agents to complete the survey is only the first step. It's equally important for you to actually do something with the results. Four steps are paramount:

1. Score the surveys and read the responses to the free-form questions.

2. Consolidate the responses and look for trends. For example, maybe the answers to many of the questions were all over the place but nearly everyone answered the question, "My contributions to the organization are valued by management," with "strongly disagree." This would seem to tell you that as a whole the group is feeling undervalued by management.

3. Determine what changes you will make to address problem areas. We recommend focusing on only one or two top-priority areas at a time. Once you've made some progress in those areas you can start working on others.

4. Share the results of the survey with your agents (so they know that the survey wasn't done in vain) and tell them what plans you have to address the areas of low satisfaction.

Following is an example of how one contact center successfully assimilated and responded to the results of an informal employee satisfaction survey:

The customer service department at Light Bulb Electrics was suffering low morale largely because its people were kept in the dark about information relevant to their jobs and their industry. Customers would often know things about the company (such as price changes) before the customer service reps (CSRs) did, management would give CSRs shipping dates that had no chance of being met, and CSRs were losing business because requests for price quotes for custom orders would sit for several days on a manager's desk.

At the suggestion of a consultant, the company agreed to conduct an employee survey as part of an initiative to improve morale and performance. Once the results had been reviewed by management, the customer service manager took the CSRs off the phones in two groups and brought in a pizza lunch. She listed on a flip chart the numerical results of the survey as well as the most common concerns raised by the CSRs. The marketing manager came in to explain that the reason the CSRs couldn't give accurate delivery dates was because the company's vendors were promising dates that the vendors couldn't meet due to a shortage of materials in the plastics industry. Once the CSRs realized that management was not intentionally lying to them and that the competition was undoubtedly in the same spot, they felt better.

To solve the problem of being left in the dark about price changes, the marketing manager added the customer service manager to a routing list for some in-house mailings so that the customer service manager would know what was going on and could share the appropriate information with the CSRs.

To address the issue of price requests sitting on a manager's desk, the group created a new position to handle just those quotes. Turnaround time for the quotes shrank from 3 to 4 days to 8 to 12 hours.

Through the skillful use of an employee survey, what started as a volley of gripes eventually became a series of meaningful, effective changes that helped improve productivity, customer satisfaction, and morale.

How Often Should You Do Surveys?

It's hard to create a general rule about how often to conduct employee satisfaction surveys. In some environments—ones that have a relatively stable climate and low employee turnover—once a year might be a good interval. In more volatile environments—for example, a center with high turnover and ongoing change—it would be advisable to conduct the survey every four to six months. Once the results start coming back with consistently high scores, the manager could start doing the surveys every year or so.

HOW DO YOU IMPROVE MORALE?

To some extent, this whole book is meant to answer the question of how to improve morale in a contact center. Good coaching practices, team building, stress relief, a sense of mission, and many other topics covered in this book will go a long way toward achieving and maintaining high morale. But since those subjects are treated at length in their own chapters, we'll focus here on a few of the more immediate measures you can take when you notice morale is heading south.

It's easy to make the assumption that the key to morale is simply to give the agents what they want. But that isn't always the case. What they want—or think they want—may be minimal work, lots of play, and plenty of pay. But we've found in a number of centers that what really makes employees thrive is a dynamic, positive environment in which agents are continually learning and their performance is continually improving. So, how do you make this happen? Good question!

It's important for you as the manager to create and continually foster a climate of enthusiasm, open communication, and active participation. It's in this kind of environment that agents will be productive and committed to your goals. You'll find that a little goes a long way: if employees see you—and the organization as a whole—making an effort to meet their needs and to treat them well, they'll be inclined to give you their best efforts.

On the other hand, if you create a climate of mistrust and uncertainty, your agents will tend to do just enough to get by. And they'll probably only do that until it becomes more appealing to get by at some other company. Of course, in almost every organization there are some "get by" people who will always be "get by" people no matter what you do to encourage, inspire, motivate, and transform them. If you're serious about improving the morale of your team, the time may come when you need to give stern warnings to those agents whose attitude is weighing down the morale of the group. Then, if they continue to create problems, it may be best to terminate them.

There are a number of important measures you can take to boost the morale of your team. Let's start by looking at Table 1-1, which details what you can do to address the previously mentioned difficulties inherent in a contact center.

TABLE 1-1 Solutions to Common Morale Problems

PROBLEM	SOLUTION
Repetitious tasks	• Give agents regular breaks from calls or keyboard work. • Let agents rotate on and off multiple projects (for example, different clients at an outsourcer) or work in a shared environment (answering the phone for different accounts/projects). • Use the stress-relief techniques outlined in Chapter 5.
Pressure to get through calls, e-mails, or chat sessions quickly	• Coach agents to skillfully shorten call length. • Slow down the predictive dialer or give agents occasional breaks between contacts so they can stretch and catch their breath.
Demanding or dissatisfied customers	• Train agents to skillfully handle challenging customers. • Rotate agents to other jobs every few hours or days so they can talk to some nice folks for a change.
Feeling of being tied to workstation	• Have one rep (or more as needed) rotate on the floor to cover people who need a break. • In addition to two 15-minute breaks, give people an additional 10–15 minutes a week when they can be logged off but not have to say why. • Let agents stand up while working. • Explain the productivity standards and ask reps for suggestions on how they can meet them and not be tied to their workstations.
Little or no job security	• Give agents more security by putting them on a career path. • Help agents plan ahead (for example, if you know a project is going to be ending in a month, let them know).
Lack of buy-in to the department or corporate mission	• Remind agents—or tell them for the first time—what's in it for them. • Translate the mission into one or more specific benefits for the employees. • Make sure agents don't feel that they're working hard just to let upper management get rich, etc.
Feeling of not being appreciated or valued by the organization	• Tell your agents—sincerely, powerfully, and continuously—that their efforts are highly valued by you and your organization. • Give agents frequent coaching with lots of praise. • Bring in senior managers for lunch once a quarter for a company update and Q&A session. • Walk around the work floor on a regular basis, talking to agents and asking how the job is going, what the customers are saying, what you can do to make their job easier, etc.
Sense of working a job rather than following a career path	• Let agents know what opportunities are available to them down the line. • Show agents how their work brings value to customers' personal or professional lives.

TIP!

To remind agents of the importance of high morale and motivation (M&M) when serving customers, make m&m's™ candies the official sugar fix of your department. You can hand out any or all of the five varieties from time to time or keep a stock on hand for morale and motivation emergencies. Here are a couple of other M&M ideas: managers can schedule M&M time, in which they sit in a quiet place eating m&m's and think about what they can do to improve morale and motivation. When the candies are gone, they go back to work and implement their ideas. Alternatively, managers can invite a peer to help brainstorm ideas (and help finish the bag).

The following list contains some additional tips to help you maintain high morale in your own environment. Make an effort to follow through with these tips on a consistent basis, and we're sure you'll see encouraging results.

Contact Center Manager's Checklist: How to Boost Employee Morale and Motivation.

- ☑ Emphasize the positive: what went right, what can be done instead of what cannot, what's going well, and so on.
- ☑ Reward agents for exceeding expectations.
- ☑ Ask for agents' input, and then use it.
- ☑ Hold agents accountable for their performance.
- ☑ Ask agents for their feedback on your performance and management style.
- ☑ Ask agents for their opinions and feelings on issues and decisions that impact the work environment.
- ☑ Offer a work schedule with as much flexibility as possible.
- ☑ Give agents all the information, tools, and resources they need to do a great job (with continuous updates).
- ☑ Regularly talk to employees about the overall mission of the business and how their efforts contribute to it.
- ☑ Provide regular and appropriate feedback on performance.
- ☑ Use proven, effective techniques for praising and correcting employee performance.
- ☑ Involve employees in decisions that affect their jobs.

☑ Establish effective and user-friendly channels of communication.

☑ Treat your employees as adult professionals—at least until they give you reason not to.

☑ Tell the truth, but gently.

☑ Be very, very, very fair with your agents.

☑ Use "we" language.

☑ Always celebrate success.

☑ Acknowledge important moments and experiences in agents' nonwork lives.

> "Businesses with a high morale factor have a competitive edge over other businesses. It is not a superior product or service offering. Nor is it related to material things. It cannot be overcome with lower prices. It is an intangible feeling transmitted from each employee to every other employee and to the customer. It makes customers respond with repeat orders."
>
> —W. J. Ransom

TIP!

Although we strongly advocate face-to-face communication between managers and agents, there's no harm in occasionally using technology to motivate your agents. Here are a few ideas:

• Send an upbeat Monday morning voice mail message to the entire team at the beginning of the workweek.

• When you notice an agent is having a particularly hard time, send a supportive message via e-mail.

• Pipe in upbeat music every so often. For example, Gateway Computers pipes in music the first thing in the morning and again late in the day. It can't be so loud that the callers can hear it, but it could be in the background.

• If possible, have music on hold for the reps so they can listen while waiting for calls.

• Arrange for employees to get birthday cards and employment anniversary cards from the big boss (these should probably be personally delivered with a big thanks).

• Use electronic wallboards to communicate and to motivate your employees throughout the day.

If you want your agents to act and perform like professionals, it's up to you to treat them that way. Among other things, this means continually sharing information with them and upgrading their own knowledge about your business, your customers, your industry, and so forth. Think about it: why should you be the only one in the department to read an article about your competitor's customer service innovations or a report on future trends in your industry? There are, of course, times when it doesn't make sense to treat your agents as colleagues. But there are also times when doing so can make them feel valued, important, and very grown up. In return you'll get their enthusiastic behavior and strong performance.

There's Always Something to Celebrate!

Find fun and creative ways to observe offbeat "holidays" such as Groundhog Day (February 2), Burundi's Independence Day (July 1), or the anniversary of the invention of television (January 7, 1927) by wearing particular clothes, bringing in special food, or otherwise celebrating in a light-hearted and respectful way. If your own memory of these dates is a little rusty, a very helpful resource is *Chase's Calendar of Events* (Contemporary Books; published annually), which lists more than 12,000 historical anniversaries, holidays, birthdays, and events.

ADDITIONAL RESOURCES

Books

Dell, Twyla. *Motivating at Work: Empowering Employees to Give Their Best.* Los Altos, CA: Crisp Publications, 1993.

Fetcher, Jerry. *Patterns of High Performance: Discovering the Ways People Work Best.* San Francisco: Berrett-Kochler, 1993.

Hiam, Alexander. *Motivating and Rewarding Employees.* Avon, MA: Adams Media, 1999.

Sloane, Valerie. *Telephone Sale Management and Motivation Made Easy.* Omaha, NE: Business by Phone, 1996.

Thomas, Kenneth. *Intrinsic Motivation at Work: Building Energy and Commitment.* San Francisco: Berrett-Koehler, 2000.

Wadhwani, Raj. *Improve the Performance of Your Contact Center.* Ontario, Canada: ContactCenterWorld.com, 2001.

Worman, David. *Motivating Without Money—Cashless Ways to Stimulate Maximum Results, Raise Morale, and Reduce Turnover with Your Telephone Sales and Service Personnel.* Business by Phone, 1999.

Worman, David. *Motivating with Sales Contests.* Omaha, NE: Business by Phone, 1999.

Companies

Nelson Motivation (a consulting and speaking company). URL: www.nelson-motivation.com.

Associations, Magazines, and Interesting Web Sites

www.goalmanager.com. A human resources portal site offering resources for motivating staff.

www.chartcourse.com. A Web site with a host of resources available.

www.motivation123.com. Tips and resources to help get and stay motivated.

www.c-interface.com. A magazine with tips on motivating frontline staff.

CHAPTER 2

The Look and Feel

Creating a Motivating
Physical Environment

Because the typical contact center employee spends most of his or her time seated at one location and glued to a phone, a computer, or both, it's important to consider the effects—good and bad—of the physical surroundings. In this chapter, we'll look at ways you can improve the physical environment of your contact center to keep employees healthier, happier, and more productive.

The physical environment of a contact center includes workstations, common areas (such as kitchens, restrooms, and meeting rooms), and architectural elements such as walls, windows, and white boards. It comprises whatever can be seen, heard, felt, and even smelled by employees when working.

Before getting too far into this chapter, give the following activity a try. Take a notepad and pen with you so you can make notes about your experience.

Go outside the building and walk in, imagining that you are experiencing the place for the first time. Open your senses and take note of colors, sounds, lighting, temperature, and anything else that strikes you.

Walk onto the call floor and sit in a rep's workstation. How does the chair feel? What do you see? What do you hear? Put your hands on the keyboard. Are you comfortable? Open a file on the computer.

> "Aesthetics, ergonomics and community spaces help create state-of-the-art contact centers. The result: calm and productive employees."
> —Penny Lunt, "Contact Centers that Work,"
> *Customer Support Management,* February 1, 2001.

Is it easy to read? Do your eyes feel strained? Do the monitor colors soothe, stimulate, or stress you out?

Look around at the walls and at anything else you see from the workstation. Is there anything about these areas that either motivates or distracts you? Can you imagine a way to better utilize these areas?

You get the picture: there are all kinds of things in the physical environment—big and little, subtle and obvious—that affect employees' morale and productivity.

> The top three complaints of call center employees are: the space is too hot or too cold, there are not enough restrooms and there is not enough parking. . . . It is not that the work is too boring or the pay is not good. If the working conditions are not pleasant then people will leave.
>
> —Susan Arledge, in an article at www.callcentermagazine.com

WHY DOES THE ENVIRONMENT MATTER?

The physical environment of your contact center impacts two major factors of your employees' work life: their motivation and their productivity. An environment that is clean, comfortable, well lit, and not overly noisy will go a long way toward making people want to work. And we all know that when this happens, quality and productivity improve.

Putting some thought and energy into the physical environment of your workplace inspires employees in another way as well: it shows them that you care. Investing in their immediate work environment means investing in their satisfaction and well-being. Frontline employees love it when the organization pays attention to them!

Following are some of the potential problems associated with not paying attention to the physical environment:

- Eyestrain
- Headaches
- Backaches
- Stress
- Fatigue
- Restlessness
- Low morale

As we all know, those conditions can lead to:

- Sickness
- Injury
- Absenteeism
- Turnover
- Disability
- Inefficiency
- Errors
- Workers' Compensation claims
- Lawsuits

> "'Employee Input DaimlerChrysler' asked its agents for their contact center 'wish lists.' Staffers suggested new divider heights and mail-slot locations, plus conference and washroom improvements. Result: Service quality rose nearly 10 percent after contact center modifications. The lesson to be learned here? Survey your reps!"
>
> —*Customer Support Management*, February 1, 2001.

WHAT CAN YOU DO TO CREATE A MOTIVATING ENVIRONMENT?

Don't worry, we're not about to tell you that improving the physical environment of your contact center takes an investment of many thousands of dollars. Many of the changes that will make a significant impact can be accomplished with minimal expense.

If you do have a budget to renovate, however, or if you're building a new contact center, contact a specialist to help you with the design. Doing everything right the first time will no doubt save you considerable misery and money down the road.

In the next section, we'll look at what you can do to optimize the following for your employees:

- Technical equipment
- Noise
- Lighting
- Air quality

- Ergonomics
- Wall space and white boards
- Common rooms
- Personal space

Technical Equipment

Having expensive, state-of-the-art technical equipment is nice, but it's not essential. What *is* essential is making sure your employees have the tools they need to do a good job. This includes monitors, keyboards, headsets, phone systems, glare screens, wrist rests, mice, and any necessary software.

Make sure the technical equipment works—always. Not only does faulty equipment lead to lower productivity and higher error rates, but think about what it says to your employees when you don't care enough to get chairs, headsets, monitors, or whatever fixed or replaced right away. If you ask reps to use error-prone equipment, don't be surprised if you get second-rate results from them.

Something else that can affect employees' motivation is the cleanliness of their equipment. Encourage them to keep their workstations and equipment clean, especially if reps share work spaces. You might try setting up a regular schedule for cleaning keyboards, monitors, phones, and so on. Keep cleaning supplies designed specifically for electronic equipment on hand and encourage your reps to use them. Their areas will look nice, smell fresh, work well, and last longer.

The human head weighs approximately 12 pounds. To keep your reps from having to work so hard to keep that 12 pounds in a comfortable position, here are two more things to keep in mind:

1. The monitor screen should be between 15° and 50° below eye level (eye level being defined as sitting straight up in the chair and looking straight ahead; see Figure 2-1).

If you ask reps to use error-prone equipment, don't be surprised if you get second-rate results from them.

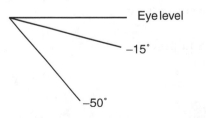

Eye level

−15°

−50°

FIGURE 2-1   Proper monitor positioning.

2. The monitor should be tilted so that the top is slightly farther away from the eyes than the bottom is. (This mimics the way our visual system has developed to view objects—think about how you read a book or a magazine while seated.)

Follow the Finger

Hold your finger at arm's length. Bring it slowly toward your nose, following it with your eyes. Notice that the closer your finger comes, the more eyestrain you feel. Keep this in mind when adjusting the distance between your monitor and your eyes.

What About Customizing Computer Colors?

On a computer monitor, high contrast between the characters and the background is desirable. Research shows that dark letters against a light background is optimal for reducing reflected light and decreasing errors. That being said, we can't altogether dismiss the "joy factor." We've seen a number of contact center employees boost their own morale by customizing their computer monitors into some wild color combinations. Our bottom line is this: if you have some valid reason to keep the colors tame, do it. If not, let your reps express their creativity and personality by customizing their colors.

Not Yet Using Headsets?

We don't know the exact statistics, but our educated guess is that only about 10 to 15 percent of contact center employees are not yet using headsets to communicate with customers. If your reps are included in that statistic, we encourage you to make the switch right away, even if they're only on the phone for a short time. Here's why:

- Headsets provide better sound quality and less annoyance than traditional telephone receivers.
- The adjustable volume allows individual reps to customize their sound levels.
- Traditional telephone receivers cause "phone neck"—at best a minor discomfort, at worst a known cause of serious musculoskeletal strain or a Workers' Compensation claim.

- Headsets improve posture, which in turn has been shown to improve voice quality and call-handling skills.

- Studies have shown that a person who spends all day on the phone can make up to 16 more calls per day with a headset. Keyboard speeds can increase by as much as 43 percent.

Noise

Nearly all workplaces (libraries and monasteries being notable exceptions) are at least somewhat noisy, and to some extent this signifies a healthy, dynamic working environment. But in the contact center environment, where most of the people are talking most of the time, noise control becomes a critical issue.

In one study, 70 percent of workers surveyed reported that noise was the number one distraction in the open-plan workplace; 81 percent reported that they could be more productive if their workplace was less distracting. After high-quality ceiling tiles and sound masking were installed, there was an increase of 174 percent in worker satisfaction levels with regard to conversational noises.*

To be effective in a contact center environment, employees need to be able to mentally block out at least some of the ambient noise, but there are limits to how much can be done simply by force of one's will. Too much noise adds to employees' stress and can lower efficiency and productivity if it inhibits clear communication between reps and customers.

Here are some things to consider:

- High ceilings, fabric-covered acoustic panels, and carpets help mitigate noise.
- Noise can be reduced by up to 40 percent by installing acoustic ceiling tiles and white noise devices.
- Wood furniture absorbs noise better than metal or glass.
- Headsets protect against noise better than traditional telephone receivers. (They also provide better sound quality.)
- Doors to areas that are adjacent to the call floor (such as a break room or a computer room) should be kept closed.
- Pictures or tapestries on the walls break up or absorb noise.
- Irregularly shaped rooms dampen sound wave reverberation.

*Source: Contactcenterworld.com.

- Agents should be sitting inside their cubicles when talking on the phone so that the sound-absorbing panels can mitigate the noise of the call floor. If call volume is low it may be alright for agents to stand or to wheel their chairs out of their cubicles, but once everyone is on the phones, it will most likely become too noisy for this.

Lighting

Good lighting in a workplace has a positive effect on mood and productivity. It has been shown to decrease eyestrain, fatigue, computer errors, and even absenteeism.

Many experts advise bringing natural light into workplaces, but unless you're building a new contact center or have a decent budget for renovating an existing one, there's probably not a whole lot you can do to bring in more natural light through new windows and skylights. If your center does have a lot of natural light, however, be sure to install high-quality glare screens on all computer monitors. (The one drawback to this otherwise optimal source of light is that it causes glare.) Another option is to coat the room windows with a glare-resistant film.

Indirect lighting (light pointing upward) can be ideal but also expensive. It eliminates glare and creates a mood of calm. Indirect lighting is created when fixtures face the ceiling and don't create glare. If you can't provide natural or indirect lighting, the next best thing is full-spectrum lighting.

> "Simply put, we designed the center around the employees. We knew from experience that the most important aspect of operating a successful call center rested in attracting, training, and retaining high-quality people."
> —Steve Higgins, president of SR&J Customer Care Call Centre in Winnipeg, Canada

Air Quality

A lack of clean air in the workplace can result in low morale, illness, and absenteeism. Following are some of the factors that contribute to poor air quality:

- Smoking
- Heating and air conditioning
- Chemicals (in carpets, cleaners, etc.)
- Ionization by electrical equipment
- Lack of good ventilation
- Dust
- Mold in carpets, walls, air conditioning filters, and ceiling vents

Most U.S. workplaces now have some form of no-smoking policy in place. This cuts down on one of the biggest causes of poor air quality. What else can you do to improve air quality? Following are a few suggestions:

- Open windows from time to time to circulate fresh air.
- Use an air ionizer.
- Put plants in the work area. They increase oxygen levels and in dry climates they increase humidity. Plus, they make the place look good!
- Have a specialist come in to check the air quality of your center and make recommendations for improvement.
- Inspect for damp areas were mold might grow.
- Clean the carpet on a regular basis.
- In dry climates, install a humidifier to regulate humidity levels.
- Schedule regular cleanings of the ventilation system.

Dead Air

One consultant reported that she went to a contact center that used morgue air filtering and managers were wondering why morale was down.

ERGONOMICS

You've no doubt heard the word *ergonomics,* even if you have no idea what it means. The term is derived from the two Greek words for "work" (*ergon*) and "natural laws" (*nomoi*). Ergonomics is the study and application of human capabilities in relationship to work demands—translation: how people and equipment work together.

Following are some tips to help you create an ergonomically sound workplace for your agents.

Who's Using the Computer?

If the computer is used by only one employee, the workstation can be optimized for that person. If it's used by two or more people (such as reps on different shifts), you'll need to create a workstation that's easily adjustable.

TIP!

Make sure you train your employees in how to use their ergonomic furniture and equipment. Buying it is only the first step.

Can't Decide Whether to Sit or Stand? Do Both!

One study showed that those who utilize "sit-stand" workstations take 10 to 15 minutes per day fewer breaks. In an eight-hour day, that's a productivity improvement that could amount to $1,300 a year per employee making a salary of $22,000 . . . when you buy an adjustable height workstation for about $800, the payback is about half a year.*

Ten Tips for Ergonomic Computer Workstations

1. Use a good chair and sit back while working.
2. Keep the top of your monitor 2"–3" above eyes.
3. Use a lumbar support cushion for the lower back.
4. Keep feet flat on the floor or on a footrest.
5. Install a high-quality glare screen on the monitor.
6. Use a keyboard tray that can be tilted backward (toward the body).
7. Use a document holder if you need to read from a book, binder, or document while entering data.
8. Center the monitor and keyboard in front of you.
9. Keep your arms and elbows close to the body.
10. Keep your wrists flat and straight.

Source: Cornell University Ergonomics Web, http://ergo.human.cornell.edu.

---

*Source: Arielle Emmett, "Better Calling by Design," *Customer Interface,* November 1, 2001.

Eye-to-Screen Distance

As a general guideline, locate computer monitors at least two feet from the eyes. If the screen can be read without strain, it's not too far away. Experts suggest that if the screen can't be read, it's better to make the characters larger than it is to move the monitor closer to the eyes. If you find that you have to be very close to your monitor or more than three feet away in order to read characters, consider having your eyes checked by a medical professional. It is possible that your eyes need a little support.

Here's what one study found:

> When viewing close objects the eyes must both accommodate and converge. Accommodation is when the eyes change focus to look at something close. Convergence is when the eyes turn inward towards the nose to prevent double vision. The farther away the object of view, the less strain there is on both accommodation and convergence. Reducing those stresses will reduce the likelihood of eyestrain.
> —Dennis R. Ankrum, Nova Solutions, Inc.

Can You Feel Your Feet?

Depending on the height and shape of both you and your chair, a footrest may help you to sit more comfortably. Here's how to determine if you need a footrest: while sitting at your workstation with your fingers on the keyboard and your forearms parallel to the floor, you should be able to rest your feet comfortably, sit with your knees in a comfortable position, and not experience any uncomfortable pressure on your feet and legs. If this doesn't describe how you feel in your chair, you may do better with a footrest. Choose a freestanding support that allows you to comfortably rest your feet while keeping your knees bent.

What About Music?

Should you allow employees to play music in the workplace? Probably not, at least if yours is a contact center where people are on the phone all or most of the time. If your reps communicate predominantly via e-mail or chat, however, music may be one of the perks you want to allow them to have.

If reps are allowed to play music at their workstations, make sure that they are very strict about not allowing it to disturb their coworkers. Also, when making their musical choices, they should err on the side of mellow. From what we've seen, it takes a pretty mature group (meaning psychologically, not chronologically) to make this practice work.

Mandatory Movement

Make sure your employees get up and move around at least a few times every day. Their brains and bodies will benefit from the action and the change of scenery. If yours is a center in which it's nearly impossible to *stop* employees from moving around too much, take solace from the fact that these microbreaks help to refresh and invigorate them.

WALLBOARDS AND WHITE BOARDS

One simple, inexpensive way to significantly improve the physical environment of your contact center is to make good use of whatever areas—such as electronic wallboards and white boards—are in view of your reps when they're communicating with customers. In this case, the improvement is more a matter of communication than of aesthetics.

Almost every contact center we've visited has a wallboard, a white board, or both, but all too often they're underutilized. We suggest you use these areas to inform, motivate, encourage, educate, and whatever else you need to do on a daily basis. Think about it: these areas are in view of your reps all day every day. What an opportunity to fill their heads with meaningful information!

Here are a few suggestions:

- Put up reminders and/or reports about team goals, sales numbers, and so on.
- Post a tip of the day—something that will help reps do their job better.
- Write inspiring quotes to motivate reps.
- Report good news.
- Remind reps to practice newly acquired skills (for example, from recent training).
- Inform reps about something that just happened, is about to happen, or isn't going to happen.

Make it a practice to continually update and change the information posted on these boards. If reps see the same message every day, they'll eventually tune it out. But if the boards are used as a communication hub, reps will look forward to seeing new messages all the time.

We think electronic wallboards are a good idea in contact centers because they:

- Let reps easily read key information
- Give all reps the same information at the same time
- Give up-to-the-minute information
- Can be used for inspirational messages as well as for informational ones
- Provide an opportunity for reps to look away from their computer screen—a recommended practice to reduce eyestrain

TIP!

Don't use buzzers or alarms with wallboards. They distract agents and add to the environmental noise.

Mug Shots

We've heard of several companies that decorate their walls with photos of their employees. Following are two creative examples.*

At Cincinnati-based Kendle International, the company's headquarters feature a special kind of art—photos of employees. The pictures, which were originally part of an ad campaign, feature employees posing happily with symbols of their favorite activities, from scuba gear to grandchildren. Chairman and CEO Candace Kendle found that displaying the photos not only boosted morale and a sense of belonging among employees, it also made the company more inviting to prospective hires.

Another entrepreneur, Herb Kelleher, cofounder of Southwest Airlines, also believes in the power of pictures. "In the hallways of our headquarters, we have photos of our employees— about 1500 pictures of our people engaged in various activities, being honored, given awards," says Kelleher. "Those pictures show that we're interested not in potted palms or in Chinese art but in our people."

*Source: Martha E. Mangelsdorf (ed.), *101 Great Ideas for Managing People from America's Most Innovative Small Companies*. Cambridge, MA: International Thomson Publishing, 1999.

Common Rooms

If your objective is to create a motivating physical environment for your employees, then you'll want to pay attention to the areas in which they spend their time away from the work floor.

Following are a few questions to ask yourself:

- Do your break rooms have what workers need: food, drinks, drinking water, places to sit, phones, something to read?
- How hard do your employees have to work to find out necessary information about personnel and other employment-related issues?
- Are the restrooms consistently clean, stocked, and well maintained?
- Are your time clocks clean? Is the time card area a welcoming one that inspires people and makes them glad they work there?
- Are your smoking areas easily accessible and kept clean?

When planning or replanning your center's layout, keep in mind the distance between workstations and the break room, restroom, telephone, and other auxiliary areas. Typically, contact center employees have short breaks. If they don't have to go very far, they'll have more time to rest or enjoy themselves and they'll be more apt to return to their workstations on time.

Don't Do It This Way

We came across one contact center that had an interesting spin on its no-smoking policy. To protect the health and attitude of nonsmokers, employees were not allowed to smoke in the building. Instead, the company installed large canister-type ashtrays outside the building. Nice gesture: the only problem was that the ashtrays were located approximately two feet from the only entrance to the building. So, every time employees came in or out of the "nonsmoking" workplace, they had no choice but to walk through the designated smoking area.

Personal Space

We all like to have our own space at work. It gives us a sense of freedom, a feeling of ownership, and a dose of independence. In some contact centers, employees do have their own personal workstations, humble as they may be. In others, reps share their workstations with agents who work on other shifts or other days.

If your reps do have their own workstations, it's a good idea to encourage them to bring in a few pictures or some artwork to personalize their space. It will help them to feel comfortable at work and may even decrease their stress.

Needless to say, these personal effects should be tasteful and inoffensive to others.

TIP!

Change things often. It brings freshness and dynamism into the work environment.

Low dividers between cubicles are conducive to teamwork and let supervisors easily see reps. This is helpful not only because supervisors can see what the reps are doing but also because they can easily spot the reps when they're asking for help on a call.

TIP!

Encourage reps to keep job aids (such as reminders of what to do or say in certain situations) posted in their workstations.

A Good Day at Work Begins in the Parking Lot

Don't let a lack of parking spaces frustrate your agents before they even walk in the door to work. It's estimated that a customer contact center requires 6 to 10 parking spaces for every 1000 square feet of space. If your center is open during evening hours, make sure your lot is well lit.

ADDITIONAL RESOURCES

Books

Bridger, R.S. *Introduction to Ergonomics*. New York: McGraw-Hill, 1995.

Brill, Michael. *Using Office Design to Increase Productivity*. Buffalo, NY: Bosti Associates, 1984.

Lagatree, Kristin. *Feng Shui at Work: Arranging Work Space to Achieve Peak Performance and Maximum Profit*. New York: Villard Books, 1998.

Myerson, Jeremy, and Turner, Gavin. *New Workspace New Culture: Office Design as a Catalyst for Change.* New York: Gower, 1998.

Peterson, Baird. *Ergonomic PC: Creating a Healthy Computing Environment.* New York: McGraw-Hill, 1995.

Petit, Ann. *Secrets to Enliven Learning.* San Diego: Pfeiffer & Co., 1994.

Sundstrom, Eric. *Workplaces: The Psychology of the Physical Environment in Offices and Factories.* New York: Cambridge University Press, 1986.

Tillman, Barry, and Tillman, Peggy. *Human Factors Essentials: An Ergonomics Guide for Designers, Scientists, Engineers and Managers.* New York: McGraw-Hill, 1991.

Yerkes, Leslie. *Fun Works: Creating Places People Love to Work.* San Francisco: Berrett-Koehler, 2001.

Companies

Engel Picasso and Associates (provides site selection and call center construction services). URL: www.engelpicasso.com; phone: 800-414-4834.

Interior Concepts (provides contact center furniture). URL: www.interior-concepts.com; phone: 800-678-5550.

Kingsland Scott Bauer and Associates (offers call center design solutions). URL: www.ksba.com; phone: 888-231-5722.

Sound-Rite Acoustics Inc. (provides sound-reducing technologies for call center environments). URL: www.sound-rite.com; phone: 800-665-3232.

Steelcase (provides office products to create a distinct office look). URL: www.steelcase.com; phone: 800-333-9939.

Associations, Magazines, and Interesting Web Sites

Ergo Web (a Web site offering interesting articles, products, and services). URL: www.ergoweb.com; phone: 888-374-6932.

Occupational Safety and Health Administration. URL: www.osha.gov; phone: 800-321-6742.

Office Ergonomics Research Committee (objective is to understand and explain the relationship between office work and discomfort). URL: www.oerc.org

Case Studies

www.neutralposture.com. Offers a case study titled, "A Low Tech, Low Cost Approach to Office Ergonomics."

www.osha.gov. Offers a case study titled, "Ergonomics: The Study of Work."

CHAPTER 3

Team Building in the Contact Center

Basic Guidelines Plus
Ten Activities to Get You Started

WHY TEAMS ARE IMPORTANT IN A CONTACT CENTER

The usefulness of teams becomes apparent when a contact center is given an objective that can't reasonably be achieved without a concerted group effort. In contact centers this tends to revolve around specific challenges related to performance and quality. An individual agent may be able to provide 100 accounts with above-average service, but it's unlikely that that same agent can meet the challenge of providing 2000 accounts at this same service level. Only a team working together to provide superior service can meet the dual challenge of quality and quantity.

Take the example of a team in a technical support contact center that was faced with the dual challenges of increasing first-time resolution scores from 83 percent to 85 percent while reducing average call length from 13 minutes to 12.5 minutes in 60 days. Because the team typically faced a wide variety of technical problems, over time its members developed a habit of sharing information with one another.

> "A team is a group of people with complementary skills who are committed to a common purpose, performance goals, and approach for which they hold themselves mutually accountable."
> —Jon Katzenbach and Douglas Smith, *The Wisdom of Teams: Creating the High-Performance Organization* (Harvard Business School, 1992)

Some team members began to emerge as specialists in particular technical areas.

To reach the goals, the team set out to become more efficient at diagnosing and solving customers' technical issues. In some cases a call would be transferred to the team specialist. Driven by the team challenge, individual members set aside their personal interests in order to be efficient and were willing to ask for help in order to become more effective.

At the end of 60 days the team reached its goal of 85 percent first-time resolution and exceeded its goal of reducing average call length. The new average call length was 12.2 minutes. By emphasizing the best that each team member had to offer, the team as a whole outperformed its members' individual efforts.

Teams can be categorized as directed or self-directed. Directed teams are appropriate in situations where the focus is narrow, the agents have limited discretion, and individual performance levels are monitored regularly. Directed teams are the most common type of teams in contact centers. On the other hand, self-directed teams are seen in contact centers where the agents have a great deal of discretion and the team, particularly the team leader, is held responsible for the overall results.

Most contact centers are regularly faced with some form of a sales or service challenge. A team challenge can drive up overall performance, create camaraderie, and make for a more stimulating environment. Contact centers charged with missions that include any of the following goals and objectives should consider using a team approach:

- Increasing company sales
- Increasing customer satisfaction
- Providing product support
- Resolving accounting disputes
- Preventing dissatisfied customers from defecting

Of course there are many other goals and objectives that can be achieved through the use of effective teams. Teams are a means to an end, and, if they are developed effectively, their average performance will exceed that of an individual in a nonteam environment.

Belonging to a team gives employees the experience of being part of something bigger than their job. There's something intrinsically satisfying about being a part of a successful whole. It's one thing to be successful as a lone wolf, but many employees will never have that opportunity. As part of a team, they can participate in success that they might not otherwise experience. And those individuals who are star performers can experience a broader success that can't be achieved by any one person regardless of how stellar he or she is.

Also, there are times when a contact center needs to get a large amount of work out of a small group of workers. A team environment can help inspire agents to rise to the occasion.

Teams do not simply sprout up wherever a group of employees are thrown together. A group of people is not a team (see Table 3-1 for details on the differences). The group may have a common objective but lack the cohesion, supportive culture, and coordinated effort evident in a team. Many contact centers have groups and departments masquerading as teams. They are teams in name only. Individuals are assigned to the groups but never feel the support, loyalty, and focus of a team. By failing to develop these groups into teams, contact centers are missing out on an opportunity for potentially dramatic performance improvement.

> "If you can't ask for help, you can't work well on a team. If you can't trust someone else to hold up their end of the bargain, they can't help you."
> —Pam Brenner

TABLE 3-1 The Differences Between a Team and a Group

IN A GROUP	ON A TEAM
Members work in isolation.	Members understand that they are one another's internal customers.
Members keep to themselves.	Members communicate openly and often.
Members feel responsible only for their specific jobs.	Members feel mutually accountable for the success of the group.
Members tend to pursue their own personal agendas.	Members work for the common goal, understanding how their personal efforts contribute toward that goal.
Members often talk about "me."	Members often talk about "we."
Members rigidly delineate roles and responsibilities.	Members maintain a high level of flexibility.
Individual successes are celebrated by the individual who succeeds.	Individual successes are celebrated by the team, which claims the success as its own.

YOU'LL KNOW IT WHEN YOU SEE IT

When a team is working well, there is a palpable feeling of high energy and productivity in the workplace. It can be felt in the air and seen on the faces of the team members. It's evidenced by the ease with which the members interact with one another and with their manager.

Following are some marks of a high-performing contact center team:

- A clear goal, challenge, or objective
- Open, easy, and frequent communication between team members
- Enthusiasm for the common goal
- Willingness to pool resources, skills, and information
- Shared understanding of priorities and of team roles and responsibilities
- Sincere concern for one another's well-being
- Willingness to teach one another and to learn from one another
- A can-do attitude when it comes to solving problems calmly and effectively
- Healthy conflict-resolution practices
- Pride in performance

DEVELOPING AN EFFECTIVE TEAM

Companies have to stand up and do two things. They have to re-create an atmosphere that demonstrates that they give a damn about workers, and they have to make it OK for employees to give a damn about each other, because it has become unfashionable, unpopular, and unhip to care about the person next to you.
—Jerome Jewell, cited in *Industry Week,* February 12, 2001

Recognizing a team is one thing, but how do you go about building a team? While there are hundreds of books and many authorities on the subject of team building, we would like to suggest a few basic concepts that will help you get your contact center teams performing at a higher level.

In order for a contact center team to be effective, it needs four basic conditions:

1. A realistic challenge
2. The skills, knowledge, and ability to accomplish the challenge
3. Accountability for results
4. The support and recognition of management

Given these basic ingredients, a team will begin to identify its strengths and weaknesses and the individuals will begin to educate one another. They will set team performance standards that will allow them to meet or exceed the challenge target. They will become accountable to each other, support each other, and care about each other. In doing so, they will become a true team rather than merely a group of individuals.

As an example, an inside sales team at a small siding company in the Midwest is challenged to sell $3.5 million in residential siding during the next 30 days. This figure represents a 6 percent increase over the team's previous record. However, the team members believe it is attainable and accept the challenge. Their incentive is that a team commission will be split equally between the team members. The company also promises to thrown in a pizza party with special recognition from the vice president of sales.

One of the team members is not particularly good at finding new prospects but is very good at closing sales once prospects have been qualified. In order to meet the challenge, the team decides to provide lots of qualified prospects to this individual and commits three members to finding prospective clients who are then referred to her for closing. Other team members will focus on their best sales opportunities and agree to refer prospects to each other if the sale requires special product expertise.

The strategy works. At the end of 30 days the team has sold $3,523,673 in residential siding. In this instance, the team members work together, using each other's strengths, to attain a goal that they could not have accomplished as individuals. While their commissions are important, the real reward is the sense of accomplishment, the team camaraderie, and the recognition of a job well done.

No Clones!

When creating and maintaining a team environment in your contact center, you may find it necessary to point out that team members aren't expected to be identical to one another in personality, work style, or anything else. In fact, most teams benefit greatly from the diversity of their members. Whenever possible, illustrate this to your team.

KEEP YOUR EYE ON THE GOAL

In order to motivate and stimulate a team, a goal must be challenging. It's also essential for all team members to know what the goal is, why it's important, when it's been attained, and when it changes. A basketball team's immediate goal is to win today's game, and its long-term goal is to do well in the season. Similarly, your team will most likely have short-term, day-to-day goals (such as staying within specified wait time guidelines or selling a certain amount of product) and long-term goals (such as completing training or raising performance levels by 5 percent by the end of the quarter).

Your team members will be inspired to meet team goals only as long as they are reaping benefits from their efforts. One of the most important aspects of your job as team leader is to keep team members motivated to work together and to move forward. To do this, make sure you're keeping agents' awareness of team goals high and celebrating accomplishments by:

- Using visual reminders such as posters and support cards
- Talking about team goals on a regular basis
- Continually sharing pertinent information and feedback with the team
- Celebrating milestones of progress
- Relating how the team goal fits into the overall success of the organization

---

Small Goals Work Too!

What if you don't have clearly defined team goals—sales, talk time, contacts handled, and so on? Does this mean you can skip this chapter? Not necessarily. Even if your agents are glued to their headsets as the predictive dialer works its magic, there are still ways for you to create a team atmosphere. Since goals are designed to challenge the team, select some items from your monitoring form and create a team goal to focus everyone on improving in that area. Here are a few examples:

- Giving accurate information
- Logging calls correctly
- Showing respect to customers
- Inputting data accurately
- Selecting the correct call map

GIVE PEOPLE THE TOOLS TO DO THE JOB

Team members are ideal candidates for training as long as they can see how the new skills can help the team reach its goals. A motivated team will generally accept new skills if there are clear benefits to be derived from implementing the skills. A motivated team will self-coach, since team members will train and encourage each other on new skills in order to accomplish the common goal. When supported by coaching from a supervisor or manager, the motivated team will accept and adapt to the new skills rapidly. Training in a team environment should involve the whole team, including the supervisor responsible for the team. Training should:

- Be skills-based
- Be relevant to the team's goals
- Have clear benefits

With increased skill levels, teams will be better able to achieve their goals and can pursue even bigger challenges.

In the sometimes impersonal world of the contact center, setting up the conditions that foster strong performance can create an atmosphere of commitment and concern between agents. This in turn helps to raise performance levels and reduce absenteeism and turnover—two big problems in contact centers.

HOW TO LEAD IN A TEAM ENVIRONMENT

Creating and sustaining a team environment doesn't mean that you as the manager will no longer have primary responsibility for the well-being and effectiveness of the group. Although the concept of self-directed work teams has proven itself successful in a number of organizations, this type of team probably requires too high a degree of responsibility and autonomy for most contact centers. So, while a team orientation is a great way to go for any number of reasons, it's likely that you'll still be at the helm. The difference between leading a team and leading a nonteam work group is that your role is more facilitative than autocratic.

As the leader of the team, it's your responsibility to help the group work together and to identify the strengths and weaknesses of individuals and of the team as a whole. For example, if two or three agents are better suited to a particular aspect of the job—for example, callbacks to dissatisfied customers—make this their role and designate a certain percentage of their time on the job to be spent accomplishing this role. You don't have to be democratic in all things. The overall strength of the team will benefit from identifying and exploiting individuals' strengths.

As a manager, your primary role is to build an environment that provides for the needs of the team and exhibits a model for communication and participation. Following are a few of your additional responsibilities as manager:

- Developing a strong performance ethic
- Selecting appropriate team members
- Providing realistic challenges and keeping the team informed of progress and milestones
- Developing a training environment that supports behavioral change
- Providing coaching support and feedback for the team as a whole and for individual members
- Holding the team and individuals accountable
- Holding brief, purposeful, and regular meetings to make sure the team is on track
- Rewarding the team as a whole for team efforts *and* individual performers for their achievements
- Eliciting support and recognition of your team from senior management
- Knowing when to take charge and when to get out of the way

> "The wicked leader is he whom the people despise. The good leader is he whom the people revere. The great leader is he of whom the people say, 'We did it ourselves.'"
>
> —Lao Tzu

TIP!

When it's needed, see that your team acts as one friend with many heads. For example, when an agent has a birthday, give him or her a card signed by all team members. If an agent suffers a loss such as a death in the family, send condolences from the whole team. These gestures reinforce the feeling that the person is a member of a bonded, caring group.

The Team Contract

One of the best things you can do to ensure the success of your team in meeting its goals is to work with your agents to develop a team contract. A team contract outlines the "rules" of team cooperation. It's not meant to replace or supersede the organization's official rules, but rather to establish a mutual agreement between team members on day-to-day issues that face the team. A team contract is also a meaningful way to actively practice the values outlined in the mission statement of your department or organization.

Because agents develop the team contract themselves—it's not some edict handed down to them from senior management—there tends to be a high level of buy-in. What this means for you is that workers feel empowered to solve problems and make decisions based on a common understanding of how things should be done. It doesn't mean that you as a manager are out of the loop entirely, but a certain level of autonomy on the part of the agents can allow you to focus your time and energy on other demands.

Once the contract has been developed (remember, it can always be revised down the road), all team members should receive and sign their own copy of the document, just as they would any other contract. By signing the contract, team members signify ownership of the contract and make a commitment to abide by its guidelines. If they can't all agree to the guidelines, they should continue negotiating until a final product emerges that does get universal approval. Otherwise, there's no genuine buy-in and members won't abide by the contract.

We recommend keeping team contracts relatively short and simple because then they have a much better chance of actually being used. Guidelines that have already been documented in an employee handbook or procedures manual don't have to be repeated in the contract. The contract offers agents an opportunity to formalize unspoken rules as well as guidelines related to issues and areas that have not already been delineated.

A good place to start is with any currently pressing issues of:

- Interpersonal communication
- Problem solving
- Conflict resolution

Following is a partial sample of a typical team contract:

TEAM CONTRACT

Rule 1   If I don't understand something my coworker says or does, I will ask for clarification.

Rule 2   If a team member deserves credit or recognition, I will give it.

Rule 3   When I have a disagreement or conflict with a team member, I will follow the approved procedures for resolving it.

Rule 4   Team decisions will be made by consensus, with the manager having veto power.

Rule 5   I agree to listen to feedback from my fellow team members.

TIP!

Let your team members come up with their own name for the team, for sub-groups within the larger team, or for specific projects. It will add an element of fun and will help them to feel a sense of ownership.

Staying Together

To make sure your team stays a team, you need to continually ask—and answer—three questions:

1. What's our common goal?

2. Are we mutually accountable for the attainment of that goal?

3. Are we making progress toward the goal?

If you can't identify the goal, don't feel mutually accountable, or aren't making progress, it's time to strengthen the cohesiveness and/or the focus of the team.

OBSTACLES TO A PRODUCTIVE TEAM ENVIRONMENT

No matter how hard you work to create a team environment, no matter how emphatically your agents say they're a team, no matter how much the center can benefit from the teamwork of its agents, there are bound to be times when the team appears to be falling apart. When this happens, don't fret. It only means your organization is just like all the others out there that are trying to succeed at the challenging game of teamwork.

Table 3-2 outlines some of the common obstacles prevalent in team environments as well as suggestions for overcoming them.

TABLE 3-2 Obstacles to a Productive Team Environment

OBSTACLE	HOW TO RECOGNIZE IT	HOW TO OVERCOME IT
Lack of unity	• Jealousy • Overzealous competition • Resistance to new hires	• Implement team building. • Emphasize and reward successes that result from teamwork. • Organize contests so that agents compete with themselves to better their own performance, rather than competing with other agents. • Create some fun team-building activities to get new members working with the team on their first day.
Lack of clear goal or objective	• Inefficiency • Confusion • Overlap of efforts • No improvement in performance	• Continually remind members of the common objective. • Make sure members know how their individual efforts contribute to team goals.
Lack of training	• People don't know how to do aspects of their jobs • Agents forget what they learned in training	• Make sure all agents are sufficiently trained. • Make sure training is consistent across the team. • Make certain that the training that is in place is relevant. • Ensure that managers reinforce training.
Cynicism	• Negative attitude • No buy-in to common objectives	• Confront cynical behavior and coach agents to improve their attitude. • Question agents as to the reason for the cynicism and fix problems as necessary.
Unfair distribution of work	• Strong feelings that "someone else should do this" • Resistance to going above and beyond • Some people constantly working while others have lots of free time	• Revisit team roles and responsibilities to make sure they're fair and well suited to each individual's strengths and weaknesses.

TIP!

What can you do about defectors, saboteurs, naysayers, or otherwise bad apples on the team? The short answer is to confront these behaviors head-on, using the appropriate coaching techniques. If you ignore them, they'll only grow stronger (and you'll look weaker). Take a look at the recommendations for dealing with difficult employees in Chapter 10.

TEN TEAM-BUILDING ACTIVITIES FOR YOUR CONTACT CENTER

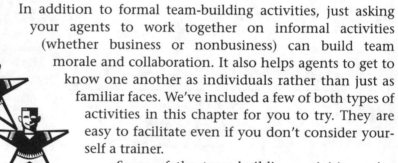

In addition to formal team-building activities, just asking your agents to work together on informal activities (whether business or nonbusiness) can build team morale and collaboration. It also helps agents to get to know one another as individuals rather than just as familiar faces. We've included a few of both types of activities in this chapter for you to try. They are easy to facilitate even if you don't consider yourself a trainer.

Some of the team-building activities we've included also have educational value, so they can be incorporated into training sessions or can even serve as informal training sessions themselves. But no matter the type of activity, the primary objective is to get your team members to interact with one another in new ways and to see that the best results occur when everyone works together.

Regularly conducting team-building activities in your center can help you accomplish the following:

- Inspire teamwork and camaraderie
- Improve morale
- Build trust and respect
- Highlight and celebrate diverse ways of thinking and doing
- Identify team strengths and weaknesses
- Reduce tension and conflict
- Create tips and techniques for improving quality and productivity

---

Aha!

Team-building activities can be effective in a number of ways, one of the most important of which is the aha! moment. The aha! moment takes place when, in the middle of what seems to be a game, a team member suddenly and powerfully realizes something very important about the job—a different way to do things, a smarter way to communicate, or something else equally enlightening.

You can elect to include one or more activities in a staff meeting or you can choose to create training sessions specifically for the purpose of team building. The 10 activities on the following pages will give you a great start. We've included a range of activities—from the simple to the more complex, from the light to the deep—that we feel meet the objective of team building. Once you've completed the activities provided in this chapter, you can seek out other activities and games (see the "Additional Resources" section at the end of this chapter) to keep your team-building efforts active and fresh.

Following are a few additional tips to help you make the activities—and your team—succeed:

- *Choose carefully.* It's a mistake to assume that all team-building activities offer participants the same learning and experience. Before conducting an activity, carefully review it to make sure it's suitable for your particular team. Take into consideration team members' skill level, job description, maturity, and whatever else seems relevant. The key is to always set your team up for success, not failure!

- *Make it relevant.* Be able to tie the activity to the actual job demands of your team members (such as the need to work together effectively) or to something that your team is currently experiencing (such as a heightened need for strong customer service). In order for a team-building activity to be successful, there has to be some connection between what team members do or learn in the activity and what they do or need to know in their day-to-day jobs.

- *Prepare.* Don't just hand out the activity and then fly by the seat of your pants. Take some time before the group convenes to plan exactly what you'll do and say to set up the activity and to debrief participants at the end of it.

- *Keep it lighthearted.* Team-building activities are meant to be enjoyable. Watch out for overly competitive or overly serious participants and remind them that the true objective of the activity is to increase teamwork, cooperation, and communication. If they're not doing this during the activity, how will they remember to do it in the real-time environment?

- *Make it a process, not an event.* Try to make team-building activities more than merely isolated events. In the days and weeks after the group has completed an activity, keep the learning fresh by talking about it and relating what team members did in the activity to what they're doing in the real-time environment.

TEAM-BUILDING ACTIVITY 1: The Commercial

In a Nutshell
Team members work in small groups to develop and present a short commercial advertising their team to customers. This activity reinforces collaboration, creativity, and commitment to service.

Time
30 minutes

What You'll Need
Blank pieces of flip chart paper, colored markers

What to Do
Divide team members into groups of three to five and give each group some flip chart paper and a few markers. Let them know that their task is to work together within their small teams to develop a television commercial advertising their team to customers. The objective is to highlight the strengths and character of their team. Encourage team members to be creative and to have fun. Almost anything goes!

You might want to preface the activity by holding a brief discussion (no more than five minutes) about how television commercials convey their message in 30 seconds or less. Following are a few discussion starters:

- What are some of your favorite commercials? Why?
- What type of commercials stick with you even if you don't like them?
- What are some popular formats for commercials (for example, a celebrity spokesperson)?

Give teams 15 to 20 minutes to create their commercials and then ask each group to present its commercial to the larger group.

TEAM-BUILDING ACTIVITY 2: Make It Personal*

In a Nutshell
In this activity, each participant uses the letters of his or her first name to inspire service-oriented actions. It explores the diversity of the team, gives team members a chance to get to know each other better, and helps team members to realize that there are literally hundreds of ways they can offer good service to customers.

Time
10 minutes

What You'll Need
Each team member will need a piece of paper and a pen. You'll need a flip chart or white board to demonstrate the activity.

What to Do
Tell each team member to write his or her name vertically along the center of a sheet of paper. Demonstrate by writing the following on a flip chart or white board:

M

A

R

Y

Tell team members that now their task is to use each letter of their name to come up with an action that they can take to offer great service to their customers. Each letter of their name must begin a word in the action phrase, but it doesn't necessarily have to be the first word of the phrase. Action can be phrased either positively or negatively. For example

Be **M**otivated to serve.
   Ask for the sale!
   Respect their needs.
Don't **Y**odel on the phone.

Encourage team members to have fun with this activity and to be wildly creative.

After about seven or eight minutes, ask for some volunteers to share what they came up with. Point out to participants that there are hundreds, even thousands of ways to give great service to their customers.

*Reproduced with permission from *The Big Book of Customer Service Training Games* (Peggy Carlaw and Vasudha Kathleen Deming, McGraw-Hill, 1999).

TEAM-BUILDING ACTIVITY 3:
Deciphering Cyber-Babble

In a Nutshell
Team members work in small groups to translate emoticons and acronyms into plain English. This activity is suitable for anyone but may be particularly appropriate for agents who correspond with customers via e-mail. It inspires group brainpower and creative thinking.

Time
10 to 15 minutes

What You'll Need
One copy each of the Cyber-Babble Quiz and its answer sheet for each group. (See the appendix for a reproducible version of the quiz.)

What to Do
Preface the activity with a brief discussion about the use of emoticons (such as the sideways smiley face) and acronyms (such as FYI for For Your Information and B4 for Before) in e-mail.

Divide the team into pairs or small groups and give each group a copy of the Cyber-Babble Quiz. Tell them to work within their groups to translate the terms and images into plain English.

After several minutes, hand out the answers to each group and ask them to check their own translations with those on the answer sheet.

Note: Although the aim of this activity is to get team members to work together on a fun and simple project, you might want to expand the activity into a broader discussion about whether or not it's appropriate to use these symbols when communicating with customers. (We recommend that with the exception of the occasional smiley face or other universally understood gesture, agents leave emoticons and acronyms out of their customer communications.)

CYBER-BABBLE QUIZ

Directions: Work with your partner to translate the following emoticons and acronyms into plain English. You may have to turn your head (or the page) sideways when translating the emoticons. :)

Examples:
FYI	*for your information*
FOAF	*friend of a friend*
O :-)	*angel*
; ^ (	*smirking face*

ATST _____

BTDT _____

CUL8R _____

FWIW _____

IDTS _____

IRL _____

: 3-] _____

P- (_____

: =) _____

= :-) _____

*<) : o) _____

*<) : o)	clown	
= :-)	punk	
: =)	orangutan	
P-)	pirate	
: 3-]	dog	
IRL	in real life	
IDTS	I don't think so	
FWIW	for what it's worth	
CUL8R	see you later	
BTDT	been there, done that	
ATST	at the same time	

CYBER-BABBLE QUIZ ANSWERS

TEAM-BUILDING ACTIVITY 4: Answer Me This

In a Nutshell
In this activity, participants answer some challenging questions that will help them get to know each other better, provide a vehicle for them to begin solving some of their own problems, and provide you with organizational issues that need to be addressed.

Time
20 minutes

What You'll Need
- One copy of the Team Questions Sheet (found in reproducible form in the appendix)
- A flip chart or white board and markers to capture responses

What to Do
Explain that this activity will help participants get to know each other better. Hand out one copy of the Team Questions Sheet. Ask team members to answer as many questions as they can within the next five minutes. Point out that they'll be discussing their answers with several other team members.

After five minutes, put people into groups of three or four. Give them 10 minutes to discuss their answers and to select one question and answer to discuss with the entire team.

After 10 minutes, ask for feedback from the groups. Post the question number and answers on the flip chart or white board. Discuss answers as needed. If team members suggest organizational improvements, either make them or let team members know why they cannot be made.

TEAM QUESTIONS SHEET

Directions: Review the following questions and answer as many as you can within the next five minutes. You will be discussing them with several of your teammates.

1. If you were manager of this contact center, what is the first thing you would change?

2. What questions do you get from our customers that you can't answer?

3. What motivates you to do your best?

4. What's the best thing about working here?

5. What do you wish your supervisor would ask you?

6. What is the most stressful part of your job?

7. What could we do to have more fun at work?

8. What one thing could we do to better serve our customers?

TEAM-BUILDING ACTIVITY 5:
A Better Way to Say It

In a Nutshell
In this activity, participants practice some key skills for communicating with coworkers when they are requesting help or information.

Time
15 to 20 minutes

What You'll Need
- Flip chart and markers
- Masking tape

What to Do
Work with the group to brainstorm 10 to 15 common requests they make of one another in the course of their jobs. They might be requesting information, help, some tangible object, or anything else. For example, one agent might go to another to request:

- A hard-copy resource such as a reference binder, a zip code guide, or something similar
- Help in solving a customer's problem
- Some needed paperwork
- Callbacks to customers
- A swap of hours or shifts

Capture the requests on the flip chart, writing one at the top of each page. Talk briefly about how the agents currently make these requests. What do they say? Do they make the request in person, over the phone, or via e-mail? Do they plan what they're going to say before they say it?

Next, tell the group members that now they're going to learn two good luck charms for getting their requests fulfilled in a way that's professional, positive, and effective. In other words, they're going to learn that there's a better way to say it. The two ways are:

1. Ask, don't tell

2. Show value

"Ask, don't tell" is pretty self-explanatory. This is a helpful way to frame a request because everyone prefers to be asked rather than told. Showing value may or may not be a familiar concept to your team. Showing value means letting the other person know what benefit will be derived from fulfilling the request. They need to consider what the value is and then point it out to the other person. For example:

> *"Your expertise would really help this customer understand how the Golden Horizons plan works. Right now she's so confused."*

> *"If I can get that paperwork from you by the end of today, we'll be able to meet the deadline for turning in our budget."*

Divide the flip charts into two sets and post each set in a different part of the room (creating two stations, each with five flip charts posted side by side). One station is the ask, don't tell station and the other is the show value station.

Divide the group into two teams and assign each team to one of the two stations (they'll need markers). Their job is to come up with a better way to say it for each request and to use the flip chart to write out exactly what they would say to make the request of a team member.

After about 10 minutes, have each group present its requests. Debrief by discussing the following:

- It's sometimes not necessary to show value (for example, if someone is requesting to borrow a book), but it's still an important skill to have for those times when it *is* necessary.

- Work is a nicer place to be if people treat each other with respect by asking instead of telling.

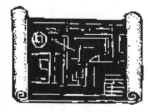

TEAM-BUILDING ACTIVITY 6: Amateur Architects*

In a Nutshell

This is a lengthy but popular activity in which participants learn to strategically use open and closed questions to get the information they need from a team member. The activity reinforces the need for collaboration with other team members and helps agents improve their questioning skills.

*Reproduced with permission from *The Big Book of Customer Service Training Games* (Peggy Carlaw and Vasudha Kathleen Deming, McGraw-Hill, 1999).

Time
20 to 30 minutes

What You'll Need

- One copy of House A for half the participants and one copy of House B for half the participants (see the appendix for reproducible versions of both houses)
- Blank paper and a pen for each participant

What to Do

Put the information from the "Open Questions" and "Closed Questions" lists pages x and y on a flip chart and review it with participants. You might ask the following questions and field answers.

Open Questions

- Solicit more than a "yes" or "no" or other one-word response
- Aim to get someone talking
- Are useful when you want general information
- Common lead-ins are *what, how,* and *why*

Closed Questions

- Solicit a "yes" or "no" or other one-word response
- Aim to limit talking or to control direction of conversation
- Are useful when you want specific information
- Common lead-ins are *who, when, did, which, would, are, can, have, do, is, will,* and *may*

- What are some examples of open questions?
- What are some examples of closed questions?
- When do you use open questions with customers?
- When do you use closed questions with customers?

Put participants into pairs and explain that the object of this activity is for one person to draw a house that matches the house his or her partner will be given. Those who are drawing can ask any questions they want and as many as they want in five minutes. Those who are describing the house should answer the questions but not volunteer any additional information.

Distribute House A to one member of each pair and ask the other member to take out a sheet of blank paper. Ask partners to sit back-to-back and spread participants out so that those drawing cannot see the houses of those who are describing.

After five minutes, have the describers and drawers compare houses. Debrief the game. Point out how open questions tend to solicit more general information than closed questions.

Have the pairs switch roles. Distribute House B to those who will be describing; the other member of each pair will need a blank sheet of paper.

After five minutes, have the describers and drawers compare houses. Debrief the game with the following questions:

- What did you learn from this activity?
- How does this relate to teamwork?

House A

House B

TEAM-BUILDING ACTIVITY 7: Information Relay

In a Nutshell

This is a relay-style activity in which each team member has to find a piece of information related to the organization, its customers, or the team itself. At the end of the relay, team members convene to share the information—and to realize that the sum is greater than the parts.

Time

The first leg of this activity is carried out by individuals and can take place over the course of a few days. The group session takes about 15 minutes.

What You'll Need

- Index cards

- For the group session, ask each participant to bring a dollar (they'll get it back)

What to Do
Part One

Inform everyone about the activity and make arrangements for the group session, which takes place after everyone has found the answer to his or her question.

Prepare questions for the information you want team members to uncover. The questions should meet three criteria:

1. Finding the information should require participants to do some legwork, but not so much that it unduly distracts them from their other work.

2. There should be no trick questions. In other words, make sure the answer does exist and can be found with a reasonable amount of effort from the agent.

3. The information to be uncovered and subsequently shared by the agent should have some relevance to the job or otherwise be useful to the agents.

Following are a few suggested questions:

- On average, how many customers does the team serve via telephone or e-mail each week?

- Who has been on this team the longest time? How long?

- How do we measure customer satisfaction?

- How did the organization get its name?

Write each of the questions provided on index cards (one question per card). You'll need one card per participant. Hand out one index card to each team member and let members know that they're expected to investigate the answer, write it on the card, and bring the card to the group session.

Part Two (Group Session)

Take out a dollar bill and ask someone to trade it for another dollar bill. Then ask that person to trade with someone else. Continue this several times and then ask the group: "Is anyone richer now that we've exchanged all this money?" Once the group members confirm that no one is richer, point out that if they had exchanged information instead of dollar bills, everyone would be richer for having learned something new. That's what they're going to do now!

Have participants take out their index cards and one by one share the information they found with the rest of the group. Wrap up by pointing out how everyone's individual efforts contributed to the overall enrichment of the team.

TEAM-BUILDING ACTIVITY 8: Secret Buddy Cards

In a Nutshell

In this activity, each team member secretly observes another for a few days with the intention of finding admirable qualities or practices. The activity builds camaraderie and helps team members to see the best in one another.

Time

The observation period of this activity should take place over the course of two or three days. Then the team gets together for a group session of about 15 minutes.

What You'll Need

Index cards

What to Do
Setup

Put the name of each team member at the top of an index card (one card per name). Spread the cards out face down either in your hands or on a table. Ask each team member to pick a card at random. (If someone gets a card with his or her own name, he or she should exchange it for another card from the pile.)

Give all team members the following instructions: "The person whose name is on your card is your secret buddy. Your task is to observe that person for the next _____ days and to find three admirable qualities. Write the three qualities on the index card and bring it to the group session. Do not let anyone know which person you are observing."

Group Session

One by one, have each person stand, look at his or her secret buddy, and tell that person directly what three qualities were observed. When complimenting one another, participants should address the secret buddy as "you," not "he" or "she." Example:

Tim, I observed you and here's what I discovered:

Wrap up by having each person give the index card with the observations to his or her secret buddy to keep.

Customers' Bill of Rights

TEAM-BUILDING ACTIVITY 9: Customers' Bill of Rights

In a Nutshell
In this activity, team members work together to brainstorm a bill of rights for their customers. The activity reinforces a strong commitment to customer service and provides an opportunity for team members to practice consensus building.

Time
15 minutes, or longer if desired

What You'll Need
- Photocopies of the Bill of Rights Sheet (see appendix for a reproducible version; one sheet for each pair or small group)
- Flip chart and markers

What to Do
Preface the activity with a brief discussion about the United States Bill of Rights.

Q: What is the Bill of Rights?

A: *It's the name given to the first 10 amendments of the Constitution.*

Q: What is the subject of the first amendment?

A: *Freedom of speech, assembly, and religion.*

Tell participants that their task in this activity is to work in small teams to come up with a bill of rights for their customers. They should think about both tasks and treatment. For example, they might determine that all customers are entitled to a short queue and that they're also entitled to be treated with respect.

Divide participants into pairs or small groups and give them 10 minutes to come up with rights. Then ask each group to report what it came up with as you capture responses on a flip chart under the heading "Customers' Bill of Rights."

Ask the group to reach a consensus as to whether or not each right should be included in the final version. Once they've agreed, elect one team member to print the bill of rights onto a fresh piece of paper and to make copies for each member of the team.

BILL OF RIGHTS SHEET

Customers' Bill of Rights

TEAM-BUILDING ACTIVITY 10: Enter a Local Race

This activity, which never seems to fail in boosting team morale, obviously takes place outside of normal working hours and outside of the normal work environment. For this reason, you'll need to be extra cautious in ensuring that team members understand that their participation in this nonwork activity is optional and that it has no bearing on their performance review or their standing in the organization. Please also check with your human resources department to see if there are any legal implications that should be considered.

If it seems like a good fit for your team, give it a try. If everyone enjoys the experience, it can become an annual or semiannual event. If they *really* enjoy the experience, some of the team members can move up to a longer distance such as 10 kilometers (6.2 miles) or even a marathon (26.2 miles).

What to Do

Encourage team members to enter a local 5-kilometer (3.1-mile) running race. Often these races have divisions for walkers as well as for runners, so it's likely that the event would be suitable for most or all team members.

The event gives team members healthy doses of fresh air, adrenalin, endorphins, challenge, and team bonding. A number of races raise money for charities or other good causes, so there's also the possibility for altruism.

Those team members who can't or prefer not to participate as athletes have the option of coming out to the race as sideline cheerleaders. To make the event more team-oriented, you can have special t-shirts made and/or include family, friends, and significant others in a group celebration at the end of the race.

We suggest you talk to your senior management about having the entry fees paid for by the organization.

ADDITIONAL RESOURCES

Byham, William, Wellins, Richard, and Wilson, Jeanne. *Empowered Teams: Creating Self-Directed Work Groups that Improve Quality, Productivity, and Participation.* San Francisco: Jossey-Bass, 1993.

Jones, Alanna. *Team-Building Activities for Every Group.* Richland, WA: Rec Room Publications, 1999.

Katzenbach, Jon, and Smith, Douglas. *The Wisdom of Teams: Creating the High-Performance Organization.* Cambridge, MA: Harvard Business School, 1992.

Newstrom, John, and Scannell, Edward. *The Big Book of Team Building Games.* New York: McGraw-Hill, 1997.

CHAPTER 4

Making It Fun to Succeed

Incentives, Rewards, and Contests

Incentives, rewards, and contests are part of almost every contact center around the country. According to a 2001 joint survey by World at Work and the National Association for Employee Recognition (NAER), 86 percent of companies have an employee recognition program and 62 percent of those that do not are considering creating one. Managers everywhere have caught on to the notion that rewarding high performers—and enticing lower ones—is important. This may be particularly true in the contact center industry, where pay tends to be consistent from one center to another and where competition for star agents is often fierce.

In most centers, incentive programs, rewards, and contests work together under one umbrella recognition program. All three initiatives can motivate agents to improve performance and to feel good about the work they do and the contribution they make to the organization. They can also bring an element of fun and excitement into the environment, help keep spirits high, and increase loyalty and company pride. If done well, they can be good for both employer and employee. What's more, they're often inexpensive—sometimes even free—and they don't have to be complicated or difficult to manage.

> "According to employers with a recognition program, more than nine out of ten say that the main objective of their recognition efforts [is] to improve employee morale. Further, about three-fourths (73 percent) of employers with recognition programs are trying to make employees feel part of the company; 70 percent are attempting to influence employee retention."
>
> —2001 joint survey by World at Work and the National Association for Employee Recognition.

In this chapter, we'll outline some basic dos and don'ts for these programs and then give you some ideas for getting started.

How Do You Know if Your Incentives Are Working?

The most common ways for employers to measure their success in these efforts are through employee satisfaction surveys, monitoring of turnover ratios, and productivity statistics.

INCENTIVES

Employee incentives run the gamut from ballpoint pens to retirement funds. They include bonuses, benefits, perks, and anything else aimed at motivating agents to take a job at your contact center and stay

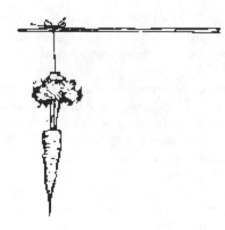

there. The idea behind these incentives is to keep agents on a track of continuous improvement and to reward them for succeeding.

So often we think that the only perks people want are more pay and then some bonus money on top of that. But that's not true. Many contact center employees are motivated to attain additional skills and knowledge so that they can look forward to the prospect of promotion or job enhancement.

We've seen a lot of studies, and they all have different results as to which incentives are most important to agents. Here, without ranking, are the most frequently cited incentives:

- Opportunities for promotion
- Additional training
- Recognition for hard work
- Better pay
- Better work environment and working conditions
- Job security
- Bonus/commission
- Employer contribution to retirement plan

TIP!
Whenever you roll out a new incentive program or contest, hold a kickoff meeting to introduce the idea to agents. The meeting doesn't have to be (and probably shouldn't be) long or involved, but it does provide a formal start to the initiative, which tends to give it more credibility with agents and can help increase their enthusiasm and buy-in.

Following are some general guidelines to keep in mind when you're creating new incentive programs or overhauling existing ones.

Make Sure the Goals Are Achievable

Most incentive programs revolve around some goal associated with productivity or quality. In order for a program to be a success, it's essential for the goal to be within reach of the agents. In Chapter 11 you'll learn four specific guidelines for identifying effective and obtainable goals. Be sure to apply these when creating incentives.

Set the bar high but not impossibly high. Remember, you *want* people to win. If the goals are set too high, people will lose heart and stop trying. What's worse, they'll feel like failures when in fact they may have made great progress from where they started.

Let People Choose Their Own Incentives

The easiest way to make sure your agents will like the perks and rewards given to them is to ask them beforehand what they want. You can include a question on an employee satisfaction survey (like that in Chapter 1) or find some other way to get agents to identify what rewards would be most meaningful to them. Chances are you'll get a variety of responses. Keep track of who wants what, and, when it's time, reward them accordingly.

Make It Enjoyable

To really get agents rallied around a goal, you have to do more than just give them a goal and then say, "OK, go out and reach it." It's equally important for the process of reaching the goal to be fulfilling for agents. This doesn't necessarily mean that at every moment the environment has to be jovial, but agents should at least feel that they're enjoying the challenge.

One way to accomplish this is to celebrate small successes along the way (more on that later in this chapter). Another is to continually remind agents of the progress they're making, the learning they're accomplishing, the professional or personal growth they're achieving, and so on. It's also important to let them know how the incentive affects them personally.

Use Incentives at Crucial Times

Incentives can be used anytime, but there are certain situations in which an incentive program is especially timely. Following are a few examples:

- At the end of training, offer incentives to agents to start using their newly acquired skills.
- When a major change occurs, use an incentive program to encourage agents to embrace the change and to make a smooth transition.
- When morale is low, try an incentive program to inject some renewed energy and enthusiasm into the team.
- At the launch of a new product or project, incentives can help rally the team.

TIP!

Why wait? On an agent's first day of work, do something that says, "Welcome to the team." Flowers, merchandise with the company logo, or cards from other agents can help considerably in getting a new agent off to a great start.

Avoid Overkill

Can you do too much? Yes, overkill is possible. Don't feel that you have to have an incentive program (or a contest) running at every hour of every day. You'll be exhausted and your agents will be too. People can't work at their peak at all times.

REWARDS

Following are some tips and caveats to help you consistently and successfully reward your agents.

Don't Rely on Rewards to Do Your Coaching for You

Tangible rewards are a great way to positively reinforce agents for their efforts, but you shouldn't rely on them to do your coaching for you. Rewards should be offered from time to time, but consistent and regular feedback on performance (in the form of praising and correcting) is indispensable. You'll learn more about how to do this in Chapter 9.

Don't Reward People for Doing What's Expected

Don't reward people simply for meeting the standards of the job. For example, if agents are required to be at work at 7:30 A.M. and only some show up at that time, you might be tempted to think that you can change the behavior of the latecomers by rewarding those who are on time. Maybe, but it's a dangerous gamble. Those who show up on time will likely be embarrassed and those who are late will eventually learn that the only drawback to being late is that they don't get a reward. Better to correct the undesirable behavior with effective feedback.

Don't Be Cheap

If people work very hard toward some company-mandated goal and are then given a ballpoint pen, they might feel less than thanked. Rewarding is not only about giving some tangible award; it's also about honoring people and treating them with dignity. Don't let cheap rewards devalue the effort of agents.

Reward More than Just Performance

Rewards don't necessarily have to be related to performance. They can also be given to agents as positive reinforcement for their behavior or for particular actions or ideas that they initiate.

Avoid Extravagance

Just as rewards can be too cheap, they can also be too expensive, flashy, or otherwise extravagant. Although it's always nice to receive big rewards, there's a danger of sending the wrong message. Agents may come to resent the fact that the organization is "wasting" big bucks on flashy rewards when they're working day in and day out for relatively low pay.

Make Sure It's Meaningful to the Recipient

Think about how people feel when, after working hard to reach a particular goal, they're given a reward that they can't enjoy—for example, tickets to a basketball game for someone who has zero interest in sports, or dinner for two at a steak house for a vegetarian. The repercussions of this kind of oversight can be even worse than giving no reward, because the agent recognizes that in your attempt to show how valuable he or she is to the organization, you've actually shown that you don't know or understand him or her at all.

Be Creative

Don't always give the same reward to agents. You'll likely have better results if you use a variety of rewards over time. If possible, make some logical or thematic tie between the reward and the performance you're reinforcing. Here's one example from a sales team:

> The manager encourages agents to land "big fish" (large, lucrative accounts): every time an agent lands a big fish or contributes in a big way to landing or keeping one, the agent gets to go fishing. There's a fishing pole and a few plastic squeaky fish with gift certificates attached. The agent who gets to go fishing uses the pole to snag a fish—and its accompanying reward—while everyone watches and applauds.

Keep It Fair

Be sure your rewards are commensurate with the efforts made by agents to achieve them. In other words, don't give out gold watches to agents for having a good sales day and don't give out movie tickets to someone whose productivity doubled during the last quarter.

Rewards should also be equitable with what other agents are getting for similar work and what their counterparts at other contact centers are getting for the same level of effort.

The Problem with Employee-of-the-Month Programs

These initiatives are well-intentioned, but if your center is one of the thousands of workplaces that honors an employee of the month, it might be time to reconsider. Here's why:

- If you're forced to choose someone new each month, eventually everyone will be chosen. And if everyone receives the award at some point, then it becomes a sort of revolving gimmick rather than a meaningful award.

- If you're not forced to choose someone new each month, it's likely that the same employees will receive the award time and again. This can cause resentment among the other employees, eventually leading to divisions in the team.

TIP!

If your center receives a letter from a customer acknowledging someone's good work, make a copy for the agent to keep. Put the letter up for everyone to see.
.

Reward Employees Who Complain

We promise, this is a great idea! Agents who inform you of what's *not* working in your organization are giving you valuable information about how you can improve workplace conditions, service levels, and other important aspects of your center. We do suggest, however, that you teach agents how to complain in a constructive, solution-oriented way.

Reward Agents for Companywide Successes

If the company wins an award or is favorably cited in a magazine, for example, let the kudos trickle down to the frontline staff.

Involve Management

Involving top management in your reward initiatives gives agents a chance to see that they're being noticed and, hopefully, valued by the company brass. You might invite an executive to come to the kickoff of a contest or campaign and then make another appearance at the completion, but ideally they'll do more than just that. Ask senior-level managers to check in with agents on a regular basis to give them encouragement and support.

Time Off?

Should you reward your agents with time off? That depends. It works in some environments, but, unless it's time off with pay, you might not be doing agents a favor. For those who are paid an hourly wage, for example, time off translates into less pay. Not much of a reward!

TIP!

Never underestimate the power of food. Pizza, ice cream, cappuccino, sandwiches, and other treats can be a simple and relatively inexpensive reward or mid-contest motivator. It's edible, it provides a break from the everyday routine, and the company is paying for it. Hey, it works!

CONTESTS

Contests can be a powerful energizer in the contact center. They give agents a break from the everyday routine, they rally them around a common goal, and they introduce some (hopefully) good-natured competition to jump-start productivity.

Following are some guidelines for running contests in your center.

Make Them Relevant

Make sure contests are appreciated and embraced by your agents. No amount of cheerleading on your part will get the agents to do something they just don't like or can't relate to. An irrelevant contest will also send the message that you and upper management aren't really in touch with the agents and the daily operations of the center.

Keep It Simple

If agents have to work too hard just to understand a contest, they'll most likely lose at least some of their willingness to embrace it. Keep the contest as simple and clear as you can.

Vary the Length

Make some contests long and others short. For example, you might hold contests here and there that last only a day, and then twice a year or so hold one that lasts two months. Shorter contests allow for immediate gratification, while longer contests give agents the chance to work toward a particular goal over time and to learn the value of patiently plugging away.

Make It Visual

Create some visual reminder—for example, a large thermometer drawn on a poster board or a person climbing a mountain—for the group members to see as they work toward their goals. The team's progress can be tracked by this graphic.

Designate a Theme

Like parties, contests tend to be more successful when everyone shows up knowing the theme. A theme provides a fun diversion from the everyday and helps agents to remain aware that they're in the midst of a contest.

There are, however, some important caveats when it comes to designating the theme. Be careful to avoid anything that might be offensive to a team member. Stay away from religious, political, or cultural themes and anything with an overly specific appeal. It's better to stay with broad themes such as eras or classic movies (keeping in mind that to some agents this means *Casablanca* while to others it means *Return of the Jedi*).

By the way, we suggest that you vary the themes of your contest. To stay motivated, people need change, freshness, and new inspiration. You probably manage a diverse group of agents, so it's a good idea to use a variety of rewards, incentives, and contests.

TIP!

Visit a party goods store for props or even to get ideas for a contest theme. These places tend to have aisles and aisles of fun, inexpensive novelties.   🔆

Avoid Overzealous Competition

Be careful not to allow the atmosphere to get too competitive. Some good-natured rivalry is OK, but if it becomes excessive, it will detract from the sense of teamwork and may create strife and acrimony among agents. At the same time, don't pretend that your agents don't have at least some measure of pride and competitiveness. It's good for people to want to win. The key is to create a balance so that the contest works for the whole group rather than just for a few key people (who, by the way, may have been winning things all their lives).

Another way to make sure your contests don't create havoc for the team is to keep them positive. In other words, avoid activities in which agents "eliminate" each other.

Reward Progress Along the Way

For incentive programs or contests that are long, celebrate significant milestones along the way.

Adjust as Necessary

If you're running a contest or campaign for the first time and once it's under way you notice that it needs tweaking, then tweak it. Changing the game in midcourse may elicit some groans from the team, but it's far better than allowing the project to fail. When you roll out a new contest, make it clear to agents that you reserve the right to adjust the rules as necessary along the way.

Make the Rules and Expectations Clear

For contests to be successful, they must be set up correctly. Among other things, this means making the rules and expectations clear from the beginning. Once you've kicked off the contest, post the guidelines in a place where agents can easily refer to them.

Keep up the Momentum

While your team is in the middle of a contest, you'll likely have to be the cheerleader. Unless you have some highly inspired supervisors or team leaders to do this, it will probably be up to you to keep up the momentum.

TIP!

If you don't have the time to thoughtfully and enthusiastically run a contest, wait until later, when you do have the time. If the contest is not given enough attention by you, it will likely be given even less attention by your team.

TIP!

For smaller contests, give out prizes that not only reward agents but also advertise your company and promote company spirit. Your company logo can be put onto t-shirts, mugs, hats, key chains, backpacks, notebooks, and any number of other items.

Cash or No Cash?

There's a lot of debate about whether or not it's a good idea to offer cash as an incentive to employees. It's certainly a universally accepted and appreciated reward, and it can work as a motivator. But it's not necessarily the best choice. Among other things, it can have the effect of devaluing other rewards. ("Susie got 100 bucks and all I got was this paperweight?") Here's what we recommend: if your center gives yearly bonuses to agents, let this be the one cash reward that they receive. Apart from that, turn the cash into some other tangible reward that will be appreciated by the recipient.

IDEAS TO GET YOU STARTED

On the following pages, you'll find several ideas for simple incentives, rewards, and contests. They can give you a place to start, and then, over time, you can develop some programs that will be custom-fit for your center.

IDEA 1: Put It in Writing

For exceptional achievements or milestones, write a personal letter of acknowledgment. It will be lasting documentation that the agent can use in the near and distant future. Following are a few tips for making this a meaningful and lasting incentive:

- Keep it brief.
- Put it on company letterhead.
- Say what, specifically, the agent did to warrant the acknowledgment.
- Tell why the agent's achievement made an impact (on the organization, on customers, on the team's morale, etc.).
- Offer congratulations and thanks for a job well done.
- Each time you write one of these letters, make it a little different. If you use a form letter, it will lose meaning.
- Specify at the bottom of the letter that you are sending a carbon copy to a senior-level manager—and then do it. It will thrill the agent and add prestige to the letter.
- Give the original to the agent and keep a copy in his or her personnel file.

IDEA 2: Visualize the Goal

Encourage agents to identify two or three items that they're working and saving toward—for example, a new couch, a trip to Yosemite, a new outfit, dinner out with the family. Encourage them to put written or visual reminders (such as pictures cut out of magazines) at their workstation.

IDEA 3: Happy Birthday

Give people their birthday (or any day within one week before or after) off work with pay. It honors agents on a special day and encourages them to do something nice for themselves.

IDEA 4: Random Rewards

Put the names of some rewards on pieces of paper and tape them under agents' chairs or in various other places on the call floor. At some point in the day, tell agents verbally or via e-mail to look under their chairs. They can then come to you to claim their rewards.

IDEA 5: Bring in a Big Shot

If it's feasible, consider inviting a local celebrity or expert to participate in a contest or campaign. The person might come to the kickoff session, send a videotaped message of support, and/or give out the awards. You might be surprised at how receptive some people will be to your invitation—it's good PR for them! Some examples of people to invite are: an athlete from a local sports team, a newscaster or weather reporter, a well-known chef, an admired politician, and so on.

IDEA 6: Greetings from Cyberspace

Go to a Web site that provides online greetings and send employees an e-card thanking them for their work. It will be a nice and different surprise—there are thousands of choices, and you can choose to include music and add a personal message. What's more, it's free!

IDEA 7: Grid Luck

Before the shift, draw a large grid on a white board or flip chart. There should be as many squares as there are agents (if your team is small, allow two squares per agent). Do not assign names to squares—agents will do this themselves during the game. Make an identical but smaller grid on a piece of paper and keep this one to yourself. Select a few prizes and write the name of each prize in a separate square. For example, if you have 16 agents (and therefore 16 squares), you might select four prizes and assign them to four random squares.

Designate a goal that you're sure everyone will reach at some point during the shift. When agents reach the goal, they can come up to the grid and write their names in whatever square they want. This continues until all agents have put their names in a square. Toward the end of the shift, match the prizes to the agents whose names appear in the corresponding squares and give the prizes out.

IDEA 8: Wanted: Customer-Pleasing Ideas

Hold a contest to see what ideas agents can come up with for pleasing customers beyond their expectations. Then put the best ones into practice. You can hold this contest on a regular basis: the ideas will just keep getting better and better.

IDEA 9: Get in the Act

This one is only for the adventurous of heart, but it's unsurpassed for its potential to make agents squeal with delight. Tell agents that when they reach a particular goal, you'll dance for three minutes to a song of their choosing. The catch is, you actually have to do it once they've reached the goal!

Alternatively, you can solicit suggestions from your group for something else you'll do if they meet their objectives. Designate appropriate guidelines (such as that it must be safe, good-natured, respectful, etc.). You can reserve the right to throw out any suggestions that you feel cross the line. Make sure that all are appropriate and that you're actually willing to do them—for example, you might not be willing to shave your head, but maybe you would dance to a hip-hop song for three minutes in front of your agents.

IDEA 10: Caught in the Act

This is a great way to reward the small everyday things that you want agents to do. Keep an instant camera on hand and try to sneak up on agents when they're doing the right thing. Take a picture and keep it on the bulletin board under a caption that says "Caught in the act of . . ." You can take pictures of agents smiling on the phones, using their job aids, correctly using ergonomic changes you've implemented, and so on. For the kickoff or completion of a specific campaign or project, you can turn the photos into a slideshow and play it along with some upbeat music.

IDEA 11: Encourage Tattling

Reward agents for reporting other agents doing something well.

IDEA 12: Pass It Along

Send a letter to the agent's closest family member (such as a spouse or parent) or significant other.

Write a nice letter praising the agent for working hard, meeting goals, and so on, and then seal it and address it to the appropriate person. Then give it to the agent and tell him or her to take the unopened letter home and have the family member or friend read it. This allows the agent to be appreciated by someone near and dear to him or her and to brag without bragging!

ADDITIONAL RESOURCES

Books

Blanchard, Ken, and Nelson, Bob. *1001 Ways to Reward Employees*. New York: Workman Publishing Company, 1994.

Hensath, David, Mcquillen, Dan, and Yerkes, Leslie. *301 Ways to Have Fun at Work*. San Francisco: Berrett-Koehler, 1997.

McCoy, Thomas. *Compensation and Motivation*. New York: Amacom, 1992.

Schier, T.J. *Send Flowers to the Living! Rewards, Contests and Incentives to Build Employee Loyalty,* Fort Worth, TX: Incentive Solutions, 2002.

Companies

Awards.com (offers different types of awards). URL: www.awards.com; phone: 800-429-2737.

Best Impressions (offers promotional products). URL: www.bestimpressions.com; phone: 800-635-2378.

Bravanta (Web-based enterprise incentive and recognition solutions). URL: www.bravanta.com; phone: 888-560-1999.

CultureWorx (provides software that allows you to design incentive programs). URL: www.cultureworx.com; phone: 847-318-9170.

Incentive Systems (helps you design and manage incentive programs). URL: www.incentivesystems.com; phone: 781-685-0100.

Lands' End Business Outfitters (products and screen printing available). URL: www.landsend.com; phone: 800-338-2000.

SalesDriver (sales force incentive programs). URL: www.salesdriver.com; phone: 877-213-7483.

Successories (motivational gifts and rewards). URL: www.successories.com; phone: 800-535-2773.

Associations, Magazines, and Interesting Web Sites

National Association for Employee Recognition (dedicated to the enhancement of employee performance through recognition). URL: www.recognition.org; phone: 630-369-7783.

CHAPTER 5

Keeping the Peace

How, When, and Why to Manage Employees' Stress

Contact center employees may be particularly vulnerable to stress because of the often frenzied pace of work, the constant demands of both external and internal customers, and countless other factors that are all too often beyond the employees' control. Most people can work at a frenzied pace for short periods of time, but if this pace becomes the status quo it will inevitably lead to employee burnout and increased turnover.

Following are some common causes of acute and chronic stress in contact centers. No doubt some of them will be familiar to you.

- Little or no control over working conditions
- Repetitive tasks, monotony
- Upset or otherwise difficult customers
- Lack of the necessary tools, information, or resources to do the job
- Unsatisfactory leadership/management
- Difficult coworkers
- Nonworking or poorly performing equipment

> "On an average work day, about one million employees are absent because of stress-related problems. Job stress costs American businesses more than $200 billion dollars a year in absenteeism, worker compensation claims, health insurance costs, and lowered productivity. Forty percent of employee turnover is stress related."
>
> —Robert Epstein, *The Big Book of Stress-Relief Activities*, McGraw-Hill, 2000.

- Pressure to move quickly through calls or electronic contacts
- Not knowing what's expected
- Too many calls or e-mail messages from customers
- Not enough work (yes, this can cause stress!)
- Job insecurity
- Noise level
- Being treated like a juvenile (for example, having to ask to use the restroom)

While some amount of stress in your employees' work environment may be inevitable, that doesn't mean you can't or shouldn't attempt to reduce it. According to the American Institute of Stress, 43 percent of all Americans suffer from stress-related health problems. That's nearly half the population!

But physical problems are only the beginning of the stress-induced conditions that can adversely affect the health of your employees and your organization. Helping your employees manage their stress goes beyond altruism. There are plenty of strong business reasons to do it as well.

By helping your employees to effectively and consistently manage their stress, you'll also:

- Reduce turnover
- Decrease absenteeism
- Improve call quality
- Achieve higher productivity
- Increase call efficiency
- Show your employees that you care about their well-being
- Show respect for your employees and for the job that they do
- Increase employee satisfaction and loyalty
- Reduce Workers' Compensation claims
- Stabilize health insurance costs
- Improve morale

And here's some further motivation for you to embark on a stress-relief campaign in your contact center: it's simple, it doesn't cost much, and it offers immediate results.

According to the Centers for Disease Control and Prevention, 80 percent of health care dollars are spent on stress-related disorders. Ailments include hypertension, migraines, ulcers, allergies, cancer, cardio-vascular disease, and a variety of other conditions. Additionally, chronic stress impedes the immune system, making the body more susceptible to common diseases such as colds and flu.

HEALTHY VERSUS UNHEALTHY STRESS

Believe it or not, some stress is "good stress." Often referred to as *eustress* (in contrast to its not-so-healthy counterpart, *distress*), good stress has an invigorating, motivating effect on people. It's what helps us meet our deadlines, inspires quick or creative thinking, and pushes us to try a little harder. So, to some extent, we all need a little stress in our lives. After all, how many of us really do our best work in the absence of stress?

Here's some more good news:

- Researchers find that deadlines, public speaking, and other stressful challenges can—when they are met and conquered—trigger the production of immunoglobins, a type of protein that strengthens the immune system. (Source: Janice M. Horowitz, "Your Health," *Time,* November 12, 2001)
- The Yerkes-Dodson principle explains that certain levels of stress-related hormones actually improve mental processing skills and physical performance.
- Steven Berglas, author of *Reclaiming the Fire: How Successful People Overcome Burnout* (Random House, 2001), found that eustress is critical for physical and mental health. The thrill of a challenge keeps a person invigorated, focused, and determined to accomplish the task at hand.

So the trick for contact center employees is to learn to optimize their stress and to turn potential stressors into stimulating, positive challenges. As a manager, there's a lot you can do to facilitate this. The first step is to recognize the warning signs of stress.

GET TO KNOW THEIR STRESS

All workplaces are at least somewhat stressful for employees, and, as we've already pointed out, some of that stress is beneficial.

Observe how your employees respond to the more stressful calls or situations at work. Try to catch them at particularly difficult moments and watch what happens. Do they strive or do they thrive?

The next step is to involve your employees in their own stress checks. Use the Get to Know Your Stress worksheet (a reproducible version can be found in the appendix). We recommend that you make copies for all employees and ask them to use it on a regular basis.

Get to Know Your Stress

Observe how you respond to the more stressful calls or situations at work. Try to catch yourself at particularly difficult moments and conduct a mental scan of your body and psyche. Notice your breathing, your body language, your thought process, and your visceral responses.

Following are some common but often unnoticed reactions to stress:

- Headache
- Stiff neck, shoulders, or back
- Tight jaw
- Furrowed brow
- Clenched teeth
- Nervous stomach
- Faster heartbeat
- Cool skin
- Cold hands or feet
- Irritability
- Fuzzy thinking
- Forgetfulness
- Emotional sensitivity
- Negative thoughts

What do you notice about your own reactions to stressful situations?

_____

_____

_____

_____

_____

_____

TIP!
Although customer contact is the heart of what your agents do, it might be wise to limit their phone time. For example, agents could be on the phone for six hours of an eight-hour shift. They could spend the other two hours completing other tasks such as paperwork, training, and so on.

According to social psychologists Christina Maslach and Michael Leiter, authors of *The Truth About Burnout* (Jossey-Bass, 1997), employee stress and its resulting inefficiency is attributable to six factors:

1. Too much work for the time allotted to do it
2. Lack of control over various aspects of the job
3. Insufficient or unsatisfactory rewards
4. Little or no sense of community in the workplace
5. Lack of trust, openness, and respect
6. Conflict between personal values and those of the organization

As a manager, you can help to control most, if not all, of these factors for your employees. Even if you don't feel there's much you can do to change the overall organizational attitude and policies, there's a lot you can do for your own department. Read the list again and make notes about what measures you can take on behalf of your own employees.

Richard Hagberg, an organizational psychologist, suggests that one way to manage stress is to remind employees how their work contributes to a shared goal or long-term vision. "When people clearly see what they're striving for and how what they're doing today relates to that, they can live with a much higher level of stress for a longer period of time. When they feel they're on a mission, their ability to cope with stress increases," says Hagberg.

TEN EFFECTIVE STRESS-RELIEF ACTIVITIES

In order to get the highest productivity and satisfaction from your employees, you need to help each one develop a stress-relief routine that works. All the suggestions outlined in this section can be effective in immediately reducing people's stress levels and helping them to keep a healthy perspective. These are quick, simple measures your employees (or you) can take whenever they feel their stress levels escalating.

Copy the reproducible version of the list from the appendix, share it with your employees, and encourage them to try out the various techniques to see what works best for them. Then make sure they use these techniques! Again and again and again.

1: Take a Walk
Refresh your mind and senses by taking a quick walk outside the building. Even if the sun is not out, the fresh air and change of atmosphere will do you good. It only takes a few minutes of exercise to reduce the level of stress hormones in the bloodstream.

2: Look out the Window
If going outside isn't feasible, go to a window for a minute or two. A study conducted by Volker Hartkopf of Carnegie Mellon University found that people who sit near a window have 23 percent fewer complaints of stress-related illnesses such as headache, back pain, and exhaustion. Even if you can't sit there permanently, an occasional walk to the window will help to expand your perspective from the small source of stress to the big picture.

3: Stand Up and Stretch
Physical exercise, even only a little bit, has been shown to help alleviate the symptoms of stress. After a difficult interaction with a customer, or some other trigger of stress, stand up and move your legs, arms, head, and back. You might also keep a stress ball or similar toy on hand to use in stressful situations. (To help chronic stress, include some kind of physical exercise in your daily routine.)

4: Breathe Deeply
There's a reason entire volumes of text have been written about the simple act of breathing—something we all do naturally and spontaneously. The fact is, the act of breathing has enormous potential to calm the nerves and quiet the mind. When you feel stressed, take a few moments to focus your awareness on your breathing. Then breathe deeply and fully, pushing the air down into your abdomen. Repeat this several times before returning to your tasks.

5: Remind Yourself of Your Wins
One of the nasty characteristics of stress is that it tends to orient your thoughts almost obsessively toward the cause of your stress or toward some other negative experience. To counter this, take a few moments to recall some recent personal achievements. Even small "wins," such as "I handled that difficult customer really well this morning," can help put you in a more positive frame of mind.

6: Laugh!
Nothing unties the knots of stress like a good laugh. Muscle tension subsides for up to 45 minutes after a good laugh. Keep some humorous books, pictures, or

articles at your workstation and spend a few minutes enjoying them when your stress level peaks. Pretend you are your favorite comedian and view the world through his or her eyes. Mostly, look for the humor around you and practice laughing at life's contradictions, at exaggerated situations, and at your own behavior and thoughts. Laughter is powerful medicine and it's free.

7: Go Within

One effective way to alleviate stress is to remove yourself mentally and emotionally from the stressful situation. When you feel your stress escalating, take a few minutes to observe a spiritual practice that will focus your attention on what inspires and motivates you, rather than on the source of your stress. Meditation, reciting aphorisms or affirmations, and reading spiritual writings are all quick, effective stress reducers.

8: Switch Mental Gears

If you find it difficult to calm your mind, at least try applying your mental energy to nonstressful tasks. Fill in a few lines of a crossword puzzle or pull out a book of brainteasers. After a few minutes, you'll be ready to return your attention to your work with renewed determination.

9: Pretend You're Traveling in First Class

One favorite stress-relief practice that's as simple as it is effective is the hot towel trick. Keep a clean washcloth in your workstation. When it's time to take a break from a tension-producing situation (stressful calls, for example), soak the towel in water that's as hot as you can stand it. Then use the towel on your hands, face, and neck. Instant gratification!

10: Resign as General Manager of the Universe

Stress is often attributed to our efforts to control situations or circumstances that are beyond our reach. Sometimes the best way to let go of stress is to let go of your need for a particular outcome or result. Be conscious of the responsibilities you accept and the limitations built into those responsibilities. Focus on the things you can affect and manage those that are not completely within your control. Accept the reality that life is a team sport. Realistic expectations about how much you can control the behavior of others may help your approach to a project and your stress about the outcome. It can be very liberating to realize that you're just fine even though things didn't go your way.

TIP!

Create a colorful poster of these 10 stress-relief activities and post it where the agents will see it when they most need to—while communicating with customers!

LOVE YOUR PROBLEMS

One sure way to beat stress in an organization is to take a proactive approach to solving problems both big and small. When workplace problems are ignored, they tend to fester and expand. This often causes unnecessary stress and has a damaging effect on morale. As a manager, do your best to create a culture in which problems are embraced as opportunities for personal and organizational growth. This approach will generate eustress that can be applied to solving problems and will decrease the distress that occurs when problems are handled poorly or not at all.

For help identifying and prioritizing the problems your employees face on the job, try out the following activity. It can be incorporated into a training session or done as part of a staff meeting or other group session.

ACTIVITY: The Problem Tree*

In a Nutshell

In this game, participants work together to identify and prioritize the challenges they face on the job. It's a useful game for airing grievances and for identifying the problems faced by your employees.

Time
15 minutes

*Reproduced with permission from *The Big Book of Customer Service Training Games* (Peggy Carlaw and Vasudha K. Deming, McGraw-Hill, 1999).

What You'll Need
Draw a large tree on a flip chart or white board. Using colored construction paper, cut out several red apples, yellow pears, and orange oranges. (Each "fruit" should be about three inches in diameter.) You'll also need masking tape.

What to Do
Divide participants into groups of three or four and give each group a few of each fruit. Ask them to discuss the various challenges they face as customer service employees and to select three challenges. They should then choose a fruit on which to describe each challenge. Apples are for critical challenges, oranges are for significant challenges, and pears are for minor challenges. They can use whatever fruit they want, but they cannot describe more than three challenges. Give participants about five minutes to do this. Then have them tape the fruits on the tree.

Next, read the challenges out loud and use a blank piece of flip chart paper to list the challenges in order of priority (apples first, then oranges, then pears). If one challenge has been given different priorities, list it under the more critical ranking. Ask the participants if the list accurately reflects their view of how the department's challenges should be prioritized.

Note: The objective of this game is to identify challenges; the next step is to put together a plan for overcoming them. Be sure to let participants know how you plan to address the problems they've identified. Let's look at two ways to follow up this activity.

Put people into small groups and divide the challenges equally among the groups. Ask each group to brainstorm solutions for several minutes and then have the small groups share with the big group. Alternatively, post flip charts of five or so of the biggest challenges on the wall. Divide participants into several groups and assign one group to each flip chart. Give them three minutes to brainstorm solutions, then rotate them to the next flip chart. Give them two minutes to brainstorm solutions to this challenge, then rotate them to the next flip chart. In the third and final round, give them one minute to brainstorm solutions. Debrief the activity with the whole group.

TIP!

Seven Tips for Staying One Step Ahead of Stress
Following are some ideas—ranging from the serious to the wacky—to help you and your team stay vigilant about stress levels. Never underestimate the power of simple ideas!

Tip 1: Create a stress-relief bulletin board in the work area. Post ideas, activities, appropriate jokes, comics, and so on, there. Update it often. You might also consider keeping a few stress-relief "toys" there, such as stress balls (soft balls that can be squeezed) or wooden massage rollers.

Tip 2:   Buy a mood ring to be shared by your work group. When you notice an employee exhibiting signs of acute stress, tell him or her to put the ring on and to wear it until it turns color to signify a state of calm. It might not be scientific, but it's fun and lighthearted—just what stressed-out workers need.

Tip 3:   Purchase a stress card for each employee. (These are credit card–size tools that gauge a person's physiological response to stress by taking a temperature reading of the thumb.) Encourage employees to consult the cards often to see whether or not they're remaining calm in the face of stress.

Tip 4:   Keep a stock of individually wrapped towelettes on hand. Every so often, circulate the call floor and hand out the towelettes so agents can use them to refresh their face, neck, and hands. If you're *really* motivated, you can write encouraging messages on the packets. Here are a couple of suggestions:

- Hang in there!

- You're doing great!

- Good job! Wipe away the stress of the day.

Tip 5:   Get a few pieces of colored poster board and use a thick black marker to write short, simple stress-relief reminders (you might even include a hand-drawn graphic). When you notice the call floor is particularly frenzied, grab a board and walk around until everyone gets the message. You might even try a sandwich board—the agents will love it! Following are a few suggestions for what to write

- BREATHE!!

- SMILE!!

- Grace under pressure!

- Don't let a bad call become a bad day!

- You people are great!

- Stretch and de-stress!

Tip 6:   Hire a massage therapist once a month (or once a quarter) to come into your workplace to give 10-minute neck and head massages.

Tip 7:   Get employees actively involved in their own stress-maintenance program by regularly asking them to suggest new stress-reduction activities. You might try holding a monthly contest for the best stress-reduction idea and then follow through on the suggestion.

CUBICLE EXERCISES

Following are some simple but effective exercises agents can do without leaving their workstations. (A reproducible form outlining these exercises can be found in the appendix.)

Searching the Horizon

When people use their computers for long periods of time, their eye muscles get tired and strained. It's important to allow these muscles to relax by letting the eyes move around and focus on distant objects. Often, the eyes also need to be lubricated. This exercise is designed to relax the eye muscles and lubricate the eyes.

Directions

Close your eyes and relax for five seconds.

With your eyes closed, roll your eyes to the left and then to the right. Hold each position for three seconds.

Open your eyes. Without moving your head, move your eyes as far to the left as possible and select an object on the horizon.

Slowly move your eyes from that point on the horizon to the end of your nose.

Repeat on the right side and straight ahead.

Relax, look around the room, and blink a lot.

Repeat the complete exercise three times.

Chin Up, Chin Down

Agents often inadvertently point at the monitor with their chin as they strain to read or enter information, putting a lot of stress on the vertebrae and neck muscles. This exercise will reposition the neck and help to find a neutral position for the head. It will also relax the upper shoulders and neck muscles.

Directions

Close your eyes and drop your chin to your chest. Hold for 10 seconds.

Gently rotate your head to your left shoulder. Hold for five seconds.

Gently rotate your head and let it gently fall back. Hold for five seconds.

Gently rotate your head to your right shoulder. Hold for five seconds.

Gently let your head drop to your chest again.

Repeat the exercise in the other direction.

With your eyes closed, bring your head to the upright position. Relax in that position for five seconds. Open your eyes.

Dancing Fingers

Typing requires a lot of motion within a limited range. Most of the typist's hand and wrist muscles are fixed in place while the fingers race across the keyboard. This exercise allows the hands and wrists to relax and stretch into other positions. It can be done while standing or sitting.

Directions

Hang your arms down by your side and relax.

Shake your arms and let your wrists and fingers flop around. Do this for five seconds.

Bring your hands together and press your fingers and palms together. Place a moderate amount of pressure on your fingers and hold for five seconds. Separate your hands and relax.

Make a fist with each hand and squeeze. Hold for three seconds.

Repeat the complete exercise.

Under-the-Desk Leg Stretch

This exercise helps stimulate blood flow to the lower limbs and also stretches the hamstrings. When a person sits for long periods of time, blood circulation to the legs is reduced and the legs may feel tired or even cramped. In addition, tight hamstrings may cause lower back pain.

Directions

Sit upright in your chair with your feet flat on the floor.

Extend your left leg so that it is straight and your toes are pointing straight up.

Lift your foot up and touch the underside of the desk. Hold for five seconds.

Bring your foot back to the floor and relax for two seconds.

Repeat with your right leg.

Repeat the complete exercise three times.

Sit back in your chair with a straight back, feet flat on the floor, and relax.

Half Moon

People who sit at a computer for extended periods often neglect to move their chest muscles and upper back muscles. This exercise is designed to stretch out the chest and back muscles and help maintain good posture. It can be done sitting or standing.

Directions

Let your arms hang freely by your sides.

Keep your arms straight and lift them slowly over your head.

Clasp your hands and push up as high as you comfortably can.

Inhale as you bend your torso to the right. Hold for three seconds.

Exhale as you return to the center. Hold for three seconds.

Inhale as you bend your torso to the left. Hold for three seconds.

Return to the center and bring your arms down.

Repeat the exercise.

Hula Hips

This exercise will stretch out tight muscles in the hips and buttocks and will increase blood flow.

Directions

Stand a few feet back from your desk with your feet slightly apart and pointed straight ahead and your knees bent.

Put your hands on your hips, extend your hips forward, and rotate to the left. Hold for three seconds.

Rotate your hips back and hold for three seconds.

Rotate your hips to the right and hold for three seconds.

Rotate your hips forward and hold for three seconds.

Repeat the exercise in the other direction.

Repeat the complete exercise twice.

TALK ABOUT IT!

To show you're serious about creating a low-stress working environment for your employees, make stress an ongoing topic of discussion. If the subject is regularly addressed, employees will see it as part of the overall vision of your department or organization, not just a momentary trend. Following are some ideas for keeping the topic alive:

- When reviewing performance and setting future goals, ask each employee what he or she is doing to deal with work-related stress.

- When introducing change, address what, if any, additional stress the change will cause for employees. Make a plan for dealing with the stress in an appropriate way.

- When you notice employees handling stress well, be sure to praise their efforts.

- If you notice aggressive communication from an agent, talk to him or her privately and probe for recent stressful circumstances on the job. Show empathy for the agent and then remind him or her of the ramifications of aggressive communication toward other agents or customers. Develop a plan to reduce the aggressive communication and get the agent's commitment to comply.

STRESS-REDUCTION PROGRAMS IN PRACTICE

Following are examples of what some companies and organizations are doing to combat employee stress.

Creative Marketing Specialties in New Jersey urges employees—most of whom spend endless hours on the phone—to exercise during their lunch hours and track what they do. Every three months, the most physically active staffer gets a prize. (Source: Stephanie L. Gruner, "Our Workplace Is Stressful. What Can I Do to Improve Morale?" *Inc. Magazine,* March 1, 1999.)

We've come across a few organizations that encourage a healthy work-life balance by offering grants to employees who seek to reduce stress outside of work by learning a new skill, pursuing a hobby, or just having some fun. Allowable pursuits include cooking classes, horseback riding lessons, yoga retreats, and running club memberships.

At Text 100, employees get two "duvet days" in addition to vacation and sick time. What does that mean? If employees don't feel like getting out of bed, they simply call in, take a "duvet day," and then sink back under the covers with no questions asked. (Source: Stephanie L. Gruner, "Hot Tip: Employee Stress," *Inc. Magazine,* November 1, 1998.)

SAP Campbell Software introduced a "Stress-Free Zone" in its Chicago headquarters. In that area, employees are asked not to talk about work. What they can do is play with toys such as squirt guns and Velcro darts. Noble-Met Ltd. encourages its employees to relieve stress in the break room by playing darts, pool, air hockey, Foosball, or ping-pong. "We've never had a problem with people abusing the privilege," says John Freeland, president of the company.

ADDITIONAL RESOURCES

Books

Allen, David. *Getting Things Done: The Art of Stress-Free Productivity.* New York: Viking Press, 2001.

Coscia, Stephen. *Tele-Stress—Relief for Call Center Stress Syndrome.* Gilroy, CA: CMP Books, 1998.

Loehr, E. James. *Success for Stress: The Proven Program for Transforming Stress into Positive Energy at Work.* New York: Times Books, 1997.

O'Hara, Valerie. *Wellness at Work: Building Resilience to Job Stress.* Oakland, CA: New Harbinger Publications, 1995.

Peterson, Dan. *Manage Employees' Stress.* Huntington, NY: Aloray Publishing, 1990.

Reinhold, B. Barbara. *Toxic Work: How to Overcome Stress, Overload, and Burnout and Revitalize Your Career.* New York: E.P. Dutton, 1996.

Companies

Stress Directions (consulting services and workshop sessions for overly stressed people). URL: www.stressdirections.com.

Stress Less (offers stress-reducing products and services). URL: www.stressless.com; phone: 800-545-3783.

Associations, Magazines, and Interesting Web Sites

American Institute of Stress (a free Web site offering information about stress, a newsletter, and tips and techniques on dealing with stress). URL: www.stress.org; phone: 914-963-1200.

EStress.com (the largest collection of online experts and original articles; from keyboard injuries, carpal tunnel syndrome, and headaches all the way to dealing with telephone stress). URL: www.estress.com; phone: 800-307-8816.

Stress Free Net (provides confidential assistance to individuals and business and occupational groups for whom stress is an important issue). URL: www.stressfree.com.

Case Studies

Call Centres.net (call center workplace stress studies). URL: www.callcentres.net; phone: +61 2 99551966.

2 MANAGING AND COACHING CONTACT CENTER AGENTS

CHAPTER 6

First, Get the Right People

*Hiring Frontline Staff for Your
Contact Center*

THE IMPORTANCE OF HIRING WELL

It's no secret that one of the most difficult aspects of contact center management is finding and keeping the right people for the job. The contact center industry experiences one of the highest turnover rates anywhere—by some estimates, upward of 50 percent. Additional factors such as a tight labor pool of quality candidates and a limited career path compound the already challenging process of hiring. Furthermore, many contact centers are adding multiple contact channels such as e-mail and chat, which only adds to the need for a more skilled workforce.

Regardless of how difficult it is to attract and retain quality agents, however, it's crucial that you take great care in hiring for your center. Hiring agents isn't something that should be done in a rushed or desperate manner.

Hiring well can save you considerable pain down the road. Not only is it expensive to replace employees who have been miscast for a job, but it's also inconvenient and unpleasant to lose agents (whether the termination is your idea or theirs).

Even if you're not the person primarily responsible for recruiting and hiring agents, you are the person primarily responsible for managing those who get hired. For this reason, your knowledge of and participation in the hiring process are indispensable. At the very least,

> "If a person is not performing, it is probably because he or she has been miscast for the job."
>
> —W. Edwards Deming

you should help define the skills and behaviors that drive job performance and participate in the selection process by speaking to prescreened candidates over the phone or in person and by participating in the final hiring decision.

TIP!

Don't be biased against applicants looking for a second job. They're often highly motivated: after all, who seeks out a second job unless they have a strong need to do so?

PREPARING TO HIRE

What do you need to do before candidates walk through the door? Lots! In order to make your hiring process effective, efficient, and fair, it's important for you to put some time and energy into planning a successful strategy. Once you've hit upon a successful formula, however, you can use it again and again for future hiring needs.

Following are seven key questions to ask yourself before you begin talking to candidates for the job. Your answers to these questions will help you to develop a winning hiring strategy.

Seven Key Questions to Ask Yourself Before Hiring

1. Why am I hiring?
2. What positions need to be filled, and what are the skills and characteristics of the ideal candidate?
3. How will I market and network to identify suitable job candidates?
4. How will I screen candidates to identify potential high performers?
5. What assessments will I use to determine high performers?
6. How will I extend offers to top candidates, and what will I say to those candidates I must reject?
7. How will I welcome new employees to the organization and help them to be integrated into the environment?

Attracting Candidates

High-performance staffing is about more than just getting the best people for the job: it's also about providing a great job for those people. It's first and foremost about being a great place to work. Here's why: studies by Manpower indicate that 60 percent of people are attracted to a particular company by word of mouth. Of all the measures you can take to attract quality contact center employees, providing a positive work setting ranks highest.

Smart contact center managers realize that the hiring process involves creating a win-win situation for the potential employee and for the company. Look at the hiring process from the candidates' point of view. They want to know:

- What is special about your company?
- What does your company offer that others do not?
- Why do people like working at your contact center?

Remember that the best candidates will be screening you and your company, just as you're screening them. As such, it's important to understand and to sell the benefits that your company has to offer. Later in this chapter, you'll learn several ways to do this.

The Job Analysis

Once you've defined some of the benefits that your company has to offer, it's time to define what the job is all about so you can find the right person to fill it. Contact center jobs are not all the same. For that reason, a person who might excel as a customer service rep might perform miserably in collections or sales. Since contact center jobs are as different as the people who fill them, it's important to understand the skills and behaviors that are necessary for success in each specific job function. Preparing a job analysis in advance is key to understanding what specific skills and characteristics are important for each job. Without a job analysis, you won't know what you are looking for in an ideal candidate.

Here's an example of how an inbound/outbound contact center corrected productivity and turnover issues by changing its hiring criteria. (Source: FurstPerson, Inc.)

An inbound/outbound contact center was experiencing increased productivity and turnover issues. Despite the use of prescreening tools, phone interviews, job simulations, and a lengthy interview process, candidate quality results were less than expected.

Discouraged by these results, the company conducted an audit of its current selection process and contracted a hiring expert to conduct a job analysis. The job analysis revealed a disconnect between the interview questions asked and the true job competencies and particular behaviors sought.

By modifying the current assessment tools to better match the new job analysis, the company increased productivity by 25 percent, reduced turnover by 69 percent, and reduced training time by 50 percent.

A job analysis includes four key steps:

1. Gather information about the job from current agents, supervisors, and managers.
2. Define an initial list of skills and behaviors that drive job performance.
3. Rate the importance of the skills and behaviors.
4. Select and validate a final list of key skills and behaviors.

A good job analysis should also include a statement of how to effectively identify and assess the desired skills and behaviors in a potential candidate—or a current employee, for that matter. With a good job analysis in hand, you'll find it much easier to identify suitable candidates. Preparing a job analysis can be a lengthy process, but it only needs to be done once and then revised as necessary whenever the job changes. Following is a sample job analysis.

XYZ COMPANY

Sample Contact Center Job Analysis: Customer Service Representative

Purpose and Importance

The purpose of this job analysis is to document the tasks and duties assigned to the position of customer service representative (CSR) and to determine the knowledge, abilities, and skills necessary for successful job performance. This job analysis serves as a guide to help in the employee hiring process and provides criteria for selecting employees who can successfully perform the work described in this analysis.

Step 1: Gather Information from Job Content Experts

Directions: Begin by selecting a team of job content experts who can effectively evaluate the key competencies and tasks of the CSR position. Through a series of questions, interview each job content expert to identify and validate competencies associated with successful job performance. Document the process for future use.

Job content experts included for this analysis:

- Customer service representatives: B. Daly, A. Fitzpatrick
- Floor supervisors: D. Stanton, P. Gupta, S. Palmer
- Quality assurance representative: M. Dewar
- Operations manager: B. Jackson
- HR generalist: C. Cheung

Detail: On January 7, 2002, a meeting was held with the preceding job content experts. The meeting was facilitated by James Hedges, using a prepared list of questions that encouraged thorough and complete discussion of the competencies associated with successful job performance. Mr. Hedges reviewed a detailed list of information about the position and the following list of questions with the job content experts:

Information reviewed:

- Job descriptions
- Sample interviews and surveys
- Customer satisfaction evaluation sheets
- Company and job expectations and guideline sheets
- Policy forms

- Monitoring report criteria forms
- Employee information sheets (used during current selection process)
- Interview summary forms (used during current selection process)

Job Description

Customer service representatives at XYZ Company are responsible for handling customer inquiries and processing sales orders through telephone, fax, and e-mail correspondences in a timely, efficient, and professional manner. To succeed in this position, representatives will be able to demonstrate and practice:

- A customer-focused attitude and willingness to serve customers
- Excellent verbal and vocal skills
- Exceptional listening, questioning, and call control techniques
- Ability to accurately and efficiently process information and tasks
- An understanding of customer needs, company products and services, and general knowledge
- Aptitude to handle challenging telephone call situations
- Ability to recommend and persuade
- Computer and telephone system application skills

List of Job Analysis Questions

- What are the core job duties of the CSR position?
- What percentage of time is spent performing each duty?
- What was the most difficult aspect of learning the job? (Incumbents)
- What do you like most about the job? (Incumbents)
- What do you like least about the job? (Incumbents)
- What technical skill or special knowledge was needed when you first started the position? (Incumbents)
- What technical knowledge or special skills could be learned on the job in a reasonable time? (Incumbents)
- What are some examples of exceptionally good performance in this position? (Supervisors, QA, Ops manager)
- What are some examples of exceptionally bad performance? (Supervisors, QA, Ops manager)
- What are some examples of why people fail or are terminated in this job? (Supervisors, QA, Ops manager)
- What are the specific job activities of the CSR position?
- What are examples of each activity?

- How often are these activities performed?
- How difficult are these activities to perform?
- How important are the representative job activities?
- Was there any information that we missed with regard to the job activities?
- How much of the job was covered by the previously discussed job activities?

Step 2: Identify Key Competencies and Identify Tasks

Directions: Begin by compiling a list of competencies developed by the job content experts in Step 1. Make sure the competencies listed in the position description are current and fully describe the duties of the CSR position. Once the competencies have been verified, identify the associated tasks.

List of Competencies and Tasks

Competency: primary job motivators (most important)	
Definition:	The attitudes, interests, and motivations correlated with job performance. Includes willingness to perform job tasks as well as all likes and dislikes associated with high job performance.
Tasks:	• Willing to perform tasks • Communicates with coworkers in a positive manner • Shows persistence in face of rejection by customers • Likes to talk with people over the phone and via e-mail • Motivated to work toward production rate goals • Accepts sitting and remaining at desk for several hours • Willing to follow policies and procedures • Enjoys work, wants to be on time, and wants to show up for work • Displays integrity • Copes with difficult or irate callers • Deals with repetitiveness
Competency: oral communication	
Definition:	Ability to orally communicate effectively. Includes proper grammar, tone, volume, rate, sentence structure, use of positive language and transitions.
Tasks:	• Speech is clear and understandable • Uses proper enunciation • Tone conveys a positive and helpful attitude • Able to speak articulately • Avoids jargon

Competency: problem solving/decision making

Definition:	Cognitive ability that involves making decisions or solving problems.
Tasks:	• Accurately determine type of customer inquiry • Determine customer's key issue or problem • Use criteria to determine correct response • Apply new product call scripts for new product launches • Apply appropriate status codes for accurate documentation • Determine correct cross-selling technique based on customer needs • Determine when call should be escalated to a supervisor • Determine when to offer customer a credit when resolving issues • Evaluate fallback options in order to save customers from canceling orders

Competency: learning

Definition:	Cognitive ability that involves learning the job, then continuously learning new information and effectively applying that information on the job.
Tasks:	• Learn to use computer, associated CRM applications, and phone system applications • Learn industry and company knowledge, product specifications, and services • Learn how to efficiently process customer orders • Learn scripts for effective cross-selling • Learn customer service skills model • Learn to accurately pronounce difficult words correctly in order to make quality calls • Learn quality criteria to perform better calls • Learn status codes to accurately document calls • Learn sales enhancement skill models

Competency: persuasion

Definition:	Interpersonal ability to influence other people to action or a new line of thinking.
Tasks:	• Question effectively to determine additional opportunities • Listen carefully and confirm needs • Influence customers to consider new opportunity • Maintain control of the call • Respond effectively to overcome objections • Ask for the sale • Close call effectively

Competency: planning and organizing work (least important)

Definition:	Planning and organizing ability that involves sequencing data and developing step-by-step plans to carry out activities.

Tasks:	• Prepare daily callback lists
	• Accurately enter customer codes into computer
	• Accurately enter customer information
	• Monitor call handle times

Step 3: Identify Selection Methods

Directions: Identify the selection methods to be used when evaluating a candidate's skill and ability level against those identified in Step 2. Use multiple selection methods in order to increase overall selection quality. Six selection methods have been chosen for the CSR position based on the job analysis. Each competency can be measured at least twice with all tools.

Competency	Measurement method					
	Computerized screening	Phone assessment	Behavioral interview	Job preview	Job tryout simulation	Face-to-face interview
	Automated prescreening for being legally able to work and having a positive attitude toward work	Personal interview used to probe for previous examples of job competencies	Survey of job attitudes, interests, and motivations and learning ability	An opportunity for the applicant to determine whether or not he or she would like the job	"Live" opportunity for the applicant to demonstrate the necessary interpersonal skills	A final opportunity to probe in depth areas important to job performance
Primary job motivators	✔		✔	✔	✔	
Oral communication		✔			✔	✔
Problem-solving skills		✔	✔			✔
Learning		✔				✔
Persuasion		✔			✔	✔
Planning and organization		✔				✔

IDENTIFYING SUITABLE CANDIDATES

After going through the job analysis process, you'll be keenly aware of the factors that contribute to an employee's success or failure in your contact center. In general, you'll want to screen for candidates who can plan and execute their work, make decisions and solve problems, exercise good judgment, connect with other people, and project a good attitude. Selecting candidates who have the right skills (or the ability to learn them) and the right attitude will help you to greatly

In general, you'll want to screen for candidates who can plan and execute their work, make decisions and solve problems, exercise good judgment, connect with other people, and project a good attitude.

increase the profitability of your contact center. You'll also develop a team of talented agents who enjoy coming to work!

It would be great to have unlimited time to personally interview every candidate who applied for a job. But, as anyone who has pondered over hundreds of resumes can tell you, identifying suitable candidates to interview can be an arduous and time-consuming process. Conducting the actual interviews takes even longer.

To save you time and significantly enhance your chances of finding great job candidates, a variety of tools are available to help screen and select potential contact center agents.

Contact center staffing specialists from FurstPerson, a Chicago-based staffing company, recommend using a "multiple-hurdle" approach to effectively screen and select candidates. By using multiple tests to screen and select candidates, they say, you can greatly increase your chances of hiring a top-performing agent for your contact center.

Some employee selection and testing tools that are currently in use are:

- Telephone screening
- Web-based screening
- Behavioral event interviews (which aim to judge how someone will act in a certain situation)
- Ability-to-learn tests (often standardized tests)
- Realistic job previews (such as sitting next to one of your current agents for awhile)
- Job simulations
- Role plays
- Psychometric tests
- Presentations
- Online chat or e-mail testing
- Data entry speed and accuracy assessments

Here's an example of how a financial services contact center significantly increased the quality of its hiring program while reducing cost per hire.*

A financial services contact center had difficulties recruiting qualified candidates to serve a growing customer account base. Their legacy recruiting system was ineffective and needed to be improved. Using a mix of internal and external resources, the company implemented a full-scale screening and selection system and focused on employment branding, which is based upon making candidates feel like the company is a great place to work.

The new hiring system proved itself immediately with exceptional results:

- Cost per hire decreased by 32 percent.
- Time to fill positions decreased by 37 percent.
- Candidates hired increased by 71 percent.
- Employee turnover decreased by 75 percent.

If you do not have the resources to perform some of these selection processes internally, consider outsourcing the screening and selection process to a qualified outsourced provider.

GETTING READY

Once you've eliminated applicants who are clearly not suitable for the job, you're ready to move on to the more personal aspects of hiring. Before going through the interviewing process, be sure you're prepared to discuss the following:

- The functions of the job
- What experience or knowledge is required
- Benefits of the job (such as a great atmosphere, team experience, enhancement of skills and knowledge, etc.)
- Details of salary, hours, flexibility, and so on
- Incentive programs
- What training will be given

*Source: Corporate Executive Board—Best Class Recruiting, 2001.

You should also be prepared to handle any questions that come your way from the candidates, and you should know how you're going to respond if a candidate wants to negotiate pay, hours, and the like.

Of course the first step in planning your interviews is to make sure that you meet all legal and ethical guidelines as well as any specific policies established by your organization. After that, hiring in a contact center should involve at least three steps:

Step 1: Telephone prescreening
Step 2: In-person interview
Step 3: Skills assessment

If the job is exclusively or predominantly electronic (meaning that the agent communicates with customers via e-mail or chat rather than the telephone), you might opt to replace Step 1 with an e-mail screening to see how candidates communicate via this medium. It's also possible in some environments that it makes sense to have the skills assessment take place before the in-person interview.

Step 1: Telephone Prescreening

A lot can be accomplished in just a few minutes over the phone. After all, in most contact centers agents spend nearly all their time on the phone with customers. By screening applicants over the phone, you'll be hearing pretty much exactly what your organization's customers would. This allows you to instantly gauge certain important criteria.

One way to save interviewing time and significantly increase the odds of getting qualified candidates is to outsource the telephone screening function. According to Jeff Furst, president of Furst-Person, "When we roll up our sleeves and begin the recruiting and selection process for our clients, we'll typically have to make contact with 2000 to 2500 people for every 100 people we hire."

Telephone interviews should be relatively short and simple. The primary objective is to screen out anyone who clearly would not be suitable for the job. What would make someone not suitable? Things like very poor verbal and vocal skills, inability to work the necessary hours, or a truly bad attitude. Keep in mind that applicants are bound to be a little nervous, however, so don't hold this against them.

At the end of the telephone interview, you should have made a decision as to whether or not to invite the candidate in for a personal interview. If you want to continue interviewing the candidate, schedule the interview appointment before getting off the phone. If you've decided not to go forward with an additional interview, let the candidate know. It's unfair and unprofessional to create a false sense of hope for someone who's seeking a job. Take extra care to be kind and honest when ending a conversation with an unsuccessful applicant, but keep in mind that no law requires you to tell applicants anything when you reject them. In fact, most legal experts advise employers to provide them as little information as possible. In most cases, you can just thank the applicant for his or her interest and time and let him or her know that you won't be extending a job offer. Following are a few suggestions for letting the candidate down:

> *"Shelley, thanks for taking the time to talk to me about the job. Because I'm looking for someone with a little more experience in telephone customer service than you currently have, I'm not able to offer you a job at this point."*

> *"Joel, I've enjoyed talking with you today and I can tell you've got a lot of energy and enthusiasm—great skills for customer service. Unfortunately, I don't think we're a good fit for you as it sounds like you need more flexibility than our company can give."*

If you choose to give more information, make sure to protect your company against discrimination claims by being factual, truthful, and to-the-point. Explain the legitimate, business-related reasons for the applicant's rejection but don't divulge any additional information. If the candidate pushes for more reasons or makes threats of legal action, end the conversation and thank the candidate for his or her time.

Step 2: In-Person Interview

Once you've prescreened a candidate over the telephone or through an e-mail correspondence, it's time for the all-important personal interview. At this stage you'll get a solid impression of the candidate's personality, attitude, intelligence, and communication skills. But once again, keep in mind that customers won't be interacting with the agent in person; it's how well the agent can convey these things over the phone (or through e-mail) that will count for the customer.

In Table 6-1 we've outlined some interview questions that can help you assess the candidate's suitability for the job. Following are some additional tips to help you lead a successful interview:

- Greet the candidate warmly and thank him or her for taking the time to come in. Do your best to build rapport and reduce the candidate's nervousness.
- Let the candidate know what to expect. At the beginning of the interview, tell the candidate approximately how long you expect the interview to last and what he or she can anticipate. Following are a few examples of this:

"Julie, let's sit down and talk for 10 or 15 minutes and then we'll move on to the skills assessment."

"Justin, thanks for coming in. I thought we'd spend a few minutes talking about the job and our organization and then I'd like to chat with you about your goals and experience. In about 30 minutes, we need to go down the hall to human resources where we'll do some call simulations."

- Once you've asked a question, listen attentively to the answer and let the candidate finish speaking before you ask something else.
- Take notes during the interview to show that you're paying attention and that the candidate's answers to your questions are being recorded.
- Be sure to ask the candidate what questions he or she has for you.

Keep Your Mission in Mind

When hiring agents for your team, keep your own professional goals in mind. You'll only be able to accomplish your own mission and objectives as a manager if you've got the right people working to make that happen.

TIP!

When interviewing applicants, be sure to ask open questions (ones that get the person to speak freely rather than just give a short, specific answer). You'll learn a lot more about the candidate if you can get him or her to open up while you do the listening. Use sentences that start with *how, why, what,* and *tell me* to get the applicant talking.

TABLE 6-1 Twelve Great Interview Questions

THIS QUESTION:	GIVES YOU INSIGHT INTO:
Tell me what your ideal life would be like. How much would you work? What type of work would you do? How much would you get paid? (*Note:* Ask this at the very beginning of the interview, before the candidate knows enough about the position to skew his or her answers toward what he or she thinks you want to hear.)	The candidate's goals, values, and personality
What motivated you to apply for this job?	• The candidate's level of interest in the job • What's driving the candidate to apply
How do you deal with difficult customers?	• The candidate's definition of difficult • The candidate's readiness to handle difficult customer situations • The candidate's attitude toward difficult customers
What was one of the biggest challenges you faced in a previous job and how did you handle it?	• The candidate's ability to identify challenges as such and to work through them • The candidate's maturity and ability to deal with stressful situations
In what ways do you hope to grow and learn in this job?	• Whether or not the candidate is thinking about the future • Whether or not the candidate is looking for a long-term job • Ways in which the candidate wants to improve
What are some qualities or characteristics that you feel customers would use to describe you?	• How the candidate thinks customers view him or her • The candidate's self-assessment of his or her strengths
Can you give me one or two examples of how you react to your own mistakes and failures?	• The candidate's willingness to be open about his or her own mistakes/failures • The candidate's maturity and professionalism in dealing with mistakes/failures • The candidate's ability to learn from past mistakes
What are the most important aspects of customer service/sales/technical support?	• The candidate's knowledge of what is required to do a good job • How the candidate prioritizes aspects of the job
How do you keep yourself motivated when your job is highly repetitive?	• The candidate's ability to be self-motivating • The candidate's understanding of the job
Think of a situation in which you had to deliver bad news to a customer. What did you say?	The candidate's ability to be honest, direct, diplomatic, and positive
Describe the best manager you ever had and what made that person so effective.	• How the candidate likes to be managed • What qualities and characteristics the candidate believes are important for a manager to possess
Do you have reliable transportation to the job?	• The candidate's ability to get to the right place at the right time • The candidate's practicality and readiness to accept a position at your location

Step 3: Skills Assessment

Depending on the needs and operations of your specific center, the third step of the interview process may involve any number of the tools we mentioned earlier:

- Behavioral event interviews
- Ability-to-learn tests
- Realistic job previews
- Job simulations
- Role plays
- Psychometric tests
- Presentations
- Online chat or e-mail testing
- Data entry speed and accuracy assessments

Step 3 is crucial because it's where candidates prove that they can do what's required of them on the job. Personality and attitude count for a lot in the first two phases of hiring, but they can't outweigh a candidate's inability to carry out the job. In order to be sure you're hiring the right candidates, it's important to carry out all three phases of the process.

What's more, some candidates may surprise—or even shock—you with how they perform during the skills assessment phase of hiring. For example, we've seen a number of job applicants whose tone of voice and attitude at the beginning of the interview process didn't give recruiters much confidence that they could do a good job. Once they got on the phone to do a role play, however, these same candidates performed beautifully! It pays to remember that how someone sounds or acts off the phones may be important for a number of reasons, but it's secondary to how that person sounds on the phone with customers.

We all have different skill sets, and while being able to interview well and test well may be an indicator of performance, it is not a guarantee. Emphasizing the practical assessment aspects of performance is the best indicator of actual performance.

When talking to candidates about this phase of the interviewing process, be careful not to refer to it as testing. That will only make candidates nervous and apprehensive. Instead, use terms like *assessment* and *measurement*. Better yet, tell candidates this is where they get to show off their skills.

Schedule hiring interviews before or after the typical 8-to-5 workday. Candidates who are looking for a second job, and those planning to leave their current job, will appreciate the fact that they don't have to take time off to come to the interview.

Should You Include Other Employees in the Interview Process?

In some centers this is a good idea. In others it won't work, either because it's too unwieldy or because it may convolute rather than assist the decision-making process. Including other employees does have at least two advantages: it can help reduce turnover by helping you be extra certain the candidate is a good match for the center, and it may be because people tend to approve candidates who are like themselves. So, if your good employees give the thumbs-up to a candidate, it may mean the addition of another good employee to the team.

What About Interviewing Former Employees?

Many contact centers experience the trend of employees leaving and then coming back months later to apply for a job. These employees may do better than before—and be more motivated to stay—now that they know the grass isn't always greener anywhere else.

HOW TO RECOGNIZE SERVICE-ORIENTED CANDIDATES

It's hard to generalize about what makes a candidate a perfect fit—or even a good one—for your job openings. A lot depends on the specifics of your environment and of the job itself. But it does seem safe to say that one of the most important things to look for in a candidate is a strong customer service orientation.

Following are some key skills and characteristics exhibited by agents who are star performers in service. Keep these in mind as you interview potential new agents for your center.

- Friendly
- Quick

- Efficient
- Eager to please
- Able to understand customers' requests
- Optimistic
- Diligent
- Creatively helpful
- Empathetic
- Poised
- Honest and fair
- Proactive
- Solution-oriented
- Emotionally stable

TIP!

Before you recruit new agents, study and interview your best performers to determine which characteristics make them successful employees. Then look for these same characteristics in candidates applying for open positions.

Waiting on Waiters

We know of at least one contact center manager who seeks out service industry veterans (particularly waiters and waitresses) to fill openings on his technical support help desk. His thinking goes as follows: the technical aspects of the job can be taught to any reasonably intelligent person in a matter of weeks or months, but the willingness to serve and the drive to satisfy customers are much more difficult to impart to new hires—or anyone else, for that matter.

WHAT TO TELL CANDIDATES ABOUT YOUR WORKPLACE

A job interview is a two-way street: you're interviewing the applicant and the applicant is interviewing you and your organization. If you want to attract the best candidates, it's not enough to simply ask them a bunch of questions. You also have to inspire them to want to work at your organization.

Following are some important things to keep in mind when talking to candidates about your organization.

- *Accentuate the positive.* Highlight the positive aspects of working in your center. Let applicants know what they can expect (beyond the obvious issues such as salary and working hours) if they accept the job: perks, incentives, opportunities for growth and advancement, and so on.

- *Be honest and accurate.* If you describe too rosy an image, it will soon become apparent to the new employee that you were dishonest during the hiring process—not a good way to start a new working relationship. Let candidates know the main points of what they can expect if they are hired.

- *Be different.* Almost everyone is drawn to environments and situations that are fun, fresh, and different from everything else out there. When talking about your workplace, highlight some of the unique or even quirky characteristics—the haunted vending machine, the quarterly "Sweats and Pizza Day," the humorous monthly e-mail newsletter. Candidates will be intrigued by the colorful mental picture that develops as you talk about your workplace, and will hopefully visualize themselves as part of it.

- *Give the big-picture perspective.* In order for contact center agents to feel good about the work they do, it's always helpful to remind them that they are part of a large and successful system, organization, or campaign. Let candidates know where your company stands in its industry, the community, or even the world. Are you the number one provider of health care services? The biggest online retailer of rock-climbing gear? The telecommunications organization with the highest customer satisfaction scores in the industry?

- *Be an attentive and upbeat interviewer.* Whether you spend a few minutes or a few hours with candidates, it's important to remember that you're making a first impression on someone with whom you may be working closely in the future. Don't jump for the phone, allow interruptions, or try to handle other matters during the interview; it will only make you look unprepared and/or inattentive to the candidate. It's also important that you convey to the applicant a positive, upbeat attitude toward your job.

- *Involve current employees.* Once you're fairly certain that you want to hire an applicant, bring in one or two current employees to roll out the welcome mat (and possibly to reel in a candidate who's not sure about accepting a position). Obviously, you should select employees who exhibit a positive, upbeat attitude toward the job and the organization and who will be friendly to the applicant.

HOW TO TURN DOWN APPLICANTS

Nobody likes to be the one to tell people they're not right for the job, but as a manager you need to be able to do just that. And it is possible to do it skillfully and compassionately. If you're honest and conscientious, there's every chance that unsuccessful candidates will leave with a favorable impression of you and your organization. This can make them good "ambassadors" for your center.

Following are a few guidelines to help you turn down unsuccessful candidates:

- Tell applicants why they're not being offered the job. This will help them to understand where they fell short and will give them a starting point for improvement.

- Let applicants know where their strengths are. Give them feedback on at least one or two things they did well during the interview process.

- Thank applicants for taking their time to talk to you and for showing an interest in your organization.

MAKING THE OFFER

Once you've decided to hire a candidate, it's important to offer the job in a polite, professional manner. Even if you suspect (or know) that the candidate definitely wants the job, you should position the offer as an invitation that you're hopeful will be accepted. Let the candidate feel successful and desirable. Following are a few suggestions:

- Tell the candidate you want him or her to work for you and explain why. This will allow the candidate to know what you think his or her strengths are.

- Disclose any important information that has not already been discussed. If you haven't already discussed issues such as salary, work hours, starting dates, and so on, now is the time to make sure the candidate knows and accepts all aspects of the job.

- Ask the candidate to accept your offer. It's always a good idea to get the candidate to say in his or her own words that he or she wants the job. The best way to do this is to invite the candidate to say, "Yes, I'll take the job."

- Let the candidate know what the next step is: report to human resources to sign papers? Go home and come back tomorrow? Also, if the candidate wants to think over the offer, be sure to give a deadline for responding.

- Introduce the new hire to some or all of your team members. Once the candidate has accepted the job, it's a good idea to introduce him or her to at least a few of the people with whom he or she will be working. Doing this right away allows the new hire to feel like a part of the team before he or she even shows up for that nervous first day on the job.

NOW THAT YOU'VE GOT THE RIGHT PEOPLE, HOW DO YOU KEEP THEM?

Employee turnover is one of the most persistent and difficult problems facing contact center managers in all industries and all locations. A high turnover rate has been largely accepted as just an inevitable reality of contact center life. But it doesn't have to be that way. If you're confident that you've got the right people for the job, it's worth your while to invest considerable time, energy, and resources in keeping these employees on your team.

In particular, the impression you and your company make to an employee on his or her first day of work is extremely important. Start out strong by having a top-notch orientation program. Following are some tips:

- Give new employees a good idea of what to expect on their first day on the job.

- Greet new employees at the front door on their first day.

- Formally introduce new employees to the team and to key coaches they can go to for special attention.

- Explain company procedures and clearly describe initial expectations.

- Inform new employees of their role in adding value to the team.

- Let new employees know where to go for help.
- Partner new employees with an experienced employee they can turn to for support.
- Ask if new employees have any special needs.
- Offer new employees a warm welcome.

Remember, your current employees are your greatest resource in attracting new candidates for your contact center.

Once you've hired the right candidates, keep them around by making your contact center a great place to work. Following are some tips to help you accomplish this.

TIP!

Tips for Reducing Turnover

- Create and maintain a consistently high-morale environment.
- Offer rewards and incentives that are based on what the agents want (versus what upper management thinks is a good idea).
- Reward managers and supervisors for retaining their best performers.
- Help agents to see their own progress and growth, and to recognize that more lies ahead.
- Offer a bonus to employees who refer friends for job openings at your center.
- Conduct exit interviews with employees who leave and then make good use of the information gathered so that you can prevent future departures.
- If a valuable employee indicates that he or she wants to leave the company, ask, "What will it take to keep you?"

ADDITIONAL RESOURCES

Books

Jordan-Evans, Sharon, and Kaye, Beverly L. *Love 'Em or Lose 'Em*. San Francisco: Berrett-Koehler, 1999.

Levin, Greg, Solomon, Laurie, Smith, Ann, Harp, Leslie Hansen, Sitzer, Wanda, Mayben, Julia, Wilber, Jennifer, Craig, Mark, Lowe, Dan, Mock, Bette, and O'Hara, Anita. *Call Center Recruiting and New Hire Training*. Annapolis, MD: Call Center Press, 2001.

O'Malley, Michael. *Creating Commitment: How to Attract and Retain Talented Employees by Building Relationships That Last*. New York: John Wiley & Sons, 2000.

Companies

FurstPerson (helps call center organizations find, hire, and keep employees). URL: www.furstperson.com; phone: 888-646-3412.

Manpower (provides staffing services). URL: www.manpower.com; phone: 414-961-1000.

Associations, Magazines, and Interesting Web Sites

American Management Association. URL: www.amanet.org; phone: 800-262-9699.

Call Center Jobs.com (Web site that helps call center employers meet with potential call center employees). URL: www.callcenterjobs.com; phone: 888-353-7529.

Equal Employment Opportunity Commission. URL: www.eeoc.gov; phone: 800-669-4000.

U.S. Department of Labor. URL: www.dol.gov.

CHAPTER 7

The Manager's Role in Employee Training

BE A CHAMPION OF TRAINING

Whether or not you're the person who actually conducts the training for your staff, as their manager your role in training is a crucial one. Agents will take their lead from you when it comes to the part training plays in the success of the team. It's essential for you to be a strong advocate and a vigorous champion of training.

It's no wonder that so many employees, in contact centers and elsewhere, dread training: it's often poorly planned and even more poorly executed. But training doesn't have to be dry and monotonous. In fact, effective training—whether it's centered around skills, product knowledge, or anything else—is active, informative, and fun. Yes, fun!

HOW BEHAVIOR CHANGES

One of the most important points we want to make with this book is the following:

Behavior changes as a result of quality training and effective coaching.

> "Compared to average call centers, leading call centers spend twice as much of the annual budget on initial training, and almost one-third more in ongoing training, according to a study by Hackett Benchmarking & Research. CSRs in the top 25 percent of centers receive formal feedback nearly twice as often throughout the year, and are 1.5 times more likely to receive informal feedback at least once a week."
> —Cited in *Call Center Management Review*, October 2000)

Both are essential, and the two must go together. Training gives agents the skills and knowledge they need to do the job, and coaching gives the all-important reinforcement that helps agents to put their training to use on the job.

The danger of not training is that agents won't be able to perform well at their job. The danger of not coaching is that agents will be able to perform well but may not. Why? Because they get the unspoken message from management that it doesn't matter, that no one cares, that there are no rewards for doing well and no repercussions for doing poorly.

Both are essential, and the two must go together. Training gives agents the skills and knowledge they need to do the job, and coaching gives the all-important reinforcement that helps agents to put their training to use on the job.

A study at Xerox showed that a paltry 13 percent of skills were retained by trainees six months after training if managers failed to provide coaching and support as the skills were being applied. And a Motorola study has found that those plants where quality improvement training was reinforced with on-the-job coaching and support from managers returned $33 on every dollar invested. Plants providing the same training with no top management follow-up produced a negative return on investment. (Source: The Clemmer Group)

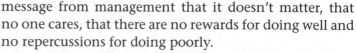

T + C = S (Training + Coaching = Success)

Agents learn new skills in a training session. Then they go back to their jobs. If the new skills aren't reinforced with coaching, the agents will revert back to the way they did things before the training, pretty much every time.

HOW TO POSITION TRAINING

In the "Trainer's Toolkit" section at the end of this chapter you'll find a form designed to help you get agents' buy-in (usually a prerequisite for active participation) during a training session. But a lot of the buzz about training happens in the days and weeks *prior to* the actual sessions.

One of the best ways you can show support for agent training is by giving it some good PR. Following are some ways to accomplish this:

- Emphasize that agents will have an opportunity to build on the knowledge and skills they already have.
- Talk about training as an investment that the company is making in the agents because the work they do is so important.

- Avoid giving the impression that training is solely remedial or corrective.

- Give training a position of high priority when it comes to scheduling. For example, don't keep postponing a training session. To do so sends the message that it's not important.

- Praise and/or reward agents who make strong contributions to the success of training sessions.

- Let agents know that training provides a great forum for them to learn helpful tips and techniques from one another.

- Remind agents that training provides a break from their often stressful daily routine.

- Set a team goal for a specific metric (along with a team reward for achieving that goal). Let agents know that the training is designed to help them meet their individual contribution to the team goal.

TIP!

Get testimonials. At the close of a successful training session, pass around index cards to participants and ask them to write a brief testimonial about their training experience. What did they learn? Did they have fun? Were they enriched with new skills? Collect the cards and use the most positive ones to inspire other training groups prior to their sessions.

SELLING TRAINING TO SENIOR MANAGEMENT

In some contact centers, upper management understands the value of training and is responsive to requests or even proactive about initiating training. This isn't always the case, however. Sometimes it can be tough to sell upper management on the necessity of training or on the added value it can bring to the organization.

If you anticipate difficulty getting approval from senior management for agent training, here are a few tips to help you make your case:

- Show a cost analysis that juxtaposes the cost of training with the potential savings that will result from agents working more productively and efficiently.

- Link the training to the strategic goals of the company and/or to statements made by upper management concerning strategic initiatives or industry trends.

- Point out the specific objectives of the training initiative: higher customer satisfaction scores, less turnover, lower error rate, and so on.

- Do a competitive comparison of your training initiative with the training programs of competitive companies in your industry. Focus on the benefits to your company.

- When talking about the cost of training, don't just give an overall dollar amount. Break down the cost to show what the per-agent investment is.

- Explain what agents will be able to do at the end of training that they're not doing now.

- Discuss what the agents are doing now that they won't be doing at the end of training.

- Tie the training objectives to the company's mission statement and/or to overall performance goals.

TIP!

Show your agents that you too are a learner. Whenever you attend training sessions to learn new skills and acquire additional knowledge for your own job, be sure to advertise this fact to your agents. Show them that you're looking forward to it. Your enthusiastic attitude will be contagious.

WHAT, ME GO?

One of the most meaningful ways to show you're a strong champion of training is to attend the sessions alongside your agents. Of course, if you're the one facilitating the training then you'll have to be there. But even if you're not the trainer, it's a good idea for you to participate.

Why? Well, we can think of three good reasons (and there are probably even more):

1. How will you know what skills to reinforce if you don't know what agents are learning, or if you don't know how to use those skills yourself?

2. Not only does your participation allow you to understand exactly what the agents are doing in the training session, it

also sends the powerful message that you're committed to learning and improvement at all levels of your department.

3. When the agents see you in the training room, learning alongside them, they'll realize that the training isn't just a feel-good event or a waste of time. "If management shows up," the thinking goes, "they must be serious about this."

Do everything possible to attend the training along with your team. If you're not able to attend all or some of it, review the training program so that you'll know what agents are learning. If possible, be there at the kickoff to show your support for training, discuss the importance of the issues being addressed, and announce your expectations. If you can be there at the end to repeat the message, that will help motivate agents to apply what they learned in class when they're on the job. The one exception to this rule is when the subject of the training is something that you're already very familiar with (for example, when new hires are being trained on how to use the phone system).

If you are able to attend the training, be a team player. Try your best to speak only if called on by the trainer, and, if you're asked to participate in a group, let the other participants voice their opinions first. When the training first begins, agents may be hesitant to speak up if you're in the room. Give the trainer time to get them over their fears, and by break time they'll see you as a regular member of the group. It's a great way to break down barriers between management and agents and it goes a long way toward making agents feel like a part of the company.

THE NEEDS ASSESSMENT

A needs assessment is the process by which you determine what training your agents need. Doing a needs assessment prior to making your plans for training is helpful for a number of reasons. It allows you to:

- Determine what skills and knowledge need to be covered in training
- Prioritize according to which needs are most urgent and which can be addressed down the road
- Recognize which areas represent strengths for your agents (so you'll know what not to train them on)

- Set a clear training objective
- Determine what needs cannot be met by training and should be addressed through other means

You can conduct a needs assessment yourself or you can bring in a training professional from your organization or from an outside training company. If you elect to do your own needs assessment, take a look at the example provided in the "Trainer's Toolkit" section at the end of this chapter.

Once you've completed a needs assessment, the next step is to plan a training program, which may take place in one or more sessions, that's driven by the needs identified in the assessment.

TIP!

Ask your agents from time to time what additional training they would like or feel they need. As with so many other aspects of management, some of the best ideas come from the frontline employees themselves.

NOT EVERYTHING IS A TRAINING ISSUE

Keep in mind that training isn't always the answer. Certain problems and issues that affect agents can only be addressed by a change to a business process or policy. For this reason, when planning your training it's important to determine whether or not the problem can be solved by training. Sometimes it can; sometimes it can't. For example, if there's not enough money in the budget for new equipment, no amount of training is going to help an agent hear customers better through a faulty headset.

Table 7-1 gives some additional examples of training and non-training issues.

In some situations there's an overlap between training issues and nontraining issues. For example, let's say an agent is having difficulty keeping up with her workload. Maybe some time management training could help address the matter, but then again, maybe the agent is simply being expected to handle too overwhelming a workload.

There's also the possibility that once a training issue has been addressed by training, it will continue to be a problem. At this point, however, the issue can no longer be dealt with by training. In most cases, it becomes a coaching issue. For example, let's say an agent is having difficulty using correct grammar and spelling in his e-mails to customers. He gets some additional training but then doesn't improve.

TABLE 7-1 Examples of Training and Nontraining Issues

PROBLEM	TRAINING ISSUE	NONTRAINING ISSUE
Faulty computer		X
Agents don't know how to use phone system	X	
Customers are upset about price increase		X
Agents are having difficulty dealing with customers who are upset about price increase	X	
Agents are consistently late to work		X
Insufficient software		X
Agents need better call control skills	X	
Commission structure doesn't support sales goals		X
Agents know how to do the job but aren't motivated to do it		X
Agents need better closing skills	X	
Agents' monitoring scores peak after training but begin to drop over time		X

He now needs to be closely and strictly coached to perform at an acceptable level.

TYPES OF TRAINING

Right about now you may be asking, "Where do I start?" Determining the type of training to provide can be overwhelming. The key is to break it down into smaller chunks. Table 7-2 describes four main categories of training and when each type is warranted.

METHODS OF TRAINING

There are literally dozens of approaches to delivering training and countless ways to categorize them. Following are several examples of common training methods:

- Instructor-led training
- Computer-based training (CBT)
- Web-based training (WBT)

TABLE 7-2 Types of Training

TYPE OF TRAINING	DESCRIPTION	EXAMPLES	WHEN TO TRAIN
Procedures	Regulations, procedures, and policies of the organization or team	• Compliance with employee handbook • Feedback and coaching guidelines of the customer contact team • How to write up an order	• New hire orientation • When a procedure is changed or when a new one is introduced
Technical skills	How to accomplish technical tasks that are necessary in the course of the job	• How to log on and off the computer system • How to use account management software	• New hire orientation • As needed for skill enhancement
Product training	What agents need to know about the products or services offered by the organization to its customers	• Features and benefits of the product line (sales or service) • How to diagnose a technical problem (technical support)	• New hire orientation • When a new product is introduced • On an ongoing basis for knowledge enhancement
Communication skills	How to communicate positively and professionally with customers and coworkers	• Up-selling and cross-selling • Verbal/vocal skills • E-mail writing skills • Handling challenging customers	• New hire orientation • When performance in these areas is low • On an ongoing basis for professional development

- Blended learning
- Distance learning
- Audiotapes
- Videotapes
- Peer training
- On-the-job training (OJT)
- Job aids
- Just-in-time training

> By varying the methods, you can keep things fresh and, hopefully, capitalize on the advantages of each approach. The mixed-bag approach is recommended for another reason as well: it reinforces the idea that learning can and does occur in a variety of ways and at almost any given time.

Additionally, there are further distinctions such as trainer-led vs. self-study and custom training vs. generic programs. The bottom line is that when you're trying to make a decision about the best way to get your agents trained, the maze of options can be pretty overwhelming!

All of these training methods can be effective. Each one has distinct advantages as well as limitations. For example, computer-based training replicates the keyboard environment of live customer communications, but it doesn't allow learners to interact with another human being as they would in a role play during a classroom training session. Similarly, relying solely on games can lead to an overly jovial environment in which very little learning occurs, whereas not allowing learners to have fun and to learn while playing can be equally counterproductive.

For this reason, we recommend a mixed-bag approach in which you find two or three delivery methods that will work well in your environment and alternate between them. For example, you might conduct a trainer-led classroom session in customer contact skills followed a few months later by an OJT course to refresh agents' product knowledge.

By varying the methods, you can keep things fresh and, hopefully, capitalize on the advantages of each approach. The mixed-bag approach is recommended for another reason as well: it reinforces the idea that learning can and does occur in a variety of ways and at almost any given time.

Whatever you decide, remember that the truly important thing is to make sure that learning occurs. Here are some points that will help you make sure your training is effective—whether you develop it in house or use an outside vendor.

Design for Adults

Adults learn differently than children, so don't rely on your high school or college experience to provide you with a model for training your contact center agents. When training working adults, keep in mind that adults learn best when:

- They feel a need to learn
- They are doing instead of just watching or listening
- They are involved in solving problems
- They are given feedback on performance
- The learning environment is informal
- The objectives are clearly defined

Consider Various Learning Styles

Engage as many senses as possible during your training. We all have preferences in how we learn, and the best learning occurs when more than one sense is engaged. In training contact center agents, the three senses to keep in mind are:

- *Visual:* Video, graphics, flip charts, slides, written text in workbooks
- *Auditory:* Tapes, leader's voice, audio conferencing, music, sound effects
- *Kinesthetic:* Touching or manipulating objects like a phone or keyboard, assembling puzzle pieces, performing role plays, demonstrations

---

When Not to Train

Plan to hold your training sessions at times when they will be the least disruptive to the team's regular work. Whenever possible, avoid holding the training during your busiest hours or when other issues or demands are especially pressing (e.g., when weekly reports are due).

Make the Connection

Throughout any training session, it's essential for participants to see the relationship between what they're doing in the classroom (or on the computer, in the ropes course, or wherever) and what they do day in and day out while seated in their cubicles communicating with customers.

HOW PEOPLE LEARN

Here's a little story about how we all learn. There are four stages of learning and we move from one to the next as our understanding progresses. Let's use the analogy of learning to drive to illustrate how we move from one of the following four stages to the next.

Unconscious Ignorance → Conscious Ignorance → Conscious Knowledge → Unconscious Knowledge

During childhood we don't drive a car. We don't even think about driving. There is always someone else to drive and it never really occurs to us that there's something odd about the fact that some people are drivers and some are not. We are in the *unconscious ignorance* stage—we don't know what we don't know. This is like an agent's first day on the job.

But then adolescence comes and somehow we become very aware of the fact that we don't know how to drive. We begin to crave that knowledge and to count the days (in some cases the minutes) until we too will be able to drive a car and partake of all that that knowledge entails. At this point we are at the stage of *conscious ignorance*—we now know what we don't know. Your job as a manager at this point is to get your agents to the place where they crave knowledge. (For help with this, see "Three Keys to Getting Buy-In from Participants" in the "Trainer's Toolkit" section at the end of this chapter.) Relating training to an on-the-job experience will also help. For example, agents will be more likely to crave training on how to handle an angry and upset customer if they just dealt with one than they would be on the first day of the job.

Back to our driving analogy: finally we reach the magical age of learner's permits and we begin to acquire the knowledge and skills necessary to drive a car, usually with the help of a coach—be it parent or driving instructor. And at first we are hyperaware of every detail. There's a running commentary going on in our mind as we go through the motions: "Foot on the gas; hands on the wheel; left turn coming up, better put on the blinker; time to check the rearview mirror . . ." This is the stage of *conscious knowledge*—we're very aware of what we now know.

Finally, at some point we begin to lose that hyperawareness. Driving becomes second nature. We assimilate the knowledge and no longer consciously think about doing something; we just spontaneously and naturally do it. This is the stage of *unconscious knowl-*

edge—we know something without being acutely aware that we know it. If we were taught and coached well, we can drive without danger to ourselves or others. Likewise, if your agents are taught and coached well, the skills required to handle customers will become second nature to them.

Although chances are good that you're not teaching your agents to drive a car, you are teaching them something. And the process is the same. As they move from one stage to another, it is the powerful combination of training and reinforcement that will result in agents having the right knowledge and using it intuitively.

How Do You Tell if Training Was Effective?

The simplest answer is also the best one in this case. To determine if training was effective, check to see if learners can do what they are supposed to be able to do at the end of training. If so, training was effective.

TIP!

Post-Training Coaching Tips

Although coaching is always an important part of the management function in a contact center, there are times when it's particularly crucial to be doing it, doing it well, and doing it often. The period of time right after agents have been trained is one of these times. Following are some tips:

- Make it easy for agents to use their new skills. Make sure they have whatever job aids, equipment, or resources they need to succeed.

- Start immediately with the new way. Learners should be expected to use their new skills as soon as the training is over. There will naturally be a period of adjustment, during which your coaching should be compassionate, but there's no point in postponing the start date for using what people have learned.

- Position training as a process, not an event. Make sure agents know that in the first few days and weeks after a training session they are still to a great extent in learning mode.

- Talk about what the agents learned in training on a continual basis. Remind them about the success they had practicing the new skills in the training, or the great idea they came up with for a new way of doing some job-related task. This will help to keep them motivated.

- Praise, praise, praise, but don't forget to correct when necessary.

Two Important Questions

When planning your training, anticipate that at the end of training you will need to answer two important questions:

1. So what?

2. Now what?

The first question addresses the transfer of learning from the training environment to the live call floor. The second question speaks to the issue of coaching. In what ways will the manager and supervisors reinforce what was learned so that the learning will stick?

TRAINER'S TOOLKIT

On the following pages are some basic training tools designed to help you (or whoever trains your staff) make training sessions effective, informative, and lively. You can photocopy the reproducible versions of these forms (see the appendix) for easy reference when you're on the job.

Here's what's in the toolkit:

- Simple Training Needs Assessment
- The Four Basic Steps: Learn—Observe—Practice—Transfer
- Ten Tips for Flips
- Three Keys to Getting Buy-In from Participants
- Tips on Leading Group Discussions
- Trainer's Checklist for Keeping Sessions Lively

SIMPLE TRAINING NEEDS ASSESSMENT

Following is a short, simple version of a needs assessment to help you efficiently plan training for your team.

Step 1. Determine what agents *should be* doing.

Step 2. Determine what agents *are* doing by gathering information through:

- Monitoring forms
- Metrics

- Interviews and focus groups
- Questionnaires
- Observations
- Customer experience management (CEM)

Step 3. Determine where gaps exist between what agents are currently doing and what they should be doing.

Step 4. Determine which of these gaps can be addressed through training.

Step 5. Plan training that addresses the gaps.

THE FOUR BASIC STEPS: LEARN—OBSERVE—PRACTICE—TRANSFER

Anytime you're trying to teach someone a new skill, there are four essential steps: Learn—Observe—Practice—Transfer. There are any number of training theories and practices that get much more complex than this, and most if not all of them have probably proven themselves to be effective. But, at the very least, make sure these four basics are covered anytime you're planning a training session.

Participants should:

- **Learn** a new skill.
  "Here's how you respond when a customer is angry or upset..."

- **Observe** the skill being practiced.
  Learners should see and/or hear several examples of how someone else carries out the skill.

- **Practice** the skill in the training environment.
  Learners should practice the skill (through simulations, role plays, exercises, etc.), understanding that they're still in learning mode. They should strive for success while knowing that it's safe to fail because this is only practice.

- **Transfer** the skill to the real-time environment.
  The learner must now use the skill on the job. It's at this point that coaching kicks in. In order for the learner to successfully assimilate the new skill and use it in the live environment, the manager or supervisor must reinforce use of the skill through praising and correcting. (See Chapter 9.)

TEN TIPS FOR FLIPS

An effective flip chart page is legible, concise, and neat. Following are some suggestions for turning your flip chart into a powerful visual aid both inside and outside of the training classroom.

1. Use lined or graphed charts to help you write symmetrically.

2. Write in block letters and make them 1 to 1½ inches high.

3. Use a combination of colored markers, but avoid using the light-colored ones for text.

4. Before drawing with markers, use pencil marks to plot sections of the chart.

5. To highlight certain points or distinguish between items, create bullets.

6. Make your charts balanced and symmetrical (for example, don't cram all the information into the top half of the chart).

7. Make sure there's a lot of white space. It's better to go onto a second page than to force too much information onto one page.

8. When creating charts that will be filled in during the session, make light pencil marks in the margins to remind you what to do.

9. When presenting a flip chart page, make sure all participants can read it from where they're seated.

10. Don't block the chart when presenting; stand to the side and point to the chart as needed.

THREE KEYS TO GETTING BUY-IN FROM PARTICIPANTS

Here's the digest version: You begin by telling participants what they'll get from the training and why it's such a good idea for them to get it. Then you end by showing them that they got it!

Here's the detailed version.

1. State the Objective of the Training Session

At the beginning of the session it's important to tell the group members what they are there to achieve. The objective should be written on a flip chart, slide, or white board (so that it can be seen by participants) and it should be verbally announced by the trainer as well (so it can be heard by participants). Keep in mind that often a training session has more than one specific objective. State them all.

To determine the objective, ask yourself, "What will the learners be able to do at the end of the training?" Then state the objective positively and concisely. Following are a few examples:

- Learn how to successfully operate the XL 22000 account management program

- Acquire skills to write e-mail messages that are clear, concise, positive, and professional

- Learn three techniques for effective cross-selling

2. Explain WIIFT

The next step is to answer the question, "What's in It for Them?" (WIIFT). Most people are motivated by answering the ever present question, "What's in it for me?" In order to get learners' buy-in and active participation in training, it's essential for you to let them know how they'll benefit by doing whatever it is that you want them to do.

There are countless possible benefits. Pick the two or three that you feel will resonate most strongly with your learners, and then point them out with enthusiasm and confidence. You can also remind the learners of these benefits throughout the course of the training. Following are some typical examples of how people can benefit from learning new skills or knowledge:

- Save time

- Reduce stress

- Handle challenging customers with ease

- Progress along a career path

- Make fewer data entry errors

3. Leave Learners with a Feeling of Accomplishment

At the end of the session, review the objective and remind learners that they've now successfully learned and practiced the new skill or knowledge. Congratulate them and encourage them to continue using what they've learned once the training is over. Although this step takes place at the end of training (at which point, hopefully, buy-in has already been achieved), it will help learners to buy into the concept of applying what they've learned. Learners will be more inspired to use what they've learned if they feel that they've worked to acquire it and succeeded in doing so.

On the next page is a concise list you can use to remind yourself of the three keys to getting buy-in from participants.

THREE KEYS TO GETTING BUY-IN FROM PARTICIPANTS

1. State the objective of the training session
2. Explain WIIFT (what's in it for them)
3. Leave learners with a feeling of accomplishment

TIPS ON LEADING GROUP DISCUSSIONS

One of the keys to a successful training session is strong participation from everyone in attendance. Following are some tips to help you get participants involved in group discussions.

1. **Make it safe to participate.** One way to do this is to avoid condemning anyone's response as "wrong" or otherwise making participants uncomfortable.

2. **Use open questions to solicit responses from the class.**
   What questions do you have?
   How might that happen?

3. **Use participants' names to help create an open, informal atmosphere.**
   Ronald mentioned something about that earlier.
   Tamara, what do you think?

4. **Thank participants for their input.**
   Thanks for your insight, Marvin.
   Thanks, Judy.

5. **Use participants as resources.**
   Who wants to answer Shelly's question?
   Where would you find the answer to that?

6. **When you're ready to end the discussion, use a closed question.**
   Are there any questions before we move on?

7. **When things get really tough, put the participants in small groups for a few minutes to discuss the topic; then reconvene the large group and ask each subgroup for a report.**

TRAINER'S CHECKLIST FOR KEEPING SESSIONS LIVELY

Regardless of the length or the topic of a training session, participants will enjoy the learning experience more if the atmosphere is lively and refreshing. Following are some tips to keep in mind when planning a training session.

- ☑ Start with a short icebreaker activity to loosen up participants.
- ☑ Include some physical movement, even if it's just getting up to walk across the room for an activity.
- ☑ If the training session is longer than two hours, include some fun, simple energizer activities.

☑ Include small group activities or discussions.

☑ Build fun and novelty into the session where possible. For example, roll a pair of dice to determine the length of a break (one minute for every eye showing on the dice).

☑ Play music during breaks.

ADDITIONAL RESOURCES

Books

Auerbach, Carol, and Silberman, Mel. *Active Training: A Handbook of Techniques, Designs, Case Examples, and Tips.* San Diego: Pfeiffer & Co., 1998.

Dainow, Sheila. *Working and Surviving in Organisations: A Trainers Guide to Developing Organisational Skills.* Hoboken, NJ: John Wiley & Sons Ltd., 1998.

Eitington, E. Julius. *The Winning Trainer: Winning Ways to Involve People in Learning.* Houston, TX: Gulf Professional Publishing Company, 1994.

Furjanic, W. Sheila, and Trotman, Laurie A. *Turning Training into Learning.* New York: American Management Association, 1999.

Jones, Phillip, and Pike, Robert W. *Creative Training Techniques Handbook: Tips, Tactics and How-To's for Delivering Effective Training.* Minneapolis: Lakewood Publications, 1994.

Companies

Impact Learning Systems (provides communications skills training for contact center agents and managers). URL: www.impactlearning.com; phone: 800-545-9003.

Associations, Magazines, and Interesting Web Sites

American Society for Training and Development (professional association and leading resource on workplace learning and performance issues). URL: www.astd.org; phone: 800-628-2783.

Human Resources.com (a human resources portal covering all relevant topics). URL: www.humanresources.com; phone: 877-212-9100.

Professional Society for Sales & Marketing Training (a nonprofit organization dedicated to accelerating business results for its members and their companies by improving sales performance). URL: www.smt.org; phone: 312-551-0768.

Training & Development Magazine (produced by the American Society of Training and Development). URL: www.astd.org; phone: 800-628-2783.

Training Magazine (a professional development magazine that advocates training and workforce development as a business tool). URL: www.trainingmag.com; phone: 800-328-4329.

Trainingsupersite.com (provides access to information on learning, training/staffing resources, and relevant editorial and other business tools). URL: www.trainingsupersite.com.

CHAPTER 8

The Measures of Success

Assessing Employee Performance

THE IMPORTANCE OF MEASURING PERFORMANCE

It may be tempting to believe that if you've hired the right people and trained them all to do their jobs, you don't have to spend a lot of time and energy measuring their performance. But the truth is that at best, hiring and training give your team a strong foundation. In order to build upon that foundation by continually improving performance and by helping agents to grow and learn, it's crucial for you to implement a well-designed measurement program.

Measurement is simply a sampling of current performance. It is typically compared to a desired result to see if the objective is being met. Companies, departments, and people measure to see if they are accomplishing their mission. Without measurement we would have no idea whether we were doing the right things to achieve our mission. It is particularly important to measure frontline interaction with customers, since most companies are dependent on customer satisfaction and goodwill for their long-term success.

If you don't regularly measure the various aspects of agents' performance, you'll probably find that even your star performers will start to show decreased motivation to do their best. And if that happens to the stars, just imagine what your less stellar performers will do! What's worse, in the absence of an effective measuring and coaching program, metrics and feedback become arbitrary, overly subjective, inconsistent, and possibly even sloppy. Not only will this be a strong demotivator for the group, but it might also cause legal and ethical problems for your organization.

Measuring and giving feedback go hand in hand and both are indispensable functions of contact center management. It does just as much harm to measure performance and not share your findings with agents as it does to give agents feedback that's not based on sound, fair, and uniform measurement criteria. In this chapter, we'll talk about why and how to measure your agents' performance (with a particular emphasis on monitoring calls and electronic communications). In Chapter 10 you'll learn how to give effective, meaningful feedback based on performance data.

TWO BY THREE

There are any number of ways to measure the performance of your team, but if you don't already have a sound program in place, or if you're looking to improve upon the program that you do have, here's one simple yet effective design you can use: Two by Three.

The Two by Three program is one in which you measure two things (productivity and quality) using three criteria (rules, Standards, and Objectives).

Productivity refers to how effective your agents are in utilizing their time and how efficient they are in balancing the various aspects of their jobs. Quality refers to how well they accomplish their tasks, especially their primary function of customer contact.

To measure productivity, you keep track of metrics generated by the automated call distributor (ACD), the computer software program, or the phone system. Typically, these statistics include the following:

- Available time (time spent waiting for calls, e-mails, or chat sessions).
- Wrap time (the amount of time an agent spends completing tasks related to one call or e-mail before becoming ready to take another). This is also referred to in some centers as After Call Work (ACW) or Post Call Processing (PCP).
- The amount of time spent on customer contacts.
- Unavailable time (time spent on break, in meetings, with a supervisor, etc.).
- Tardiness and absence.
- Service level (percentage of calls answered in a given amount of time).
- Response time (the time it takes agents to respond to transactions that do not have to be handled immediately upon arrival, such as e-mail).

Productivity measurement works like this:

Step 1: Set clear rules, Standards, and Objectives (you'll learn more about these later in this chapter).

Step 2: Communicate the rules, Standards, and Objectives to the agents and check for their understanding and agreement.

Step 3: Regularly review metrics such as those stated earlier and any others that are germane to your team.

Step 4: Let agents know how they're doing, work with them to improve where needed, and take disciplinary action if necessary.

Quality measurement is slightly more complicated and challenging, but it's also a lot more fun. Whereas productivity measurement is very cut-and-dried, quality measurement is where you can really see your agents engaged in the heart of their job—communicating with customers. Quality measurement gives you an opportunity to see meaningful progress on the part of your agents. For a caring coach, it's a lot more fulfilling to see an agent improve his or her ability to question customers about their needs than it is to see the agent spend 8.7 seconds less in wrap time. (That being said, we also understand that 8.7 seconds less in wrap time can, in some organizations, lead to a healthier bottom line and a higher customer satisfaction rate.)

So now you have the two in the Two by Three. Let's move on to the three criteria used to define productivity and quality measurements.

RULES, STANDARDS, AND OBJECTIVES

In order to be an effective manager, you need to have a set of clear, fair, and relevant guidelines against which to measure the performance of your agents. We tend to work with three types: rules, Standards, and Objectives. All three of these criteria can be used to measure both productivity and quality.

Rules are the most stringent of the three. They're the actions for which an employee faces disciplinary action and may even be terminated. Some rules are uniform across the organization— things like no drugs, no stealing, and so forth. Other rules may be specific to your department—no swearing when talking to customers, no personal calls when logged into the computer system, no hanging up on customers, and so on.

Standards describe the minimum acceptable level of performance for all reps. They refer to the "bones" of the job—what's required of every agent in every customer interaction. If an agent does not meet a Standard, he or she is falling below the line for acceptable performance. Standards are also quantifiable, meaning they're either met or they're not—there are no ifs, ands, or buts with Standards.

Following are some examples of Standards randomly selected from sales, service, and support teams:

- Gives appropriate greeting
- Verifies customer name and address
- Confirms understanding of customer's service issue
- Uses correct keycode
- Offers to send preview package (if customer qualifies)
- Asks for an order

Read through the list of Standards one more time, noting how easy it is to determine whether or not a Standard has been met. The answer to each criterion is either yes (the agent did it) or no (the agent did not do it). That's what makes a Standard a Standard.

Basically, if a team member accomplishes all Standards on a call or in an e-mail—even if it's not done with a lot of skill or pizzazz—he or she will meet the minimum acceptable level of performance. Of course, you want agents to do more than this—that's where Objectives come in.

Performance Objectives are somewhat less distinct than Standards, and as such, are measured more subjectively. Objectives are qualitative; they describe something that you want agents to accomplish but that you understand will be accomplished to different degrees depending on the agent's skill level and on the unique properties of the call, e-mail, or chat session. Whereas when measuring Standards you determine whether or not they were met, when measuring Objectives you assess *how well* they were met.

Shouldn't Those Words Be Lowercase?

Why are we capitalizing *Standards* and *Objectives*? Because as they're used in this chapter, they're proper nouns. We don't want to confuse you by implying, for example, that objectives of your senior-level management are the same thing as Objectives for your customer service quality program. So, when you see the terms *Standard* and *Objective* capitalized, it means we're referring to the criteria related to your monitoring program.

Following are some typical Objectives:

- Builds rapport with customer
- Handles challenges effectively
- Uses empathy as appropriate
- Exhibits strong verbal and vocal skills
- Uses active listening skills
- Minimizes dead air
- Keeps customer informed

Arguably, you could use "yes" or "no" to determine whether these Objectives were met, but you wouldn't really be making a valuable assessment. The real aim is to determine how well the agent accomplishes the task. A yes/no measure is too short-sighted for Objectives. We've found it's better to use a sliding scale. Here's an example of what we mean:

New agents might have long periods of dead air—clearly not satisfactory, but also understandable as they are struggling with a new system and new product information during their first few weeks on the job. If you were using a yes/no scale when monitoring an agent like this, you would probably check "no" to indicate that the Objective was not satisfactorily met.

As agents become more comfortable with their knowledge and tools, however, they become better able to converse with the customer while researching information or while waiting for the computer to display data. They are now satisfactorily handling dead air by saying things like, "Let me look that up for you . . . let's see here . . . I'm still checking," or "I'm sorry this is taking so long . . . I understand it's snowing back there where you live." Would that be "yes" or "no" on your yes/no scale? It would be "yes" because the agent is filling up the dead air.

But how would you score an agent who said, "I'll be happy to look that up for you . . . now earlier you said that you were trying to pay off all your credit cards. While we're waiting for your account to come up, I'd like to tell you about a wonderful offer we have that will allow you to consolidate your debt and reduce the amount you pay each month in interest. . . ." Would you score a "yes" or a "no"? Clearly a "yes." And would it be a bigger "yes" than for an agent who was talking about the weather? If you were working for a credit card company and wanted to promote balance transfers, the answer would be a resounding "YES." And that's why we prefer a sliding scale: it recognizes the difference between adequate and excellent.

Here are two other reasons for differentiating Standards from Objectives: consistency and fairness. It should be relatively easy for all supervisors to score Standards consistently because they're cut-and-dried: "yes" or "no." But what does the Objective "sounds professional" sound like? You probably have an idea and would know it when you heard it. But could you explain it in detail to an agent or to another manager? If three supervisors listened to the same call, do you think they would agree on whether or not the agent was "professional"? How about an Objective like "exhibits strong verbal and vocal skills"? Do you think everyone in your contact center would agree on what that means? That's the ideal situation, but we've found that in the real world it happens less frequently than desired. It's much easier to agree on Standards since they're "yes" (the Standard was met) or "no" (the Standard was not met); it's easy to identify whether the appropriate greeting was followed and whether accurate information was given. Since Standards are by definition the minimum accepted level of performance, it's not fair to discipline an agent for doing something that different supervisors might not score consistently.

Of course, the ideal situation is when all supervisors who hear a call score the call the same. That way, an agent receives consistent feedback no matter who is giving the feedback, and the agent knows what good performance looks like. The only way for that to happen is for you to consistently hold call calibration sessions with your supervisors. In these sessions (and weekly is not too often!), groups of supervisors listen to calls, fill out monitoring forms, and then discuss why they scored the calls a particular way. This will help ensure the consistency and fairness that are essential if you want the agents in your call center to exhibit high morale.

Now let's recap the Two by Three method.

The two categories of performance measurement are:

1. Productivity
2. Quality

The three types of measurement criteria are:

1. Rules
2. Standards
3. Objectives

WHAT TO MEASURE

Now that you know *how* to measure, you're faced with one of the more difficult challenges of contact center management: knowing *what* to measure. Naturally, there will be a trade-off between measuring as many performance criteria as possible and making sure you don't spend your whole working life doing it. As with just about every other aspect of your role as manager, you need to prioritize. The aim is to measure enough criteria to get a true assessment of how your agents are performing but not so many that the process becomes unwieldy.

Keep in mind that you can always adapt your measurement criteria later if you realize you've left something out or included something that really doesn't need to be a priority.

When deciding what to measure, the most important thing to remember is that agents will take their lead from you—what you measure is what they'll do. If you include "shows empathy" among your Standards and Objectives, be prepared to hear a lot of empathy going around. If you decide to leave out "controls call" (or chat session), don't expect that agents will expend a lot of energy attempting to do this.

TIP!

Sometimes, a shorter call is not a better call! Many contact center managers automatically assume that keeping talk time to a minimum is an absolute rule. This isn't always true. In a number of situations, longer talk time increases both the bottom line and customer satisfaction. For example, taking time to hear and understand what callers want instead of cutting them off may take a few additional seconds but may save considerable time down the road (if, for example, the agent was solving the wrong problem because he or she didn't understand it clearly). Also, it may take an agent a few extra moments to explain to a customer what he or she can expect to happen after the call is completed, but this extra step may eliminate callbacks to the center from customers who have wrong expectations.

WHAT NOT TO MEASURE

Sometimes the easiest way to determine what aspects of your agents' performance to measure is to start with a list of what not to measure.

Following are a few things we think you should leave out of your measurement protocol:

Rules

Rules don't really lend themselves to being measured. Agents either adhere to rules or they face termination. That's what makes a rule a rule.

Nonperformance Issues

Things that aren't relevant to performance—for example, how agents dress, whether their workstations are tidy, and so on—don't belong on your list of Standards and Objectives.

Administrivia

Things like whether or not agents get their health insurance application to personnel on time or whether they log off the system when going to lunch may be important (that's up to you to decide), but they're best handled separately from customer contact issues.

Issues You're Not Willing to Press

Let's say you're inclined to include the official greeting on your list of Standards but you know that two or three of your top salespeople don't use this greeting. Will you discipline them for not meeting the Standard? If not, then don't make it a Standard. It wouldn't be fair to the other agents.

Objectives You Cannot Define

Suppose you want to include "sounds professional" as an Objective for your agents. If you and the other managers or supervisors cannot agree upon what "sounds professional" means and how it is illustrated in the live call or e-mail environment, either keep refining the term until you do get agreement or leave it out.

Customer-Driven Statistics

To be fair to agents, metrics have to be dependent on agent behavior, not customer behavior. For example, you wouldn't want to measure the number of incoming calls or e-mails, because it's a metric over which the agents have no control.

Once you've determined which performance issues to measure, and which ones not to measure, the next two steps are to commit them to paper and to communicate them to your team. Earlier in this chapter you saw a four-step model for measuring productivity. On the pages that follow you'll learn about the various aspects of monitoring, the predominant method of measuring quality.

MONITORING PERFORMANCE

The best way to accurately assess the quality of your agents' interactions with customers is to monitor their calls or electronic communications. Fortunately, in the e-mail or chat environment, you'll automatically get both sides of the "conversation." The best way to accurately assess an agent's performance in the telephone environment is to listen in on both sides of the call.

Table 8-1 describes the different types of monitoring as well as the advantages and disadvantages of both.

Is It Live?

The primary advantage of monitoring live calls rather than listening to recordings of calls that ended an hour, a day, or a week ago is that you can intervene and save a bad call from getting worse. A second advantage is that you can give immediate coaching on calls. This way, the agent will be able to easily recall details of the call (such as how the customer responded to something the agent said).

If it just isn't possible to monitor live calls and give immediate feedback, we recommend either using call monitoring software that allows you to send an audio clip along with comments to the agent, or replaying the call for the agent so that the call is fresh in the agent's mind when he or she receives the feedback.

TABLE 8-1 Types of Monitoring

TYPE OF MONITORING	DESCRIPTION	ADVANTAGES	DISADVANTAGES
Remote	Takes place in real time but away from the call floor.	Offers a "true" result because the agent doesn't know the supervisor* is listening.	• The supervisor can't give immediate help to the agent (except in cases where the supervisor uses a two-way radio to communicate with a supervisor on the call floor or the phone system has a "notify" function that signals the agent to put the caller on hold and speak with the supervisor). • The supervisor hears the call but doesn't see how the agent is using the computer and other reference materials in the workstation.
Shadow	Takes place in real time and away from the call floor, but the supervisor uses a computer monitor to follow along with the agent.	• Offers a "true" result because the agent doesn't know the supervisor is listening. • The supervisor can observe the accuracy and appropriateness of the agent's keystrokes.	The supervisor can't give immediate help to the agent (except in cases where the supervisor uses a two-way radio to communicate with a supervisor on the call floor or the phone system has a "barge in" or "notify" function that signals the agent to put the caller on hold and speak with the supervisor).
Side-by-side	Takes place on the call floor. The supervisor listens through a headset plugged directly into the agent's phone.	• The supervisor can observe the accuracy and appropriateness of the agent's keystrokes and use of other reference materials. • The supervisor can communicate with the agent through notes and gestures, if necessary. • The supervisor can interrupt a call (for example, to give assistance to a struggling agent) or even take it over if necessary.	The agent may behave differently because he or she knows he or she is being monitored.
Taped call	The supervisor assesses the quality of the taped call hours, days, or weeks after it occurred.	The agent can listen to the taped call to hear how he or she handled it.	• There's no opportunity for the supervisor to save a live call that's going badly. • Lag time between call and monitoring session means that the agent does not get immediate feedback.

*Supervisor in this table refers to anyone monitoring the call.

How Often and How Long?

The frequency and length of your monitoring sessions depends on a number of factors, including:

- Average length of call, chat session, or e-mail thread
- Volume of calls or electronic communications
- Similarity (or dissimilarity) of one contact to the next
- Ratio of supervisors (or managers) to agents

Not surprisingly, there is no hard-and-fast rule for how often reps should be monitored. In some environments (for example, the subscriber services division of a newspaper), once a week per rep is enough, whereas in other centers (such as an independent contact center to which a company has outsourced a three-month sales campaign), all reps should be monitored every day.

Following are a few scenarios of how different coaches use monitoring on the job.

Coach 1

Colleen is a supervisor for a customer service team at a large financial institution. The reps on her team take calls from customers with a variety of questions and needs—everything from checking into why a particular automated teller machine (ATM) fee was assessed to asking questions about refinancing their homes. Colleen spends five hours out of every eight-hour shift monitoring calls and giving feedback to reps. She monitors calls from a workstation that is right on the call floor; this way she can walk over to a rep's desk to give immediate help on a call if necessary.

Coach 2

Paolo is the manager of 30 sales representatives and three team supervisors at a software company. His supervisors take primary responsibility for monitoring and giving feedback to the reps (they each handle a team of 10 reps), but because Paolo knows it's important that he know firsthand how his reps are doing on the phones, he monitors at least one call per rep per week. With his new reps and those who are struggling, Paolo gives immediate feedback. With his more seasoned reps who are consistently high performers, he uses examples from their calls (anonymously) as training points in staff meetings and training sessions.

Coach 3

Isaac is a tech support manager for the online division of a computer retailer. He monitors the quality of the more than 15,000 weekly e-mail correspondences between his team of 18 service reps and their customers. Isaac monitors by reviewing e-mail threads within three days of their resolution. He reviews about 10 e-mails per rep every two weeks and then sits down with each rep to give feedback.

For new team members who are still learning the ropes, focus your assessment and feedback on:

- Basic skills
- Basic product knowledge

Once a team member has mastered the basics, start to look for and discuss:

- Skill improvement
- Increased product knowledge
- Smooth and efficient call flow
- Rapport with customers

When team members consistently demonstrate proficiency in these areas, focus your monitoring and coaching on:

- Improved decision-making capabilities (such as up-selling and cross-selling)
- Solutions to challenges
- Mastery of service skills and product knowledge

TIP!

There are two occasions when you might want to monitor more often than usual:

1. When reps are new to the job (whether the rep is a new hire or has been promoted). The extra attention and support will encourage reps at this challenging time.
2. When a new procedure or Standard is initiated. Even seasoned professionals can struggle when asked to adapt to a new way of doing things.

But We Have QAs to Do That!

Depending on the size and structure of your contact center, you may have a quality assurance (QA) department whose hushed denizens are, as their title suggests, responsible for ensuring the quality of reps' interactions with customers.

In many ways, this is a great thing. Organizations rely on the QA department to give them all kinds of numbers, statistics, scores, analyses, indicators, percentages, and ratings that help the big chiefs make important decisions about the health and future of the company.

However . . . with all due respect to the important purpose that they serve, we've yet to meet the company whose QA department is able to meaningfully and immediately improve reps' performance.

In order to improve their performance, your agents—just like everyone else in the world—need someone to give them more than just some markings on a sheet of paper. They need someone to give them:

- Immediate feedback
- Lots of praise
- Attention, support, and concern
- Specific suggestions for improvement
- Constructive, skillful criticism
- An opportunity to be heard

So, by all means count on your QA people to do the kinds of things they're very good at (see the preceding text), but not to improve the performance of your agents. That's your job.

That being said, please don't get the impression that we believe you and the QA department aren't mutually dependent. There are numerous occasions when you need each other. If, for example, you're concerned about an agent's performance, you can check with QA to see if their data backs up your assessment. If it does, great. If it doesn't, figure out where the discrepancy is. The best way to ensure that the QA department and the supervisors are all monitoring with the same outcome is to include the QA department in your call calibration meetings.

PREPARING YOUR AGENTS FOR MONITORING

Monitoring is standard practice in contact centers, but that doesn't mean that agents are always comfortable with the practice. If your team is not accustomed to monitoring, or if the monitoring and coaching program has been carried out badly in the past and now you're turning it around, be sure to address the agents' concerns. If monitoring and coaching are done well, agents will learn to appreciate what these procedures can do for them.

Table 8-2 outlines some common objections to monitoring and offers advice for overcoming them.

TABLE 8-2 Common Objections to Monitoring and How to Address Them

AGENT'S OBJECTION	HOW TO ADDRESS IT
"It's not fair because I don't get a chance to defend myself."	• Make sure agents know that monitoring and coaching go hand in hand and that when they receive feedback, they'll have an opportunity to discuss the call or e-mail. • Make sure that agents have a complete understanding of the standards and objectives and exactly what performance is expected. • Give agents a monitoring form and allow them to score their own customer contact.
"You just want to catch me doing something wrong."	• Remind agents that the aim of measuring performance is to improve quality and productivity, not to catch them doing something wrong. • Be sure that agents get lots of praise for the things they do well.
"I'm always being singled out."	• Make sure all agents know that every member of the team is regularly monitored. • Be sure to spend approximately equal time monitoring all agents—even your best agents want to improve.
"The person listening to me doesn't understand what kind of pressure I'm under."	• Show empathy for agents. • Schedule mandatory time for the supervisor to handle calls or electronic communication each week.
"People are harder on me than they are on others."	• Assure agents that everyone will be held to the same Standards and Objectives. • Use frequent call calibration meetings to be sure that supervisors are being consistent and fair in their monitoring.
"I'm expected to do things I don't know how to do."	• If there's any truth to this, make sure agents get appropriate training. If it's not true, make sure they know what good performance looks like.
"My every move is being watched and I don't like being micromanaged."	• Point out that every employee's work—even yours—is assessed by management. The only fair way to assess agent performance is to listen to both sides of the call.
"I don't like to be compared with others; it creates a competitive environment."	• Assure agents that everyone will be measured against a set of uniform performance criteria, not against other agents.

TIP!
Don't neglect your star performers. They need monitoring and feedback too!

WHAT'S IN A MONITORING FORM?

Once you've set Standards and Objectives for your team, the next step is to create a monitoring form that's customized to the unique properties of your department. A monitoring form is what you use to assess the quality of an agent's performance on a call or in an online communication.

Typically, a monitoring form includes the following elements:

- Administrative information such as agent name, time and date, and so on
- Scale of measurement (for example, Yes/No/Not Applicable for Standards and 1, 2, 3, 4 for Objectives)
- Standards
- Objectives
- Plenty of room for comments

On the following pages are several sample monitoring forms, each from a different type of contact center environment.

SAMPLE MONITORING FORM #1
For an inbound customer service call

Supervisor _____

CSR _____ Date _____ Time _____

Customer account number _____ Name _____

Standards (X = Standard met   O = Standard not met
         N/A = Standard not applicable)

| **Opens the Call**   **Comments** |

_____ Gives scripted greeting
_____ Gathers account information
_____ Acquires/spell-verifies caller information
_____ Uses support cards if caller won't give info
_____ Responds to caller's first statement

Takes/Gives Accurate Information

_____ Reads help screens as appropriate
_____ Gives accurate info to answer caller question/s

_____ _____
_____ _____
_____ _____

Closes the Call

_____ Offers additional information/education to caller
_____ Gives correct scripted closing

Objectives (1 = Needs improvement   2 = Satisfactory   3 = Excellent
         N/A = Not applicable)

_____ Questions to gather information
_____ Listens for key words and phrases
_____ Confirms understanding
_____ Does not ask for info already provided
_____ Handles challenges
_____ Responds professionally
_____ Builds rapport
_____ Demonstrates verbal/vocal skills

Notes

SAMPLE MONITORING FORM #2
For multiple-call monitoring for outbound sales prospecting calls: can be used for up to five calls

Sales rep _____

Date _____

Call Standards (N = No, standard was not met   Y = Yes, standard was met)

Confirms prospect	N Y	N Y	N Y	N Y	N Y
Uses prospect name	N Y	N Y	N Y	N Y	N Y
Uses intro script	N Y	N Y	N Y	N Y	N Y
Responds to first statement	N Y	N Y	N Y	N Y	N Y
Questions for info	N Y	N Y	N Y	N Y	N Y
Tells what to expect	N Y	N Y	N Y	N Y	N Y
Thanks prospect	N Y	N Y	N Y	N Y	N Y
Closes appropriately	N Y	N Y	N Y	N Y	N Y

Professional Demeanor (1 = Needs improvement   2 = Satisfactory 3 = Excellent)

Attitude	1 2 3	1 2 3	1 2 3	1 2 3	1 2 3
Tone of voice	1 2 3	1 2 3	1 2 3	1 2 3	1 2 3
Use of language	1 2 3	1 2 3	1 2 3	1 2 3	1 2 3
Builds rapport	1 2 3	1 2 3	1 2 3	1 2 3	1 2 3

Comments

SAMPLE MONITORING FORM #3
For an inbound technical support call

Technician _____   Date _____

Supervisor_____   Time of call start _____

                                        Time of call end _____ .

Tech Support Standards   Comments
(X = Completed   O = Not completed   N/A = Not applicable)

_____ Uses scripted greeting

_____ Echoes caller's problem statement

_____ Reassures caller

_____ Questions to diagnose problem

_____ Takes notes

_____ Accurately diagnoses problem/s

_____

_____

_____ Solves problem or calls for supervisor

_____ Confirms caller's understanding

_____ Confirms caller's satisfaction

_____ Offers additional assistance

_____ Uses scripted closing

Tech Support Objectives   Comments
(1 = Below average   2 = Average   3 = Above average   N/A = Not applicable)

_____ Listens to caller

_____ Empathizes with caller

_____ Walks caller through problem solving

_____ Explains tech terms in plain English

_____ Educates caller

_____ Exhibits CFE (courtesy, friendliness, enthusiasm)

_____ Handles challenges

Overall Rating

_____ Poor   _____ Fair   _____ Good   _____ Excellent

Figure 8-1 shows a monitoring form that's been filled out by a manager or supervisor.

CSR	*David Asack*	Supervisor	*Martina Wilson*
Date	*5/27*	Time	*2:10 p.m.*

Standards | **Comments**

(N = Not met   Y = Met   N/A = Not applicable)

N	Y		Comments
		Opening the call	
___	X	Gives proper greeting	
___	X	Gives full name	
___	X	Offers assistance	
		Accuracy	
X	___	Verifies information	*Verified spelling of name, but not street name, zip, or phone.*
___	X	Exhibits accurate product knowledge	*Product knowledge much improved.*
		Etiquette	
___	X	Uses caller name	
___	X	Asks permission to transfer/put on hold	
X	___	Explains purpose for transfer/hold	*Said "hold please," and*
X	___	Thanks caller for holding	*didn't thank when returning.*
		Closing the call	
___	X	Confirms caller satisfaction	*"I know you're in a hurry, but I want to*
___	X	Tells caller what to expect	*take just one more minute to let you*
___	X	Thanks caller	*know what will happen next."*

Objectives | **Comments**

(1 = Below expectations   2 = Meets expectations   3 = Exceeds expectations)

1	2	3		Comments
			Service Skills	
___	X	___	Questions for information	
___	X	___	Uses active listening skills	
X	___	___	Confirms understanding	*Forgot to confirm quantity. Created*
___	___	X	Builds rapport with caller	*misunderstanding that took time to sort out.*
			Verbal/Vocal Skills	
___	___	X	Rate of speech	
___	___	X	Volume	*Excellent verbal skills, very professional*
___	___	X	Tone	*tone!*
___	___	X	Grammar	

FIGURE 8-1   Example of filled-in monitoring form.

Five Easy Pieces

If you don't already have a monitoring system in place, or if it doesn't seem to be working as well as you'd like, here's a quick, easy plan for setting up an effective system:

Step 1: Develop performance Standards and Objectives for your team.

Step 2: Create a monitoring form and an accompanying Contact Quality Guide (based on the Standards and Objectives).

Step 3: Share the monitoring form with team members. Be sure to define what each requirement means as well as what constitutes excellence in each area.

Step 4: Monitor calls or e-mails for a few weeks. (Be sure to give feedback to team members.)

Step 5: Revise the form if necessary and continue the ongoing cycle of monitoring and feedback.

A Strong Case for Not Scoring Your Forms

You may have noticed that in the sample forms we've provided, there's no cumulative score for the agent. That's because scoring forms, although a common practice, can be very problematic in the contact center environment. As soon as agents hear the score they received, they tend to mentally register only whether or not they "passed" and then tune out anything the coach says after that. But if continuous improvement is the true aim, then the specific details of the call, and not the score, are what's really important.

In our view, it's just too simplistic to say that some calls pass while other calls fail. If a coach invests time and energy making a careful assessment of a call or e-mail, it only seems right that the result should be a meaningful learning opportunity for the agent. Here's an illustration:

> At PDQ Contact Center, agents are required to achieve a score of 70 or above on the monitoring form. If they don't, they may face disciplinary action. So manager Bob listens to one of agent Susie's calls, and she scores a 71. Bob's not too surprised because Susie generally scores in the low 70s. But since this isn't golf, it's fair to say that Susie isn't doing very well. So, off Bob goes to Susie's cubicle to give her some feedback on the call. The first thing she wants to know is whether or not she scored at least a 70. As soon as she hears or sees (by peeking at the

monitoring form Bob is holding in his hand) that she got a 71, she breathes a sigh of relief. And then she tunes out everything else Bob says, because in her mind the only thing that really matters is whether or not she received a passing score.

You may be thinking that not everyone is like Susie; many agents are self-motivated to continually improve. And you're right, some agents are. But those who perform in the low 70s most often are not.

Scoring does tend to be important for the purposes of the QA department, and we're not suggesting that you don't allow the QA people to do their job. But when it comes to feedback (which, remember, is *your* job), we suggest that you either don't mention the score or mention it only after you've given specific feedback to the agent.

CONTACT QUALITY GUIDE

Your monitoring form is the cornerstone of your monitoring and coaching, as it will be your main tool to use in giving feedback. But to help you in your quest for consistency and fairness, you also need to have a Contact Quality Guide. This is a one- or two-page document that provides a brief explanation of each Standard and Objective.

Why do you need to go to this trouble? Well, what if you've consistently scored an agent a 2 in professionalism and the agent wants to know what, specifically, he or she needs to do differently in order to score a 3? As we discussed earlier, the ideal situation is that everyone in the contact center agrees on what "professional" looks or sounds like. That's where your Contact Quality Guide comes in handy.

Developing a Contact Quality Guide may take some time, but it will be well worth it because you'll be able to clearly communicate Standards and Objectives to your agents and you'll be able to monitor them in a consistent manner.

Take a look at Sample Monitoring Form #1 and the Sample Contact Quality Guide that follows. (See the appendix for a reproducible version.) Notice how the Contact Quality Guide gives much more detail than the monitoring form.

SAMPLE CONTACT QUALITY GUIDE

Standards

Gives scripted greeting	Uses greeting on screen, captures media code
Gathers account information	Asks for account number and explains why
Acquires/spell-verifies info	Key-spells caller info and asks caller to confirm
Uses support cards if necessary	Uses appropriate statements if caller won't give info
Responds to first statement	Leads into call by taking care of caller's question first
Reads help screens as appropriate	Does not read too much or too little info; checks in with caller
Gives accurate info	Gives full and correct answer to caller's specific question
Offers additional info/education	Gives whatever additional info is appropriate to call
Gives correct scripted closing	Follows correct closing screens; logs call correctly

Objectives

Questions to gather information	Uses open/closed questions appropriately
Listens for key words and phrases	Shows by response that agent understands caller
Confirms understanding	Asks for confirmation that understanding is correct
Does not ask for info provided	Does not ask caller to repeat what he/she said earlier
Handles challenges	Uses appropriate skill model to handle challenges
Responds professionally	Is positive, polite, and skilled at all stages of call
Builds rapport	Uses caller's name, shows appreciation, responds to caller
Demonstrates verbal/vocal skills	Uses right tone, pace, grammar; avoids slang/jargon

As you create your Contact Quality Guide, ask yourself at each step, "Have I given enough information so that my agents will know exactly what is expected of them?" If not, add a few more words.

Once you've completed your Contact Quality Guide and have conducted some calibration sessions to be sure everyone agrees, hand out copies to your agents along with a copy of the monitoring form so that they know what is expected of them.

TIP!

If a few different people monitor and coach a single team of employees, make sure they get together from time to time to calibrate their results. This ensures that the reps' performance is being fairly and consistently assessed. It also keeps those who are monitoring on their toes!

About All That White Space . . .

You need to write a lot of comments and specifics about the call, because if you go to give feedback and all you've got is marks and numbers, your feedback is going to sound (at best) something like this:

> *"Julie, you exhibited great listening skills in that last call. I also thought you did a good job at building rapport."*

But wouldn't the feedback make more of an impact if it went something like this:

> *"Julie, you exhibited great listening skills in that last call. I could tell that the customer was really impressed when you said, 'Let me just confirm what you've told me so far . . .' and then you restated the three needs she had divulged up to that point in the call. I also thought you did a great job at building rapport. Mrs. Sapian really warmed up when you started using her name, plus it was such a nice touch when you told her who to contact for a copy of the grant application guidelines . . ."*

TIP!

Tips for Writing Comments on Monitoring Forms

- If you want to point out something the rep said during the call, write the exact comment and put it in quotation marks.

  "I can get that done for you right now."

  "That's definitely not the kind of service we want to provide."

- Draw an arrow or a line to tie your comment to the Standard or Objective it relates to.

- Put a plus or a minus sign in front of comments to indicate whether the comment relates to something you want to praise or something you want to correct.

  + Sounds very natural, not as if reading a script

  — Hurried the customer, often interrupted her

- Never write comments that you wouldn't want someone else to read.

  Wrong: *Gave idiotic response to caller's question about shipping options*

  Right: *Brush up on knowledge about shipping options*

See the appendix for a reproducible, concise version of these tips.

Where Does the Customer's Opinion Come In?

What should you do about including customer satisfaction as a criterion in your measurement procedures? It's a tricky subject. The problem with measuring customer satisfaction is that it's very unpredictable and very subjective. If an agent does everything he or she is supposed to do but the customer is impossible to please, are you going to take action against the agent? Conversely, if the customer seems delighted but you happen to know (because you can see behind the scenes) that the agent did something wrong, are you going to go with the customer's opinion? Here's where we come down on the matter: create a customer feedback loop somewhere in your organization, but don't use it as your primary measure for giving performance feedback to agents.

ADDITIONAL RESOURCES

Books

Deblieux, Mike. *Supervisor's Guide to Employee Performance Reviews.* Charlottesville, VA: Lexis Law Publishing, 1999.

Phillips, J. Jack. *Handbook of Training and Evaluation Methods.* Houston, TX: Gulf Professional Publishing Company, 1997.

Rae, Leslie. *Trainer Assessment; A Guide to Measuring the Performance of Trainers and Facilitators.* New York: Gower Publishing Company, 2002.

Robinson, G. Dana, and Robinson, James C. *Training for Impact: How to Link Training to Business Needs and Measure the Results.* San Francisco: Jossey-Bass, 1989.

Zigon, Jack. *Employee Performance Measurement Workbook.* Holmes, PA: Zigon Performance Group, 1998.

Companies

ACD Call Center (offers a call center measurement toolkit). URL: www.call-center.net; phone: 800-700-2831.

Satmetrix (Satmetrix *Employee* measures employee satisfaction and loyalty and tracks employee feedback suggestions). URL: www.satmetrix.com; phone: 888-800-2313.

ZPG (offers train-the-trainer workshops for measuring employee performance). URL: www.zigonperf.com; phone: 800-244-2892.

Associations, Magazines, and Interesting Web Sites

ZPG (provides resources for measuring, managing, and improving employee performance). URL: www.zigonperf.com; phone: 800-244-2892.

Case Studies

United States Office of Personnel Management (offers a free case study entitled "Handbook for Measuring Employee Performance: Aligning Employee Performance Plans with Organizational Goals"). URL: www.opm.gov.

CHAPTER 9

Coaching to Improve Performance

The Fundamentals of Effective Feedback

THE KEYSTONE OF COACHING

The term *coaching* in its broadest sense can be used to describe many of the managerial and motivational functions outlined in this book, but in its most common usage *coaching* refers to the practice of giving feedback to employees in order to help them achieve improved performance. This is fundamentally what coaching is—helping people to do a better job.

Giving feedback goes hand in hand with the practice of measuring performance. First you monitor an employee, then you coach, and then you monitor again. It's an ongoing process. If you're doing it right, you should be seeing your employees' performance continually improve.

Coaching can be one-way (meaning you do the talking) or two-way (meaning you and the rep have a conversation about performance). Typically, one-way coaching occurs right after you've heard a call or otherwise measured performance. It might also occur after you've monitored several calls or e-mails over a period of time and want to give feedback on trends in the rep's performance. In one-way coaching, you go out to the call floor and give quick verbal feedback to the rep or you send a coaching comment through your call monitoring software's feedback mechanism. One-way coaching works well when circumstances don't allow you to take agents off the floor for more extensive discussions. In contact centers where e-mail is the primary form of communication, the majority of your feedback may be via e-mail with only occasional face-to-face feedback. Voice mail is also a quick way to give spot feedback.

Two-way coaching refers to more in-depth feedback sessions where you and an agent sit down to talk about trends in performance, a particular situation that's troubling the agent, or some other issue. Two-way coaching also takes place during quarterly performance reviews or "chats" about why a particular behavior has not changed. Two-way coaching should take place in your office or in some other location away from the contact center floor.

Typically, one-way coaching occurs on a daily or weekly basis—it's an ongoing and intrinsic function of daily life in the contact center. Two-way review sessions may take place every week, month, or quarter, or simply as needed. Of course, sometimes a one-way coaching session can escalate into an impromptu two-way session—usually because the rep disagrees with your feedback or for some other reason wants to discuss a performance issue at length.

In this chapter you'll learn several principles of feedback that can be applied to both one-way and two-way coaching sessions. In Chapter 10, you'll learn more about how to address behaviors or performance issues that aren't improving despite your repeated feedback.

It Only Takes a Second

Hopefully, you're already in the habit of giving quick verbal feedback to your reps on a regular basis. It can take the form of praise, constructive criticism (which we call *correcting*), or both. Following are some examples of one-way coaching.

"Great way to handle that upset customer, Renee! Your calm persistence really turned her attitude around."

"Johnny, you really helped that caller understand how our insurance plan is a great fit for her family. And I could tell she appreciated the fact that you took the time to explain everything to her in plain English. Good job!"

"Thanks for your help with the systems today, Pat. I know how busy you are. With your help, though, we'll be able to get the client's project up and running in time, and I just want you to know how much I appreciate you finding time to pitch in."

"Zack, in your correspondence with the customer from Gideon Electronics, you had a great opportunity to use open questions to gather information about his needs. That would have helped to simplify and expedite the order. Don't forget to use that Open Questions job aid we created during our last training program. Do you think you can make a commitment to refer to that list during the rest of your correspondence today?"

> "As progressive call centers recognize that they can no longer rely on traditional training techniques to raise performance levels and continually re-skill their workers, they are adopting and developing a genuine coaching culture."
>
> —Perry Zeus, "Coaching in New Call School Centres," *Customer Contact World*, November 1, 2000.

WHY COACHING IS SO IMPORTANT

Giving feedback to your employees isn't a luxury. It isn't a maybe. It isn't a one-of-these-days-I'll-get-around-to-doing-it aspect of your job. Giving feedback to your reps is one of the two or three most critical things you do as a contact center manager. Several studies have shown the dramatic results of pairing coaching with training. One, for example, found that training alone increased productivity by 22.4 percent. But when training was followed up with coaching, the figure soared to 88 percent. (Source: "Executive Coaching as a Tool: Effects on Productivity in a Public Agency," *Public Personnel Management*, vol. 26, issue 4, winter 1997, p. 461)

To prove this point, all you have to do is take a very short, very easy pop quiz.

COACHING 101 POP QUIZ

1. What happens when an employee's undesirable behavior isn't addressed?
   a. It continues.
   b. It continues.
   c. It continues.

2. What happens when an employee's desirable behavior isn't noticed and praised?
   a. If you're a little lucky, it continues for a while.
   b. If you're not so lucky, it stops.
   c. If you're insanely lucky, the employee is self-motivated enough to continue the behavior whether or not you give positive feedback.

(Answers: All are correct.)

OK, you get the point. In the absence of coaching, the best result you can hope for is the status quo. In our experience, the most successful contact centers are those in which managers have put in place a meaningful, effective, and consistent practice of coaching.

But there are other reasons why giving feedback is so important. It shows your reps that you're on top of things, that you're keeping yourself informed, and that you're dedicated to a course of continual improvement. What's more, coaching shows your employees that you care about them, about their performance, about the customer, about service levels, and about running a top-notch contact center.

In the absence of coaching, most employees become demotivated. It becomes irresistibly easy and comfortable to just slide by, to put in the minimal amount of effort. "After all," the thinking goes, "why should I care about doing a good job when nobody's watching (or listening)?"

Here's a question we often want to ask managers who don't give feedback to their reps: if you're not telling them how they're doing and how they can do better, through what magical, mystical means do you expect their behavior to change?

> *Here's a question we often want to ask managers who don't give feedback to their reps: if you're not telling them how they're doing and how they can do better, through what magical, mystical means do you expect their behavior to change?*

OK, get ready, because we're going to hit you over the head with it one more time: if you're not regularly giving feedback, you're skipping out on one of the most essential aspects of your job as a manager. Contact center employees rely on you to let them know what they're doing well and where their performance needs to be improved.

The worst kind of feedback isn't negative feedback, it is *no* feedback. This forces the employee to guess, to have doubts.

—John T. Self

Why Some Managers Don't Give Feedback (or Seven Famous Excuses for Not Coaching Employees)

You're probably wondering why, if it is such an important part of the managerial function, some people still don't make a practice of coaching their reps. Following are seven famous excuses (each of which we've heard countless times) as well as our attempts to overcome them. *Warning:* The following section is not one of the more warm and fuzzy portions of this book.

Excuse 1: "I Don't Know How to Give Feedback."

Fair enough. If you don't know how to do it, we're not surprised that you're currently not in the practice of coaching your employees to improve their performance. (We are a bit surprised that you were hired to be a contact center manager and weren't then taught how to give feedback, but that can be a chapter in our next book.) This book is where you learn to give feedback. Later in this chapter, you'll learn some very simple yet effective models for praising and correcting behavior. Here's the bottom line: if you want to keep using this as a legitimate excuse, you'd better stop reading now.

Excuse 2: "I Don't Have Time to Give Feedback."

Really? You don't have the same 24 hours in a day that the rest of us have? Fascinating, but probably not true. We know that managing in a contact center involves many important functions, all of which take time, energy, and talent. But what we don't understand is that some managers fail to view coaching as one of them. It's crucial for you to be able to manage your time and your tasks so that you can incorporate coaching into your daily routine as a manager.

Need some further inspiration? Think of how much more time you'd have in a day or in a week if you didn't have to:

- Hire new reps to replace the ones who left because they felt unappreciated
- Put out fires that could have been prevented if you had addressed them (via coaching) when they were only sparks
- Pull teeth to get your reps to perform well

Excuse 3: "Feedback Doesn't Work."

This comes as news to the thousands of contact center managers for whom feedback is an indispensable tool in driving improved performance. If you believe that feedback doesn't work, then chances are good that there are problems either with the validity of the feedback or with the approach of the person giving it.

Excuse 4: "Employees Aren't Receptive to Feedback."

This is sometimes true. But it can be changed. One of the things that may need to happen is for you to remind your reps of one of the universal truths of the workplace environment: that having a manager means being managed. Don't get us wrong, we're not fans of heavy-handed management, but the truth is that this is how successful contact centers operate. Employees should expect to receive feedback; if it's done well, they'll start to crave it.

Here's a true story from one of our colleagues. It shows how much progress can be made in the course of just one workday.

Kate Jennings (not her real name) is a talented trainer and consultant who frequently works with contact centers. She was contracted to monitor and coach a group of "high-end" customer service representatives—the well-paid, educated, experienced, well-dressed type. Initially, the reps felt they had nothing to learn from a consultant and they resisted Kate's presence in their work environment. The last thing they wanted to do was sit and listen to some outsider tell them how to perform better at their job.

But, being the wise soul that she is, Kate had a plan. She began by monitoring calls and giving only praise. She would monitor a call, then walk over to the rep's desk and praise the rep for one or two things he or she did particularly well on the call. Kate did this with everyone, and after a while it warmed them up.

Then she moved on to correcting. Along with the praise, she would give reps one or two suggestions for something else they might try on their next few calls. Then she would monitor again and once again give feedback. If the reps had done what she suggested, she praised and thanked them for their efforts. It didn't take long before these reps, who had initially been very icy, were pushing their chairs out into the aisle to catch Kate's attention. By the end of the day, enthusiastic requests such as "Hey, Kate, did you hear that last call?" and "Kate, will you monitor me again?" had become commonplace.

Excuse 5: "I Don't Want to Be Negative."

So don't be. There's no law that says correcting has to be negative. In fact, when done skillfully, correcting shows reps where they have an opportunity to improve and leaves them feeling inspired to try. (You'll learn more about how to do this later in the chapter.)

Excuse 6: "I Don't Know What I Should Coach Them On."

Sorry, but we have to say it: to us, this excuse is deeply troubling. To be successful, a contact center manager has to play a hands-on role. We don't mean to sound flip or critical; we're just saying that in order for you to do a high-quality job as a manager, it's key for you to know what to look for in your agents' performance. If you're new to the job or for some other reason haven't yet learned how to assess agents' performance, then the best thing is to start immediately (Chapter 8 is a good place to start). You might also ask for help from another manager, your own manager, or someone else in the center whose expertise might be useful.

Excuse 7: "I Trust Them to Manage Themselves."

It's great when you get to a point where you have agents you can trust to always do a great job. But chances are good that not all members of your team are able or ready to successfully manage themselves. Plus, everyone—even your consistently stellar performers—needs praise, and praise is the cornerstone of coaching. And then, of course, there are new agents joining your team; how can you expect them to manage themselves? And what about when a major change gets implemented? This is another example of when coaching from a manager becomes indispensable.

THE SEVEN FUNDAMENTALS OF FEEDBACK

Later in this chapter, you'll learn some simple yet effective models for praising and correcting. In that section, you'll learn what to say. For now, though, let's talk about what to do when giving your feedback to reps. The seven guidelines outlined in this section will help you to master this delicate but essential function of the management role. They'll also help to ensure that your feedback is well received by your reps.

The appendix contains a reproducible, condensed version of the seven fundamentals.

Fundamental 1: Be Specific

When giving feedback, it's important to focus on specific details. Not only does this show that you were paying close attention when monitoring, but it also helps the rep to understand exactly what he or she did right or wrong. Notice how much more effective the second of the two following statements is in comparison with the first:

Take One

"You did a great job on that last call."

Take Two

"You used some great open questions to get the customer talking."

Now the rep knows what specific behavior he or she exhibited that made the call successful and is eager to continue it. The same holds true when you're correcting. Notice the difference between the following two statements:

Take One

"You could have tried harder on the call with the prospect from Smithson Electronics."

Take Two

"When the customer from Smithson Electronics resisted your attempt to close the sale, you had a great opportunity to use the two steps for overcoming resistance that we learned in the sales training course."

In this case, the rep now knows what "trying harder" looks like and is much more likely to do it in future calls.

Fundamental 2: Focus on Performance, Not Personality

Your feedback should always focus on issues of performance, not on traits of a rep's personality. If you feel that a character flaw is to blame, then translate it into a performance issue before giving feedback. Like this:

"Pat, your tendency to speak so quickly when asking customers for their account information sometimes gives the impression that you're being curt."

Fundamental 3: Focus on Behavior that Can Be Changed

There's really no point in giving feedback to someone if there is nothing he or she can do to change the behavior. For example, if a rep speaks with a strong accent, chances are he or she has always spoken that way. By giving feedback on the accent you won't accomplish anything—except possibly to make the rep self-conscious and insecure.

Fundamental 4: Keep It Simple—And Sincere

Just like the rest of us, your reps will be overwhelmed if asked to improve in more than one or two areas at a time. If you identify 10 areas in which you want a rep to make progress, point out 2 of them. Then, once the rep has made progress in those areas, introduce something else for him or her to work on (after praising the previous progress, of course).

Also, keep it concise. This will prevent you from wasting unnecessary time and from convoluting the true performance issue. If there's too much "fluff," the rep may not be able to discern what's really important.

Managers who aren't very comfortable giving feedback to their employees often surround the true message with a lot of extra words, especially when correcting. There are two potential problems with this tendency: (1) it devalues the feedback and (2) it makes the manager look unskilled.

> Words that come from the heart enter the heart.
>
> —Anonymous

Fundamental 5: Give Feedback as Soon as Possible

As a general rule, it's best to give feedback as soon as possible after monitoring a call, an e-mail, or a chat session. This way, the rep will be able to recall specific details about the communication. If you aren't able to give feedback right away, have a tape of the call, or a copy of the e-mail thread or chat session, with you when coaching. Not only does this help refresh the agent's memory, but it also provides "evidence" in case there's a discrepancy between your assessment and that of the agent.

Fundamental 6: Pay Attention to Your Body Language

Your body language when giving feedback to a rep—particularly if it's done out on the contact center floor—can make a big difference in how well the feedback is received. Following are a few tips:

- *Keep it private.* One-way coaching typically takes place on the call floor, and for obvious reasons it's important to do what you can to keep it private. Approach the rep with a smile as you enter his or her cubicle or workstation and then get down to the rep's level either by kneeling or sitting. Speak just loudly enough for the rep to hear you.
- *Maintain eye contact.* Whether you're praising, correcting, or both, look the rep in the eye. This conveys an attitude of sincerity and professionalism and shows the rep that he or she has your undivided attention.
- *Watch your tone of voice.* When giving feedback, be careful to use a calm, supportive, and upbeat tone. When addressing undesirable behavior, it's often necessary to be firm, but that doesn't mean you have to be aggressive. If you let your own impatience or frustration creep into your tone of voice, you'll cause the rep to be far less receptive to what you have to say.
- *Smile!* If you're praising a rep, your smile conveys your appreciation and support. If you're correcting, a smile might send a visual cue that negates the verbal message, but after you've finished correcting, you might smile and thank the rep for his or her willingness to make a commitment to improve.

Fundamental 7: Avoid the Ambush Approach

Don't just race over to a rep's desk after hearing a call or seeing a problem in a chat session and immediately jump into your feedback. We've found that you'll have much better results if you ease into the session by giving the rep a moment to mentally prepare for the feedback. This shows your concern and respect for your employee and it sets up the session as a professional exchange—the kind of thing that happens all the time in a successful contact center environment.

Following is a script from the first few moments of a typical one-way coaching session:

> Coach (smiling):   Hi, Casey.
>
> Casey: Hi.
>
> Coach: I just monitored a couple of calls, and I wanted to take a moment to discuss them with you. Can I ask you to put your phone in "make busy" mode so you won't get a call while we're talking?
>
> Casey (adjusting phone):   Yeah, sure.
>
> Coach: Thanks. OK, Casey, let's talk first about some of the things that really impressed me on your call with the woman from Texas . . .

This setup only takes a few seconds but it provides a good transition into the one-way coaching session.

Two Basic Colors

Feedback comes in two basic colors: praising and correcting. Praising means positively reinforcing behavior that you want the employee to continue. Correcting means curtailing behavior that you want the employee to discontinue.

"Mistakes are the usual bridge between inexperience and wisdom."
—Phyllis Theroux, *Night Lights* (Penguin, 1988)

PRAISING

Praising your employees is the single most important thing you do as a coach. People will perform their best when they feel good about themselves and the contribution they're making to their organization. And it's pretty hard to feel good when all they hear is what they're doing wrong.

In order to consistently perform at the highest levels, your reps need to hear words of praise and encouragement from you. Again and again and again. Believe us, they'll never grow tired of it!

When you praise your employees, you profoundly influence their self-esteem and their performance on the job. As behavioral scientists have proven time and again in the laboratory, positive feedback increases the frequency of a desired response. When negative feedback is given (or when no feedback is given), the desired behavior tends to occur less and less frequently.

> The deepest principle in human nature is the craving to be appreciated.
> —William James

How to Praise

There are a number of effective models for praising employees. Outlined in this section is one very simple way that we've found to be effective in any environment. It's called the Behavior—Effect—Thanks (BET) Model. It's as easy to do as it is to remember, and it can greatly impact the performance and morale of your team. All three steps of the BET Model serve an important purpose. Let's take a closer look at each one.

B Behavior

Tell the rep what, specifically, he or she is doing that is valuable. This identifies the desirable behavior so that the rep can continue it.

E Effect

Tell the rep how that behavior made a positive contribution to the outcome of the call, the company's bottom line, or anything else. This step explains to the rep why that specific behavior is so valuable.

T Thanks

Thank the rep for his or her contribution. There are lots of ways to do this: the important thing is to show your appreciation and to encourage the rep to keep up the good work.

See the appendix for a reproducible, concise version of the BET Model.

Special Effects!

Feeling stuck about how to let reps know what the effect of their behavior is? Try one of these:

- *"That shows the customer that we care about getting it right."*
- *"That's a great way to let our subscribers know that we have many services they might not be aware of !"*
- *"By doing that, you really cut down on the call length."*
- *"You made the customer feel important."*
- *"That will help us meet our department's goal of a 10 percent increase in renewed memberships."*

Following are several examples of the BET Model:

*"Joey, I really liked the way you handled that upset customer. When you showed empathy for his situation, (**BEHAVIOR**) you really won his trust. (**EFFECT**) Good job! (**THANKS**)"*

*"Delia, you did a great job informing that last caller about the prescription drug program. It seemed like she was ready to end the call, but your closed question, "Do you take any medication on an ongoing basis?" (**BEHAVIOR**) uncovered a real need for the home delivery pharmacy. (**EFFECT**) It sounds like the caller will be able to save a lot of money with our plan. Great work! (**THANKS**)"*

*"Amid, you've really mastered the art of up-selling. I could tell that Mr. Hammond hadn't even considered bumping up his order, but once you pointed out the benefits of purchasing a year's supply, (**BEHAVIOR**) he was thrilled. (**EFFECT**) A few more calls like that will take us a long way toward reaching our sales goal this month. Thanks for your strong contribution! (**THANKS**)"*

*"Grace, you've done such a nice job of working with the team leaders to manage the agents during our spring sales campaign. I also want to complement you on the inspiring way you've decorated the contact center floor. (**BEHAVIOR**) Our numbers are coming in much higher than we expected. That makes our entire department look good and will help us earn that bonus we're shooting for. (**EFFECT**) Thanks so much for your hard work. I really appreciate it. (**THANKS**)"*

*"Julio, I'm so excited about the way you've been able to improve the attendance record in your unit. (**BEHAVIOR**) By having people here—and having them here on time—your team is now 12 percent over standard in the number of customers you serve each day. (**EFFECT**) That's just fantastic! I really appreciate the way you took a*

personal interest in those two or three problem agents and got them back on track and excited about coming to work. I'm really impressed with your work. **(THANKS)** "

> "In my wide association in life, meeting with many great men in various parts of the world, I have yet to find the man, however great or exalted his station, who did not do better work and put forth greater effort under a spirit of approval than he would ever do under a spirit of criticism."
>
> —Charles Schwab

OK, Coach, it's your turn to give it a try. Read the following two scenarios and write a BET statement to praise the rep in each situation.

Scenario 1

Harold is a technical support representative assigned to take calls for a large software company that outsources its service calls to your contact center. When you monitored his last call (from a home user named Ann Whelan), you noted several things he did well, including the following:

- He asked some great questions that helped to quickly and accurately diagnose the customer's software problem.

- While the customer was describing the problem, Harold listened attentively and took notes. Before moving on to a diagnosis, he repeated the main points of what the customer had described to make sure that he had correctly understood what she said.

- Before ending the call, he confirmed that the customer was satisfied with the way he handled the call and he asked if she had any other software or service issues.

Choose any one of the bulleted points and write a BET statement to praise Harold. Be sure your statement covers all three steps: Behavior—Effect—Thanks. You can use the lines provided.

Now try one more.

Scenario 2

Debra is a customer service representative who handles chat sessions for the subscriber services department of a large daily newspaper. When monitoring one of her sessions (with a subscriber who was upset because his newspaper had not been delivered), you observed that she did the following:

- She empathized with the customer.

- She maintained a poised and positive demeanor.

- She apologized and said, "That's certainly not the kind of service we want to provide."

- She offered the customer a choice between having the paper delivered within an hour (to his home or office) or receiving a one-week credit on his subscription.

Choose any one of the bulleted points and write a BET statement to praise Debra. Be sure your statement covers all three steps: Behavior—Effect—Thanks. You can use the lines provided.

_____

_____

_____

_____

_____

_____

_____

_____

_____

How did you do? There are lots of different possibilities. Here are some BET statements that we liked.

BET Statement 1 for Harold

"Harold, your questioning skills in that last call were excellent! The caller was rambling, and your question, 'What specific information are you looking for?,' got her right back on track. When she still wasn't clear about the outcome she wanted, you said, 'There are a couple of things you can do. Do you want the print function completely disabled or would you like to be able to print out a record of all transactions at the end of the day?' **(BEHAVIOR)** *Both of these questions helped you quickly and accurately diagnose the customer's software problem. That helps keep your talk time down and our profits up—and it helped save the customer time as well.* **(EFFECT)** *Thanks for doing such a great job on that call.* **(THANKS)"**

BET Statement 2 for Harold

"Hey, Harold, it sounded like that last call was a complicated one! I noticed that you were taking some great notes and that you took the time to confirm your complete understanding of the customer's problem prior to making a correct diagnosis. **(BEHAVIOR)** *That really made Ann feel confident that you understood her issues and could solve her problem, which is a key reason why we always get repeat business from her.* **(EFFECT)** *Nice touch!* **(THANKS)"**

BET Statement 1 for Debra

"Debra, you did a nice job handling that angry customer. He was threatening to cancel his subscription, but as soon as you empathized by saying, 'I can appreciate that it's frustrating not to have the news available before you leave for work, **(BEHAVIOR)** *he calmed right down. I think you saved a customer today!* **(EFFECT)** *Good job! I really appreciate you putting what you learned in training into practice.* **(THANKS)"**

BET Statement 2 for Debra

"Debra, that last caller sounded pretty upset, and I thought for sure he was going to cancel. When you emphasized the positive by stating, 'Mr. Jones, up till now we've had a perfect delivery record in your area for the last five years. We intend to be perfect for at least another five,' you proved our value and helped him realize that this was a one-time event, which made all the difference. **(BEHAVIOR)** *I think we can count on Mr. Jones as a customer for another five years because of that.* **(EFFECT)**. *Thanks for the awesome work!* **(THANKS)"**

Praise like a Professional

Praise shouldn't be confused with a compliment. Telling a rep her hair looks nice is paying a compliment. Telling her how she saved a customer from defecting to one of your competitors is praise. Know where to draw the line.

When to Praise

When should you praise your employees? As often as possible. There is always something to praise—every day, with every employee. The more you praise, the more willing your reps will be to receive feedback from you. And this means that when you have to correct something they're doing wrong, they'll be much more open to hearing it from you than they would be if they didn't frequently receive praise.

> "Deal with the faults of others as gently as with your own."
> —Chinese proverb

CORRECTING

Oh, how we wish the only task we had as managers was to praise employees all day long—it's just so much fun! But in the real world of contact centers (at least in the real world of all the contact centers we've ever been in), managers are faced with the responsibility of continually improving the performance of frontline employees. And the only way to do that is to combine all that praising with equal doses of correcting. Even your strongest reps can improve, and it's your job to help them know how.

In order to be an effective manager, you must be willing to venture out of your comfort zone to correct behavior that directly or indirectly affects the productivity or well-being of your team or organization. When you give constructive feedback to your employees, you give them an opportunity to improve and the encouragement and support they need to do it. When you don't address poor performance or incorrect behavior, you set your employees up for eventual failure. No good coach wants to do that!

As you learned earlier in this chapter, correcting refers to the practice of giving feedback on the skills or areas in which a rep is not performing as well as he or she could be. Correcting should not be reserved only for your lowest-performing reps. All employees need to be coached toward improvement, and we've found that if it's done well, even the highest performers will come to crave your feedback on their calls (or e-mails or chat sessions). If they get enough praise, your employees will be open to correcting. They'll learn to trust you and know that you want them to succeed.

Of course, there are some managers who correct much more than they praise. This can be even more harmful than praising without correcting. (If you tend to be one of these, stay tuned for Chapter 11, in which we share with you a number of creative ideas for remembering to give agents liberal doses of praise.)

Whereas praising is a simple enough practice that you can usually deliver it without a lot of forethought, correcting takes homework. You need to be prepared to tell your reps exactly what they can do to improve. How can you expect them to perform better if you don't tell them how?

TIP!

Ask your employees for feedback about your performance as a coach. Then thank them for their feedback and make any necessary adjustments to your own performance. We guarantee you'll learn a lot, plus you'll model the fine art of receiving feedback.

How to Correct

As with praising, there are any number of effective models for correcting employees. One that we've found to be simple yet highly effective in contact centers is the Behavior—Effect—Expectation—Secure commitment (BEES) Model. Here's how it goes:

B   Behavior

Point out the behavior that you want to correct. Remember to be specific.

E   Effect

Explain what effect that behavior had on the customer, the outcome of the call, the company's goals, and so on.

E   Expectation

Tell the rep what you expect him or her to do differently. (This is where your preparation comes into play.) Be sure to keep your expectations realistic.

S   Secure Commitment

Secure a commitment from the rep to try what you've asked. This step is essential because it's where you get the rep to verbally commit to what you're asking him or her to do.

The appendix contains a short, reproducible version of the BEES Model.

Let's look at some examples of a coach correcting an employee using the BEES Model.

> *"Jamie, I think you could have made that call even stronger by using closed questions to control the call.* **(BEHAVIOR)** *That woman just rambled on and on, and as a result the call was about twice as long as it had to be.* **(EFFECT)** *As you know, decreasing call length is one of our performance goals this quarter, so I'd like you to focus on that for your next few calls. You can refer to the job aid we created that lists closed questions and other techniques for controlling call length.* **(EXPECTATION)**. *Give it a try and I'll listen to some more calls. Then we can talk again before you leave for the day. Does that sound like something you can do?* **(SECURE COMMITMENT)**"
>
> *"Rebecca, there was one thing in that call that really concerned me, and that's the way you were talking to the customer about benefits without consulting the help screens.* **(BEHAVIOR)** *In this case, you were lucky and the information you gave the caller was accurate, but, as you know, the help screens are continually being updated, and if you don't consult them when talking about benefits, you run the risk of giving the caller the wrong information.* **(EFFECT)** *I'd like you to focus on this for the rest of the day, making sure you go to the help screens in every call, even if the question is very simple.* **(EXPECTATION)** *Can I get you to commit to this, and I'll listen to some more calls throughout the day?* **(SECURE COMMITMENT)**"

See? It's simple—and effective! Now it's your turn to give the BEES Model a try. Just as you did with the BET Model, read the two following scenarios and then try your hand at crafting a BEES statement for each one.

Scenario 1

Antonio is a telephone sales representative who makes outbound calls to businesses in the manufacturing industry. His objective is to sell subscriptions to several industry-related magazines and periodicals. You just monitored one of Antonio's sales calls and you noted a few areas of concern:

- Antonio didn't use the standard call opening. He skipped the last step ("Ask your first question") and as a result had a hard time getting the customer engaged in a dialogue.

- When the prospect resisted the offer of a trial subscription to *Metropolitan Machining*, Antonio missed an opportunity to point out benefits that could have outweighed the customer's objection.

- Your overall impression of the call was that Antonio wasn't really trying. You'd like to see him exhibit a more enthusiastic and upbeat attitude when on the phone with prospects, as you've seen this can make a big difference in the outcome of sales calls.

Choose any one of the bulleted points and write a BEES statement to correct Antonio's performance. Be sure to include each step: Behavior—Effect—Expectation—Secure Commitment. You can use the lines provided.

_____

_____

_____

_____

_____

_____

_____

_____

_____

_____

Following are some sample BEES statements for Antonio.

BEES Statement 1 for Antonio

"Antonio, in the last few calls, you opened the call with, 'This is Antonio with MarKay Media Group. I'm calling today to follow up on your inquiry about advertising in Metropolitan Machining.' *You omitted the last step, 'Ask your first question.'* **(BEHAVIOR)** *Because you omitted that step, you had a hard time engaging the customers in a dialogue. This added to the length of the calls and allowed the customers to take control of the calls.* **(EFFECT)** *I'd like you to pull out your opening script and use it for the next few calls. Be sure to focus on the last step.* **(EXPECTATION)** *Will that work for you?* **(SECURE COMMITMENT)** *"*

BEES Statement 2 for Antonio

"Antonio, one of the benefits of Metropolitan Machining *is its independent ratings of various machine suppliers, which saves our customers a lot of research hassle. On the last call, I noticed that this benefit was missing from your conversation.* **(BEHAVIOR)** *As a result, the customer didn't understand the value of the offer and failed to subscribe.* **(EFFECT)** *I'd like you to focus on delivering a complete subscription script to every caller.* **(EXPECTATION)** *Do you feel you can do that?* **(SECURE COMMITMENT)** *"*

Scenario 2

Amanda is a customer service rep in the contact center of a large banking institution. She handles e-mail from customers with a wide range of questions, concerns, and problems. While reviewing one of Amanda's e-mail threads, you noticed that:

- Because of the customer's writing style, Amanda assumed he was a senior citizen and had a Golden Horizons savings account (designed exclusively for senior customers) but never actually confirmed this with the customer. Therefore, she may have given him wrong information about the features of his account.

- Throughout the e-mail thread, Amanda never used the customer's name. This is a performance standard in the contact center and all reps are required to use the customer's name at least once.

- Amanda neglected to inform the customer about the bank's low mortgage rate. As part of a promotion for the newly adjusted rate, all customer service reps have been asked to mention it to customers and ask if they're interested in learning more about it before ending the interaction.

Choose any one of the bulleted points and write a BEES statement to correct Amanda's performance. Be sure to include each step Behavior—Effect—Expectation—Secure Commitment. You can use the lines provided.

_____

_____

_____

_____

_____

_____

_____

_____

_____

_____

Here's our take:

BEES Statement 1 for Amanda

*"Amanda, in this e-mail thread we're reviewing, you neglected to use the customer's name. (**BEHAVIOR**) As you know, that's a standard in the unit. When you neglect to use the customer's name, not only are you not up to standard, but you're also missing a great opportunity to build rapport with the customer. (**EFFECT**) I'd like you to use the customer's name in all your e-mail correspondence. An easy way to remember to accomplish that standard is to use it in your opening or*

closing . . . something like, 'Thanks for your inquiry today, John.' **(EXPECTATION)** *Will you do that?* **(SECURE COMMITMENT)**"

BEES Statement 2 for Amanda

"Amanda, in your last e-mail communication, there was no mention of our new low mortgage rate promotion. **(BEHAVIOR)** *It's a standard that you mention the promotion, and the new rate can really save our customers a lot of money. If customers don't understand that we have lowered our rates, they often jump to the competition.* **(EFFECT)** *I need your commitment that you'll mention the promotion on every call.* **(EXPECTATION)** *Can you do that?* **(SECURE COMMITMENT)**"

When BEES Becomes BESS

In some situations, you may decide to change the third step of the BEES Model—Expectation—to Solicit suggestions, meaning that you ask the rep for suggestions about how his or her performance issue can be improved. This can be helpful in several ways. First, some agents may respond better to a plan that was their idea than they will to one that you're suggesting. Second, by asking agents for suggestions about how they can improve performance, you empower them as instruments of progress (it's always a good idea to encourage employees to come up with initiatives that will result in performance improvements). Finally, when you ask agents for suggestions as to how they might do something better, you often get insights into why they're doing that thing in the first place. This provides you with valuable feedback about agents' personalities and about what they're dealing with in their calls and e-mails.

In fact, in some environments, BESS is the standard approach and coaches switch to BEES when the center is very busy and there's no time to solicit agents' input. Decide which model will work best according to the particulars of your environment and the relative maturity and willingness of your agents.

The appendix contains a short, reproducible version of the BESS Model.

Here's an example of the BESS model:

Coach: Eric, I know you're taking a lot of calls these days because we've been so busy, and I understand how exhausting that can be. I'm concerned that on a few of the calls I've heard this week you haven't been taking notes and confirming your understanding of what the caller says. (**BEHAVIOR**) As a result, it's easy to get off track and give the wrong information, like you just did on that call with the man who wanted to include a leg to Tampa on his flight itinerary. If he hadn't been paying such close attention, he might have agreed to pay for a ticket that he didn't actually want. (**EFFECT**) What ideas do you have for keeping yourself energized and attentive during your calls? (**SUGGESTION**)

Eric: Well, I'm just taking so many calls and I don't have any time between them to prepare myself for the next call or even to breathe! I think I need to have a little more wrap time between calls just to get myself ready, to reorganize the materials on my desk—including my notepad, which keeps getting buried under things. Can I just stay in wrap mode for another 20 or 30 seconds after a call? That way I'm pretty sure I can keep up with everything I'm supposed to do on each call.

Coach: Alright, Eric, I think that's fair. Let's try having you take an extra 20 seconds between calls; you can keep your phone in wrap mode during that time. I'll listen to some more calls over the next few days and you'll focus on taking notes and confirming your understanding, right? (**SECURE COMMITMENT**)

Eric: Right.

One more thing about BESS: when soliciting suggestions from agents, use an open question (such as "What ideas do you have?") rather than a closed question (such as "Do you have any ideas?"). It's too easy for agents to simply reply "No" to the latter question. If they're not given the option of saying no, they'll work harder to come up with a suggestion for improvement.

> A number of studies have shown that most people think of themselves as top performers!

HOW TO DO TWO THINGS AT ONCE

Two-way coaching sessions almost always involve both praising and correcting. And, for a number of reasons, sometimes you'll need to accomplish both praising and correcting in a single one-way coaching session. When this is called for, we like to praise two or three things and correct one or two things per session. This leaves reps feeling encouraged and inspired about what they've done well but not overwhelmed about what they can do better.

When you praise and correct at the same time, there are a few additional things to keep in mind:

Praise First

When it comes to one-way coaching, we've found that the familiar adage "Save the best for last" does not apply. The session is bound to go better when the praising is done right at the beginning. This puts reps at ease—they'll breathe a sigh of relief to know that at least they're doing *something* well—and they will be in a more receptive frame of mind to receive whatever correcting you have to bestow upon them.

Avoid Using But

Once you've praised an employee's performance, *but* is the very last word in the English language that he or she will want to hear. As soon as an employee hears *but* (or its stepsister, *however*), the praise you just delivered has a tendency to fly out the nearest window. You can avoid this by using a transition phrase that moves the conversation along while allowing the rep to feel valued and supported (see the next section).

Make a Smooth Transition from Praising to Correcting

Once you have made your BET statement (or statements), stop talking and pause for a few seconds. This allows the praise to settle in and shows the rep that you're not just rushing through the praise in order to get to the correcting. Then, use a positive, professional transition statement as a segue into your BEES statement. Following are some that can work well:

- *"Now let's talk about some of the areas where I think you can be stronger . . ."*
- *"Jed, let's take a look at some of the things that didn't go so well on that call . . ."*
- *"I have some ideas about how your performance can be further improved . . ."*

- *"Let's look at some of the things that might have been stronger in that call..."*
- *"What I'd like you to work on now is..."*
- *"I noticed a couple of areas where I think you can be stronger..."*
- *"Let's look at a couple of things that seem to be giving you trouble..."*

Don't Sandwich Your Feedback

We're not sure why, but for some reason the praise-correct-praise model is a very commonly used feedback method in contact centers. No doubt the intention behind this model is a well-meaning one: let the first thing and the last thing the employee hears be good. One problem with this technique, however, is that the correcting isn't given equal importance. Instead, it gets buried. The other problem is that the agent doesn't get to bask in the praise. We've heard from a number of contact center agents that they're so accustomed to the sandwich approach that when they hear praise they're just waiting for the other shoe to drop. It can do wonders for their morale and motivation to give them praise and—for the moment—nothing else.

If you have a valid performance issue to address, there's no need to feel insecure about discussing it. It's better to convey your concern and support through your attitude than through "protecting" an employee from hearing unpleasant news.

TIP!

One way to show a supportive attitude when giving feedback is to use "we" language (especially when correcting). Words such as *we, our,* and *let's* (instead of *you, you,* and *you*) remind reps that improving performance is a team effort. Here are a few examples:

- *"One of the things we can do to correct that is..."*
- *"Our goal on these calls is to..."*
- *"For the next few days, let's try to focus on improving data entry errors..."*

Coaching involves bringing about change in the individual's thoughts, attitudes, and behaviors. It is a psychological-based process and coaches, therefore, require an understanding of the psychology of change.

—Suzanne Skiffington

ADDITIONAL RESOURCES

Books

Boughton, Nathaniel, and Gilley, Jerry W. *Stop Managing, Start Coaching!: How Performance Coaching Can Enhance Commitment and Improve Productivity.* New York: McGraw-Hill, 1995.

Collins, M. Michelle. *The Thin Book of 360° Feedback.* Plano, TX: Thin Book Publishing Co., 2000.

Crane, G. Thomas. *The Heart of Coaching: Using Transformational Coaching to Create a High Performance Culture.* San Diego, CA, FTA, 2001.

Flaherty, James. *Coaching: Evoking Excellence in Others.* Stoneham, MA: Butterworth-Heinemann, 1998.

House, Henry, Kimsey-House, Henry, Whitworth, Laura, and Sandahl, Phil. *Co-Active Coaching: New Skills for Coaching People Towards Success in Work and Life.* Palo Alto, CA: Davies-Black Publishing, 1998.

Mink, G. Oscar. *Developing High Performance People: The Art of Coaching.* Cambridge, MA: Perseus, 1993.

Tornow, Walter, and London, Manuel. *Maximizing the Value of 360-Degree, Feedback: A Process for Successful Individual and Organizational Development.* San Francisco: Jossey-Bass, 1998.

Whitmore, John. *Coaching for Performance (People Skills for Professionals).* London: Nicholas Brealey, 1996.

Companies

Get Feedback.net (a Web-based human performance profiling, reporting, and feedback company). URL: www.getfeedback.net; phone: +44 870-011-6300.

Web Surveyor (offers tools to create, publish, announce, and analyze results from online surveys). URL: www.websurveyor.com; phone: 800-787-8755.

CHAPTER 10

Dealing with Difficult Employees

Coaching Negative, Unmotivated, and "Problem" Agents

> "You get the behavior you tolerate."
>
> —Plato

One of the unpleasant but seemingly unavoidable aspects of contact center management is the need to deal firmly and fairly with difficult agents. Just as there are any number of reasons why an agent can become a problem—bad attitude, inability to do what's required, unresponsiveness to feedback on performance, and so on—there are various ways to handle the issues and the agents who create them.

In this chapter we'll look at effective models for coaching agents when there's a problem with either their behavior or their performance. In most cases, this two-way coaching takes place after a manager has used BET, BEES, BESS, or a combination of the three (see Chapter 9). This chapter outlines the more in-depth feedback sessions that are called for when simpler coaching efforts have not been effective in changing the behavior or performance of agents. The suggestions made in this chapter are not meant to replace your organization's disciplinary protocol. Rather, we'll deal here with the people side of coaching problem agents.

That being said, we do want to advise you to make sure that your center has a disciplinary protocol in place and that it's communicated to agents *before* they find themselves being subjected to it. Ideally, this information (which behaviors are unacceptable and what happens when an agent exhibits them) should be communicated during an agent's new-hire orientation. Typically, this protocol includes a four-step process: (1) verbal warning, (2) written warning,

(3) sanctions, and (4) termination. Later in this chapter you'll learn about a coaching process called warning. You may find that it has some overlap with whatever procedure you have in place for giving agents a verbal warning.

Could You Be Part of the Problem?

Sometimes an agent's poor attitude or inappropriate behavior is an unconscious effort to get attention in a destructive way because he or she can't get attention in positive ways. Surprising as it may sound, this may be partly your fault as a coach. To avoid this, make sure that you give plenty of positive reinforcement when agents exhibit desirable behavior.

CAN'T OR WON'T?

There are several reasons why people may not perform to expectations; before you can effectively coach these agents, it's important to determine whether the problem is occurring because the agent *can't* do something or *won't* do something. These can be two very different issues, and should be handled accordingly.

Determining where the root of the problem lies is key to figuring out the best way to communicate with a problem agent. Following are several examples of reasons why an agent can't or won't do something that's expected.

Agent doesn't want to do something:

- He or she isn't sufficiently motivated.
- He or she doesn't agree with the reasons why it should be done.
- He or she is intimidated by potential failure.
- He or she feels pressure from coworkers.

Agent can't do something:

- There are circumstances beyond his or her control.
- He or she doesn't have the necessary information or support.
- He or she lacks the required knowledge, training, or experience.
- He or she doesn't know what's expected.

As you can see, in order to change the behavior it's important that you first get to the true source of the problem. The best way to accomplish this is to make sure that your communication with agents is genuinely two-way. One important step is to make sure you ask the agent for an explanation of his or her behavior (you'll learn more about how to do this in the sections that follow). Another key is to make sure that agents are comfortable talking to you about the various factors that affect their performance and behavior.

TIP!

If an agent complains about something in the center, ask for specific, recent examples. Then ask the agent to suggest some constructive ways to solve the problem. This helps to empower the agent as a problem solver rather than merely a problem reporter.

Translating Attitude Problems into Performance Issues

Inevitably, there will be times when the problem created by an agent is clearly attributable to a poor attitude. But in order to effectively coach employees with attitude problems, you need to translate the problem into a performance issue. If you address the attitude directly, it's likely the agent will take it as a personal attack. To turn the attitude into a performance issue, identify some specific examples of how the attitude is manifested in the agent's work. Following are a few examples:

> *"Your curt responses to the customer's questions made the customer feel that he was being a nuisance to us."*

> *"Your unwillingness to carefully and accurately document service issues on the XK2700 contributes to lower customer satisfaction scores because customers have to re-explain their issues to the next agent when they call back."*
>
> *"When you don't take the time to write clear and concise e-mail responses to our customer queries, customers get a very unfavorable impression of our organization and of the service we provide."*

TIP!

Ten Tips for Communicating with Problem Employees

Following are some general guidelines to keep in mind when communicating with problem employees.

1. *Deal with the issue right away.* If you delay your response or ignore the issue altogether, you may look weak and ineffective as a manager. You'll also send

a message to other agents that they too can get away with this inappropriate behavior.

2. *Discuss the issue privately.* If you talk to the agent in front of his or her peers, he or she may become more defensive or aggressive. It may also make the other agents uncomfortable.

3. *Stay calm and poised.* Because you're the one in the position of power, you'll set the tone of the discussion. Always maintain a professional demeanor and convey the message, "This isn't working. How can we fix it?"

4. *Allow the agent to vent.* Just as you would an upset customer, give the agent a few moments to air his or her grievances. Sometimes this venting is exactly what a person needs to do before calming down and discussing the issue more rationally.

5. *Empathize.* If an agent is upset or disgruntled, let the agent know that you're aware he or she has strong feelings about the issue and that you're interested in helping him or her resolve them. Empathizing is not the same thing as agreeing. It just lets people feel heard and acknowledged.

6. *Focus on the issue, not the person.* No matter how strongly you believe that the agent's behavior or attitude is at the root of the problem, don't make the issue a personal one. You want to communicate that you are for the employee but against the behavior.

7. *Find common ground.* In order to get the agent to move toward a resolution, get him or her to acknowledge one or two areas in which you're both in agreement. For example, "Michael, we both have a stake in making this a good place to work and we've both been affected by the unusually high call volume over the last two weeks. Wouldn't you agree?"

8. *Point out alternative ways for the agent to express him- or herself.* If the agent has lashed out in anger or otherwise made an inappropriate display of emotion, point out that there are more constructive ways to express him- or herself and give one or two examples of what he or she might do in the future.

9. *Always give the agent an out.* It will only further upset agents if they feel that they're being backed up against a wall. When working to resolve an issue, be sure to give the agent an opportunity to choose the correct outcome of the discussion.

10. *Focus on a solution.* When emotions are running high, it's all too easy to get stuck in a continuous cycle of discussing the problem. Once the issue has been clearly identified, move the discussion forward by focusing on ways to resolve it.

See the appendix for a compact, reproducible version of these tips.

TWO-WAY COACHING

Two-way coaching allows you to have a conversation with the agent about a specific area of performance or a problem behavior. It typically occurs after a one-way coaching session has failed to change behavior. On occasion, however, a manager may use one of the two-way models without having attempted to correct behavior with one-way coaching.

The objectives of two-way coaching are to determine why a particular behavior or performance issue is occurring and to make a plan for solving it. Unlike the one-way models you learned about in Chapter 9, which take place on the call floor, two-way coaching sessions should take place privately. They can either be held in the manager's office or in some neutral location located out of earshot of the other agents.

Table 10-1 describes the three models of two-way coaching. In the sections that follow, you'll learn about each one in detail and see examples of it in practice. The appendix contains a short, reproducible overview of all three models.

Troubleshooting

Once you've addressed a particular performance issue with an agent and then seen that the issue has not been resolved, it's time to escalate to the more in-depth two-way coaching technique known as Troubleshooting. Troubleshooting aims to send a more serious—but still supportive—message to the agent that the issue must be resolved. What makes it different from the correcting models you saw in Chapter 9 is that Troubleshooting aims to get at the

TABLE 10-1 Two-Way Coaching for Performance and Behavior Issues

TWO-WAY COACHING MODEL	DESCRIPTION	WHEN TO USE IT	SAMPLE SCENARIOS
Troubleshooting	Aims to prevent a problem from continuing and possibly escalating into disciplinary action.	• For performance issues, if one-way coaching has not resulted in satisfactory change • For behavior issues, if this is the first time they are being addressed	• After repeated feedback from the manager, the agent is still making too many data entry errors. • The agent repeatedly forgets to clock out during lunch break.
Negotiating	The manager works with the agent to come up with a plan for solving the performance or behavior issue.	After Troubleshooting, if the issue is negotiable	• The Troubleshooting session wasn't successful in getting the agent to correct the tendency to talk too fast on the phone. • After the Troubleshooting session, the agent is still spending too much time small-talking with customers.
Warning	The manager makes a last attempt to address the issue before the agent faces disciplinary action.	After Troubleshooting, if the issue is not negotiable	• The agent is giving customers inaccurate information and has not responded to the manager's attempts to correct this. • After having the issue addressed by the manager, the agent continues to speak disparagingly of customers.

cause of the problem and to get the manager and agent working together to develop an action plan for improvement.

Troubleshooting can also be used to address behaviors that are related to attitude rather than performance. Furthermore, a simple one-way coaching session (such as using BEES to give quick feedback to an agent right after a call) can sometimes spontaneously escalate into a Troubleshooting session—usually because an agent disagrees with the feedback or for some other reason wants to discuss the issue further.

Following are three scenarios that call for Troubleshooting:

Scenario 1

Lee (the coach) has just shared feedback with Emma (the agent) about her questioning skills on outbound sales calls. Lee tells Emma that when he monitors her calls, he finds that she often misses opportunities to uncover customers' needs because she doesn't make skillful use of questions. Emma feels that she does question adequately, and she gives examples of questions she used in her last few calls. Lee acknowledges Emma's perspective but maintains his belief that she needs to use more strategic questioning in her calls.

Scenario 2

Petra (the coach) gave one-way coaching to Dominic (a technical support agent) about his tendency to use slang and jargon when helping customers. Dominic agreed to work on curbing this tendency, but after listening to several more calls, Petra has not noticed any improvement.

Scenario 3

Nolan (the coach) has been working with Gabrielle (the customer service agent) to improve her performance in building rapport with customers. Despite her agreement to do the things Nolan has asked, Gabrielle hasn't actually made any noticeable progress in this area.

The Troubleshooting Model doesn't have a catchy acronym to help you remember it (like BET, BEES, or BESS), but it does have a simple, logical progression:

Step 1: Describe the behavior. Provide one or two specific examples, and show documentation (such as a monitoring form) if necessary.

Step 2: Explain the effect of the behavior. Tell the agent how the behavior affects the customer, the team, or the organization.

Step 3: Ask for an explanation of the behavior. Keep an open mind as you listen to the agent. Remember that the agent isn't always at fault.

Step 4: Suggest/solicit solutions and show support. Let the agent know that you're determined to find a solution that will change the behavior and that you're available for assistance and support.

Step 5: Develop an action plan for correcting the behavior. Summarize key actions and designate a future date to review progress. Be sure to allow adequate time for the agent to make a lasting change.

Here's an account of the Troubleshooting session between Lee and Emma:

Lee: Emma, I know that you are using open and closed questions throughout your calls, but the question is whether you're using enough of them and using them at the right times. As you've seen time and again with the sales that you've closed, strategic questioning can make all the difference when it comes to getting prospects to open up and talk about their needs.

This week I've monitored four of your outbound calls and on three of them I observed that you missed key opportunities. For example, when you were speaking to the buyer at Hamilton-Frederick, I noted that he said, "We mostly buy our supplies at an office goods warehouse store." That would have been a great time to ask something like, "How much time does that typically take?" or "Wouldn't it be nice to have the supplies delivered right to your company?" Instead, you immediately moved on to the presentation stage of the call. **(Step 1: Describe behavior)**

As it turned out, he said he wasn't interested, and I got the feeling that this was largely due to the fact that in his mind, no need or problem had been identified that we might be able to address. **(Step 2: Explain the effect of the behavior)**

Do you see how questioning might have improved that call?

Emma: Well, maybe, but you never know.

Lee: Why do you think you didn't use a question to uncover a need in that call? **(Step 3: Ask for explanation)**

Emma: He just seemed like he was in a hurry and wanted to get off the phone. It seemed to me that he didn't have any interest in hearing more about our services.

Lee: I know it can be difficult when the prospect seems to be in a hurry, Emma. What suggestions do you have for an action plan to help you use more questions in your calls? Is there something I can do to help you do this more effectively? **(Step 4: Suggest/solicit solutions and show support)**

Emma: Well, I don't really know. I mean, as I said, I thought I was using plenty of questions in my calls. It just seems like you always want me to use more.

Lee: I do want you to use more, but only because I am certain it will get you better results. This means more sales and higher commissions. Isn't this something you also want?

Emma: Yes.

Lee: I have an idea. During our recent training session, all the agents created a job aid to be used in their real-time sales calls. On the second page was a list of questions to use at key points in the call. Do you remember doing that?

Emma: Yes. I liked doing that in training, but I haven't really used it since then.

Lee: So, how about if you dig yours out and then post it up in your cubicle? Try to use at least three of those questions in each sales call. In many cases, I'm sure you'll be able to use more, but let's set a minimum of three. Then, I'll listen to more calls this week and we'll review your progress on Monday. Can you agree to that plan? **(Step 5: Develop a plan)**

Emma: All right. That seems doable.

Lee: Great, Emma! Go ahead and take a few minutes to find your job aid right now before going back on the phones. We'll talk again on Monday.

Then what?

If Troubleshooting doesn't work, it's time to take more drastic measures. In the case of most attitude or behavior problems, this may mean disciplinary action. For performance issues, the next step is either Negotiating or Warning. Determining which route to take depends on the following criteria.

Negotiating is called for if the issue is negotiable. For example:

- Austin is falling behind in his goal of documenting the outcome of tech support calls immediately after the call has ended.
- Barbara's performance level for handling challenging calls has slipped significantly.

Warning is called for if the issue is nonnegotiable. For example:

- Ciara doesn't verify spelling of customers' names and addresses.
- Eduardo consistently fails to respond to customers' e-mails within the allotted time frame of 24 hours.

The chart in Figure 10-1 will help you understand how the process works.

Negotiating

Negotiating provides an opportunity for you to show that you care about the agents' feelings and that you're willing to listen to their perspectives on the performance issue. Negotiating includes four steps:

Step 1: State both sides of the issue
Step 2: Ask for suggestions
Step 3: Accept solutions or offer alternatives
Step 4: Reach agreement

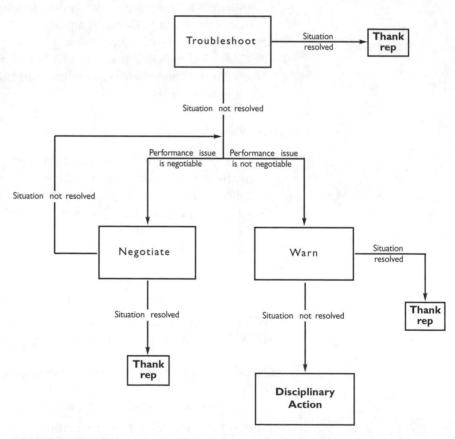

FIGURE 10-1 Two-way coaching.

Let's look at a Negotiating session between Chris (the coach) and Pat (a service and support agent) at an ISP (Internet service provider). Previously they participated in a Troubleshooting session centered around Pat's reluctance to offer customers additional information about what's available to them when they open an ISP account.

Chris: Pat, we talked before about the fact that you aren't letting customers know about the services we offer them through their home page. As I recall from our last meeting, even though our team has established a goal of 20 percent more service upgrades this quarter, you don't want to offer them because you feel they're not a good value for subscribers. **(Step 1: State both sides of the issue)**

Pat: That's right. We have this mission statement about acting with integrity and putting customers first, but then we try to sell them this stuff that they don't need. They can get it all for free at other Web sites—ones that specialize in those specific services. For example, why should they pay extra each month to have access to our financial services and travel links? I just don't think we're doing the right thing.

Chris: Well, Pat, I appreciate your commitment to our mission statement. At the same time, I believe that we are offering added value to our subscribers by giving them these other services. Remember, not everyone is as Internet savvy as you; many of our subscribers don't know how to get around to find what they need. Our service upgrades make that really easy for them. What's more, our job is just to offer it to them. Then we let the subscriber make the decision as to whether it's a good value.

Pat: I know, but I'm still uncomfortable doing it.

Chris: We seem to be at an impasse. What do you suggest we do? **(Step 2: Ask for suggestions)**

Pat: I don't know. I like my job here, but I don't want to sell something just so the company can get rich.

Chris: How about if we compromise—you agree to offer the service upgrades to all subscribers this week while I find some research on how our subscribers feel about the added value upgrades? I'm pretty sure we already have some data on this. If feedback from subscribers indicates that they find the upgrades a good value, then you'll continue to sell them. If the subscribers aren't satisfied, I'll agree to talk to upper management about it. Will that work? **(Step 3: Accept solutions or offer alternatives)**

Pat: OK, I'll do it. I'm not thrilled about it, but I appreciate you looking into this. It seems fair.

Chris:　Great! Let's get back together in two weeks and I'll let you know what I've found out. In the meantime, I expect to hear you letting all your callers know about everything that's available to them. **(Step 4: Reach agreement)**

It's important to remember that agents, as direct links to your customers, often have valid concerns and input. It's also possible that you're both right. When you negotiate, focus on finding a solution rather than on pulling rank.

> *When you negotiate, focus on finding a solution rather than on pulling rank.*

If your Negotiating results in improved performance, be sure to thank the agent for his or her efforts to improve. If Negotiating doesn't result in a change of behavior, it's back to the Negotiating table for another round of talks.

When is Nonnegotiable Negotiable?

Although performance Standards (such as the ones listed on the monitoring forms in Chapter 8) are usually nonnegotiable, there are times when you might want to loosen up on this rule—such as when a Standard has just been introduced or when an agent is new to the job.

Warning

To correct performance or resolve conflict surrounding a nonnegotiable issue that hasn't been resolved through Troubleshooting, you move on to the two-way coaching process known as Warning. This is usually the last effort before a disciplinary measure or even termination takes place. Depending on the protocol and structure of your contact center, it may be appropriate to involve a member of the human resources department in this kind of coaching session. After a Warning session, it's essential that you document the discussion and follow through with whatever actions you've committed to.

Warning involves four steps:

Step 1: State the issue
Step 2: Ask for an explanation
Step 3: Describe the consequences of noncompliance
Step 4: Secure commitment

See the appendix for a reproducible version of these steps.

Because Warning takes place after a Troubleshooting session, it isn't necessary to describe the behavior and its effects—the agent is already aware of this. Usually at this point, the tone of the coaching session is more serious than it is during Troubleshooting or Negotiating. That's appropriate, because the repercussions of not meeting a performance standard can be very serious.

Let's take a look at a typical Warning session. Here's the situation:

Albert has been a tech support agent at Wyomia Electronics for two years and in that time has generally performed satisfactorily. Winnie, his manager, finds him to be motivated, pleasant, and knowledgeable. On several occasions, however, Albert has been coached to remember to restate the customer's technical issue in the form of a problem statement. This is a performance Standard at Wyomia, and during a recent Troubleshooting session Albert and Winnie agreed to some action steps that have not been carried out. Here's how the Warning session goes:

Winnie: Albert, as you know, creating a problem statement and confirming it with the customer is a Standard for our tech support team. As such, it's not an optional element of the call; it's something that every agent needs to do in every call. Since we last talked about this issue, it doesn't appear you've done any better at echoing customers' issues as problem statements. **(Step 1: State the issue)** I'm eager to hear your opinion about why this is happening. **(Step 2: Ask for an explanation)**

Albert: I'm aware that it's a Standard, but it's just not the way I approach technical problems. I feel that I almost always understand what the customer is saying, and it doesn't seem necessary to restate it as a problem statement.

Winnie: Albert, there are a few good reasons why we determined that problem statements should be a Standard, and although you often do very well with solving issues, there are times when a problem statement could have expedited the resolution. If you aren't willing to meet this Standard, I'll have to look at transferring you into a position where you are able to meet the Standards. I'm going to listen to some more calls today and I expect you to be 100 percent in compliance on this issue. **(Step 3: Describe the consequences of noncompliance)**

Albert: A hundred percent right away? That's harsh!

Winnie: Is it something you can agree to do, Albert? **(Step 4: Secure commitment)**

Albert: Yes, I'll do it. I don't want to be transferred.

Winnie: Great, Albert. Thanks for your time. I'm glad to hear you're ready to commit to this.

Warning sessions are typically brief. By the end of a session, your question about why the agent's behavior hasn't changed should have been answered and you should have a new plan for correcting the behavior. All that's left after that is for you and the agent to stick to your commitments!

TIP!

When agents (even the difficult ones) leave your center, thank them for their work and wish them luck in their future endeavors. At this point, there's nothing you can do to keep them, and there's no point in having them go away with a sour impression of you or your organization.

ADDITIONAL RESOURCES

Books

Bramson, Robert. *Coping with Difficult People.* New York: Dell, 1988.

Branham, Leigh. *Keeping the People Who Keep You in Business: 24 Ways to Hang on to Your Most Valuable Talent.* New York: Amacom, 2000.

Brounstein, Marty, and Manber, Beverly. *Handling the Difficult Employee: Solving Performance Problems.* Los Altos, CA: Crisp Publications, 1993.

Smith, Gregory. *Here Today, Here Tomorrow: Transforming Your Workforce from High-Turnover to High-Retention.* Chicago: Dearborn Trade, 2001.

3 DEVELOPING YOUR LEADERSHIP SKILLS

How to Be the Right Person for the Job

CHAPTER 11

The Successful Contact Center Manager's Bag of Tricks

Ten Key Practices

> "You can buy people's time; you can buy their physical presence at a given place; you can even buy a measured number of their skilled muscular motions per hour. But you cannot buy enthusiasm . . . you cannot buy loyalty . . . you cannot buy the devotion of hearts, minds or soul. You must earn these."
>
> —Clarence Francis

Your job as a manager is not only to support and enforce high standards of quality and productivity on the part of your agents, but also to model those standards in your own work and character. There's no formula for perfect coaching: it calls as much for intuition as for technique, and what works with one agent might not work with the next. But there are some characteristics and skills that successful contact center managers seem to have in common. In this chapter you'll learn about 10 key practices that, if faithfully applied, will take you a long way toward success in your center, in your career, and even in your life outside of work.

TEN KEY PRACTICES OF SUCCESSFUL CONTACT CENTER MANAGERS

The 10 key practices of successful contact center managers are as follows:

1. Set effective and realistic goals
2. Create action plans

3. Use positive language

4. Listen

5. Maintain a sense of humor

6. Praise

7. Observe your environment

8. Interact with agents on a daily basis

9. Solicit feedback from agents

10. Empower your agents

See the appendix for a reproducible version of these practices.

The first two practices involve ongoing activities that will help you to continually improve your own performance and that of your team. The third through fifth items on the list are indispensable practices for any manager who values being a great communicator. And, as you'll see later in this chapter, the last five practices comprise POISE, a set of five practices that we encourage contact center managers to accomplish every week.

Set Effective and Realistic Goals

Goals are what inspire us to go beyond—to transcend previous accomplishments and to feel the satisfaction of continuous improvement, whether personal or professional. As a coach, you're responsible for setting goals not only for yourself, but also for your team as a whole. Goals can help you all to work more efficiently and to maintain a sense of mission and purpose.

In order for a goal to be effective and realistic, however, it must be more than just a wish or a hopeful intention. The most meaningful goals meet four key criteria. (See the appendix for a concise, reproducible version of these criteria.)

First, goals must be *specific and measurable*. That means that goals must answer three important questions:

1. What will be improved?

2. By how much or how many?

3. By when?

For example, let's say you develop a goal of getting your paperwork in on time. The intention is clear, but how will you know if you've accomplished your goal? And how much of an improvement will you make over what you're currently doing? A better way to write this goal would be to make it specific and measurable:

I'll catch up on all outstanding paperwork by this Friday. From then on, I'll turn in my reports and department time sheets by the specified deadline.

The second criterion for goals is that they should be *positive*. Notice the difference between the following two goals:

I won't keep procrastinating on the monitoring form rewrite.
I will finish the revision of the monitoring form by June 12.

The second goal is more powerful because it says what will happen rather than what will not. The first example calls to mind the failure of not getting things done on time. The second example is more motivating because it helps a person to visualize a successful outcome.

The third criterion for goal-setting is to create goals that are *directed toward results rather than attempts*. Notice the difference between the following two examples.

We'll mention the warranty to all customers.
Our team will increase the number of warranties sold by 5 percent.

In the first example, there's a danger of obtaining a false sense of success: if you mention the warranty to all customers but nobody buys it, will you really feel you've succeeded with the intention behind the goal? The second example, however, is aimed at a particular result: an increase in warranties purchased by customers.

> "Try not. Do, or do not. There is no try."
> —Yoda, speaking to Luke Skywalker

Finally, goals should have a *reasonable chance of being obtained*. To ensure this, start with small improvements. Note how much more reasonable the first of the following two examples is.

I'll decrease the turnover rate for my team by 20 percent over the next six months.
I'll decrease the turnover rate for my team by 80 percent this quarter.

In order to maintain your motivation to continually set and reach goals, it's important to keep them obtainable. If they're too lofty or unrealistic, you'll eventually become demotivated and disinterested. Remember, you can always set new goals once you've reached your original ones.

So, let's recap. Effective and realistic goals are:

- Specific and measurable
- Positive
- Results-oriented
- Obtainable

Following are a few more examples of well-written goals. As you read through them, note where each of the four criteria is met.

> *In the next quarter, I'll get price quotes back to 90 percent of callers within four hours.*
>
> *Each agent on our team will meet his or her primary call objective on 60 percent of prospecting calls this quarter.*
>
> *Our Customer Elation Task Force will compile all results from the online customer survey and make a report to the rest of the team by June 30.*
>
> *I'll finish the self-study version of the mentoring training program and achieve a Level III rating within the next two months.*

Four Keys to Effective and Meaningful Goals

- Specific and measurable
- Positive
- Results-oriented
- Obtainable

Create Action Plans

Creating action plans for improvement is a key practice that shows you're sincere and dedicated to being the best manager you can possibly be. An action plan is exactly what it sounds like—a plan for putting into action a particular goal or objective. Action plans can be related to goals you have set for yourself (or your team), or they can be targeted toward other areas of your personal or professional growth. They outline a reasonable, logical plan for reaching the goal.

As we've all no doubt experienced, setting goals is an inspiring, energizing practice, but it does not magically transport us to a time or place in which the goals have been achieved. Rather, the only way to get there is through focused effort and considerable determination.

The process of creating action plans is straightforward and simple. The difficulty comes in following through with your plans. To create an action plan, you break down the goal into a set of specific and manageable steps for getting from point A to point B.

Following are some examples of action plans. The first two are for two of the sample goals you saw in the goal-setting section of this chapter. In the appendix you'll find a reproducible form you can use again and again to create your own action plans for improvement.

> **Goal:** *I'll finish the self-study version of the mentoring training program and achieve a Level III rating within the next two months.*
>
> **Action plan:** *I'll set aside two hours every Tuesday and Friday for the next four weeks to complete the self-study coursework. I'll then spend two to three weeks applying the skills from the course while carrying out my everyday duties on the job. Once I feel ready, I'll complete the test.*
>
> **Goal:** *I will finish the revision of the monitoring form by June 12.*
>
> **Action plan:** *I'll create a draft form by the end of this week and then all team supervisors and I will use it while monitoring during the next week. We'll have an end-of-shift meeting that Friday to calibrate results and revise the form as necessary. I'll get Nancy's approval on the final version by June 10 and then I'll roll it out to the agents on the 12th.*
>
> **Goal:** *To help our TSRs meet their new sales goal, I'll find and implement a telephone sales training program by July 30.*
>
> **Action plan:**
>
> - *Develop a list of evaluation criteria. Due date: April 30*
> - *Develop a list of training vendors. Due date: May 5*
> - *Develop a request for proposal (RFP). Due date: May 7*
> - *Send RFP to vendors. Due date: May 15 (Note: proposals to be due by June 8)*
> - *Review proposals and interview potential vendors. Due date: June 25*
> - *Check references and select winning vendor. Due date: June 30*
> - *Schedule training. Due date: July 25*
>
> **Goal:** *Create reasonable standards for the customer service team by August 5.*

Action plan:

- *Compile a list of current performance standards and job responsibilities. Due date: June 1*
- *Assemble a team of job experts who will help analyze and define standards. Due date: June 10*
- *Hold an information meeting with job experts to propose and discuss new standards. Due date: June 20*
- *Finalize list of new standards. Due date: June 23*
- *Submit list of standards to management team for approval. Due date: June 25*
- *Revise standards based upon recommendations from the management team. Due date: August 1*
- *Present final list of new standards to human resources and quality assurance departments. Due date: August 4*

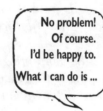

No problem!
Of course.
I'd be happy to.
What I can do is ...

Use Positive Language

Positive language is the art of using words and phrases to communicate a positive, supportive tone to your agents, customers, and anyone else you come into contact with. Positive language is a key communication skill that can help you create a professional, easygoing rapport with people and head off potentially adversarial interactions. We think it's important to get into the positive language habit for all aspects of your role as a manager, but it's especially crucial when you have to say no or communicate bad news.

Note the difference between the following two statements:

"There's no way I can review your proposal today. It will have to wait until later in the week."

"I've got your proposal on my desk and it's making its way to the top of the pile. I should definitely be able to review it by the end of the week."

In both examples the core message is the same—the manager will review the proposal later in the week. But in the second example, the manager conveys the message in a constructive, upbeat way by using positive language.

Here's another example:

"Julie, unless you make callbacks to those customers right away, they're all going to have the wrong information about the dates of the Super Saver Promotion."

"Julie, I think we can still save this. If you can make callbacks to all those customers within the next few hours, we can get the right information to them before it's too late."

To communicate with positive language, look for ways to incorporate the following guidelines into what you say.

- Project an attitude of sincerity and respect.
- Highlight the positive.
- Emphasize what you can do, not what you cannot.
- Give options or alternatives whenever possible.
- Avoid statements that can put people on the defensive.
- Show willingness to find a solution.
- When you have to say no, explain the reason and, if appropriate, show empathy.

One of the great things about positive language is that it tends to be contagious. If your agents see and hear you continually using positive language, they'll pick up the habit themselves.

Listen

One of the best things you can do for your agents, your customers, your colleagues, and yourself is to learn to be a good listener. It's a rare and valuable skill in any situation, but the ability and willingness to be a good listener are particularly helpful for anyone in a management position. Learning to listen actively and carefully can radically transform your relationships, your productivity, and your effectiveness as a leader.

Following are some tips for helping you to become a good listener. (See the appendix for a condensed, reproducible version of these guidelines.)

Focus

When someone is speaking to you, either in person or on the phone, focus your attention on the conversation. Don't do other things at the same time, don't look away, and don't take another phone call. If you're communicating face to face, look the person in the eye, turn your body forward, and maintain a relaxed but attentive countenance. By focusing your attention, you'll not only absorb the message more fully, but you'll also increase the other person's confidence that you are indeed listening attentively.

Listen for Key Information and Key Feelings

Good listening is a function of the ears, the mind, and the heart. Of course you should listen for the important details of what the person is saying, but it's also essential to listen to how it's being said. Every time agents speak to you, they're giving you clues about their state of mind, degree of urgency, communication style, and attitude. This can provide you with valuable insights about how to respond for the best results.

Let the Other Person Finish Speaking

When having a discussion with someone, always let the other person finish speaking before you respond. Don't interrupt, don't rush the person, and don't start thinking of what you're going to say until the other person is finished speaking.

Pause before You Respond

Once the other person has finished speaking, pause for a few seconds before you respond. This allows the message to sink in, gives you time to formulate your response, and shows the other person that you're actively listening to what he or she has to say. You might be surprised at what happens when you do this—we've found that most people are shocked to discover someone listening with such patience and attentiveness.

Show Your Support

Whenever it's called for, empathize with your agents and show your support for them. Even if you don't fully agree with what they say, it's important to make sure that they feel they've been heard. Showing that you care and understand will help you to maintain a good relationship with them. Here are a few lead-ins to empathy statements:

> *"I can appreciate . . ."*
> *"I understand . . ."*
> *"I know what you mean . . ."*
> *"I don't blame you for being upset about that . . ."*

Confirm Your Understanding

If what the other person is saying to you is at all complex or lengthy, confirm your understanding of what he or she has said. To do this, you can verbally summarize the main points of what you've heard and then ask if your understanding is correct. Confirming is important not only because it shows you're paying attention, but also because it gives the person an opportunity to hear his or her statement echoed. This gives the person an opportunity to correct you if the information is not accurate.

> "If you want to understand management, read books and go to classes that teach it. If you want to know how to manage your employees, go to them and listen to what they have to say."—Jack H. Grossman and J. Robert Parkinson in *Becoming A Successful Manager* (Contemporary Books, 2002)

Maintain a Sense of Humor

No matter how stressful, pressured, and demanding your work is, there's always room for some good-natured humor on the job. A sense of humor is a universally appreciated quality. There's no reason why you can't take your job seriously and at the same time know when lighthearted moments are called for. Humor defies a concrete description, but we all know what it is and we all know when we're in the presence of it. And we know how cathartic it can be to laugh.

Studies of humor as a leadership strategy have shown that it makes a person more persuasive, motivating, and interesting in the eyes of other people. As a manager, your ability to keep a sense of humor at work makes you more approachable, more likable, and more human to your agents. Humor can lift the tension off the high-pressured call floor and can help you to reduce your own stress and that of your agents. It may also help you to rally the troops when necessary and bring problems under control. What's more, agents will go home with the feeling that although the center is a place where they work hard, it is also a place where they have laugh and fun.

There are, of course, a few important caveats. Humor in the workplace must always be appropriate and innocent. It should never be offensive or embarrassing to any individual on your team. If your personal sense of humor tends to be sarcastic or aggressive, you'll have to create a second sense of humor that's appropriate for you to exhibit on the job. Also, humor should provide an enjoyable distraction during difficult moments; if everything on the job is carried out in a humorous way, the integrity and productivity of your team's work will most likely suffer and there's a good chance many of your agents will be annoyed by the overly jovial climate.

Tips for Maintaining a Sense of Humor at Work

- Encourage a climate of reciprocal humor. If you can joke about work, then your agents should be allowed to do the same.
- Share amusing stories from your own experiences or from magazines and newspapers.
- When agents are especially frazzled or when the call floor is particularly frenzied, introduce some good-natured humor to ease the tension.
- Send out a joke of the day, provided that it's suitable for everyone to read.
- Encourage agents to share stories of humorous calls and other situations at work.

MANAGING WITH POISE: FIVE STEPS TO MAKING EVERY WEEK SUCCESSFUL

POISE is an acronym, each letter of which stands for an important coaching function:

Praise
Observe your environment
Interact with agents on a daily basis
Solicit feedback from agents
Empower your agents

> We suggest you make POISE an active part of your ongoing work as a contact center manager. These are practices you can carry out day in and day out to make your center a hub of continuous improvement. In fact, we suggest you check in with yourself on a weekly basis to make sure you're putting POISE into practice. Once you've conscientiously applied these concepts for a while, they'll become second nature to you and you'll find yourselves carrying out these actions spontaneously and consistently.
>
> The appendix contains a reproducible version of the elements of POISE.

Praise

In Chapter 9 you learned why it's so important to give feedback to your agents on a regular basis—and praise is a big part of that under-

taking. We'd like to expand on the subject of praise here to give you some additional insight and advice.

When employees receive sincere and relevant praise on a regular basis, they feel valued and supported by management. And when employees feel valued and supported, they become dedicated to their work and eager to meet the needs of the organization. As was pointed out in Chapter 9, they also become receptive to feedback that doesn't take the form of praise.

Should you praise just to praise? Well, yes and no. We're not suggesting that you make up things to praise or that you praise employees for minute or trivial activities (for example, remembering to turn in their time sheets). That would only serve to devalue the praise and make employees suspicious of your motives. But we do suggest that you get into the habit of giving praise whenever you recognize that doing so can lift a burden or make someone's day.

TIP!

Tips for Remembering to Praise Your Agents

- Put five coins in your right pocket. Every time you praise an agent, move one coin over to your left pocket. Every morning and every afternoon, try to transfer all four coins.

- Create a reproducible form with an alphabetized list of your agents on it and at the beginning of each workweek start with a clean copy. As you go through the week, highlight each name to indicate that you've praised that individual for something. Try to have every name highlighted by the end of each week.

- Every week or two, select some aspect of the team's work that deserves a pat on the back. Send an e-mail or a voice mail to the group praising them for their collective success.

- Make the first thing and the last thing you do every workday be to praise someone for a job well done.

- Review your list of top performing agents and be sure you praise them too. It's easy to focus on the agents who need help improving and forget your top performers.

There's one more reason we're so insistent on praising your agents: it's good for you! Think about it—don't you feel a lot better at the end of the day, the week, and the year when you've spent a good amount of your time and energy making people feel good about themselves and the work they do? Frequent praising forces you to look for the good in people. Over time, this can have a powerful and positive effect on your own psyche.

Observe Your Environment

It's pretty near impossible to successfully manage in an environment with which you're not intimately familiar. And the only way to become intimately familiar with your environment is to make a strong effort to continually observe what goes on in your center. Carefully and frequently observing your agents at work will help you to be proactive about issues that require change, rather than waiting for a problem to emerge.

Being a good observer does something else as well: when you're a daily presence on the call floor, it sends a message to agents that you're present, involved, and interested. This can work in your favor for a couple of reasons. For one thing, agents will come to see that not much gets by you and as a result they'll stop trying to get things by you. Second, agents will realize that you're right there in the trenches with them.

It's also important, however, that agents don't feel you're spying on them. When you make observations about your team and your workplace, make sure they feel that you're there to help and support them.

TIP!

Tips for Observing Your Team and Your Workplace

- Sit at your desk and, without looking out at the call floor, draw a diagram of it. Who sits next to whom? What equipment is in the area? Where are the walls, windows, and doors? If you're not able to do this, you're probably not as familiar with your call floor as you should be.

- Spend at least some part of your day out on the floor with your agents. Listen to the hum of people talking. What other noises are there? Is there anything that distracts people from their work? Observe how each agent sits when on the phone or on the computer with customers. Watch how agents make use of reference materials or whatever other resources they keep at their desks. We're not saying you have to change these things; we're just saying it's good for you to know what's going on out there.

- Take note of how agents interact with one another. Who interacts with whom the most? Does anyone tend to be alone out there? If so, is this by choice or because the others aren't engaging this person?

- Is there fear in your environment? If so, when do you notice it? Is the fear directed toward you?

- Notice how agents communicate with one another. Listen to the words you overhear and to the tone in which they're spoken. This can give you valuable insight into the vibe of the workplace and also into potential issues to be addressed by training or other measures.

- Block out actual time frames in which you'll concentrate primarily on observing.

TIP!

Keep a journal of your ongoing observations about your group and workplace. It will help you to chart your progress over time.

The Power of Personal Attention

"One motivational experiment isolated two groups of workers. One group was treated differently than other workers at the company; the other was treated just like everybody else. The results? Both groups performed better simply because they had been singled out to be involved in an experiment, which made them feel special."

—Nancy Stevenson, *10-Minute Guide to Motivating People*
(Alpha Books, 2000).

Interact with Agents on a Daily Basis

At first this suggestion may seem obvious. You may be thinking, *Doesn't every contact center manager interact with his or her agents on a daily basis?* But what we're talking about is really *interacting,* not just noticing agents are there and occasionally talking to them when the need arises.

It's not enough just to have cursory interactions with your agents as they're out on the call floor plugging away. It's not even enough just to greet them on their way in (although that is a good idea) or to approach them when you have a specific issue to discuss.

Think about what the word *interaction* really means. The 10th edition of *Merriam-Webster's Collegiate Dictionary* defines it as "mutual or reciprocal action or influence." By meaningfully interacting with your agents, you'll get to know them as individuals with unique talents, capacities, interests, and perspectives. You'll be able to build a strong rapport with the people you manage, which in turn will help them to feel comfortable opening up to you. It also reminds agents that you are a part of the team, not someone who is above or beyond it.

Interacting with your agents sets a tone of dialogue and open communication in the department. It shows that you're active and involved in the everyday functions and events in your department. Building rapport creates a sense of team, energizes the environment, and lends agents your expertise. They can learn from you and you from them. The more you know the agents in your department, the more insight you'll have into what makes them tick. This is valuable for managers.

TIP!

Tips for Interacting with Your Agents

- Get to know your agents' interests, backgrounds, and previous accomplishments.
- Remain approachable. Make sure agents feel comfortable coming to you.
- Strive to create mutually rewarding relationships with your agents. In a healthy workplace, there's always some give-and-take between managers and employees.
- Think of your agents as internal customers and treat them with the same respect as you do external customers.
- Help your agents to be successful and to feel special.
- Explain the reasons for decisions made by you or by upper management, and for procedures.
- Regularly share information about yourself with agents—but be sure to use very good judgment about what to share.
- Praise agents behind their backs (for example, when talking to other agents on the team). Make sure, however, that everyone gets praised from time to time rather than just a few stars.
- Make a point of asking noticing something special about a particular rep and ask a question about it rather than offering a comment.

"Managing a department effectively is an ongoing process that consists of developing mutually rewarding relationships with your employees. You will be required to create healthy partnerships with each of the people under your influence."—Jack H. Grossman and J. Robert Parkinson in *Becoming A Successful Manager* (Contemporary Books, 2002)

Solicit Feedback from Agents

One of the best ways to get information from your agents is also one of the simplest—ask them for it. Soliciting feedback from your agents on a regular basis gives you valuable information about what's going on with them and with your customers. It provides an opportunity for you to learn information that might not otherwise come your way. It's also a mechanism by which the agents *help you help them.*

Your frontline staff people are in direct communication with the customers of your contact center. By definition, this makes them experts, and as such they are great sources of information. But often that information won't get back to you or to upper management unless you ask agents for it. You can also solicit feedback on any number of other subjects—how you're doing, how they're feeling, what ideas they have for change, and so forth. The idea behind this objective is simply to get your agents to talk to you regularly and comfortably.

Here are some important guidelines:

- Use open questions (ones that elicit more than just a "yes" or "no" response).
- Listen!
- Thank people for their feedback, input, insights, and whatever else they give you.
- Use different methods to solicit feedback: ask directly, send out questions via e-mail from time to time, initiate some form of a suggestion box, and so on.
- On occasion, answer a question with a question. For example, when an agent asks for your opinion on something, say, "Well, I'm not sure. What do you think?" When doing this, however, it's important not to come across as flip and not to withhold information that the agent really wants to have. Once the agent has responded to your question, you can give your own opinion.

Seven Great Questions to Ask Your Agents

1. What was the most satisfying experience you had at work this week?
2. What's your favorite type of customer interaction? (You'll notice they won't all say "the easy ones." Some agents thrive

on challenging calls and e-mails. This question will give you insight into what motivates each agent.)

3. What could I have done better? (Or, How could I have handled that better?)

4. What are you hearing from customers?

5. What would you like to be able to do for customers that you're not able to do?

6. What inspires you to do your best work?

7. What are you learning? (Or, Where do you see improvement in your work?)

Of course, once you start and keep soliciting feedback from agents, it's important for you to actually do something with the results!

Empower Your Agents

Empower is one of those words that tend to be overused in business circles, and yet the concept, if anything, seems to be underutilized. Empowering your agents means giving them some measure of authority, some degree of ownership over their jobs and work lives. This can be a particularly important management practice in contact centers because of the degree to which agents' jobs are repetitive and monotonous.

Empowering agents can increase their motivation, their self-discipline, and their ability to learn from their mistakes. It also shows that you're willing to trust them—at least until they've given you reason not to. Most importantly, empowering agents allows them to feel that they are responsible for their own success.

Take a page from the coach of ice skater Sarah Hughes. At the 2002 Winter Olympics, when Sarah finished her gold medal performance, her coach told her to quietly pause for a moment and focus her awareness of how this success felt. She told Sarah to breathe deeply, to listen to the ecstatic fans, to look at all the flowers and gifts being showered onto the ice, and to realize that *she* had created this moment. It was a mental snapshot that Sarah is sure to remember for the rest of her life. Even if you view your agents' successes as less than Olympian, you can still inspire them to remember the moment, to remember what success feels like. It will provide a powerful memory that they can call on the next time they're working through difficult, demanding experiences.

Naturally, the degree to which you empower your agents will depend on various factors of your particular contact center. In some environments agents can work fairly autonomously, whereas in other centers a high degree of regulation and supervision is required. There is always some room for empowerment, however. Following are some tips to get you started.

TIP!

Tips for Empowering Your Agents

- Always make your agents feel that they are professionals.
- Figure out what aspects or functions of your job can be delegated and then find the right person(s) to delegate them to.
- Allow agents to take some risks.
- Give agents the responsibility for making certain decisions that affect their work.
- Ask agents how they would do something (for example, solve a problem) rather than telling them how to do it. Then, if you like a suggestion, encourage the agent to proceed with that course of action.
- On occasion, respond to agents' questions by saying, "I don't know. Where would you find the answer?"
- Take time to teach agents what you know.

News Flash!

You're a manager; your employees are not. You already have the upper hand, so don't push it too hard. Be a humanistic, compassionate, firm, disciplined, and caring coach to your team.

ACTIVITY: Walk the Talk

This two-part exercise is useful in translating intentions (the talk) into actions (the walk). It's always nice to say that you're committed to supporting and empowering your agents, but it's equally important to show that you mean it. How do you do that? Through your management style and the actions you take on a daily basis to support and empower your team.

Part 1

Take a few moments to think about the various functions of your agents' job and about your own management style. Despite what you say or what you intend, what are the messages you actually communicate to them?

Write down three actions or habits that tend to be patterns in your management style and that you suspect may be sending the wrong messages to agents. We've provided two examples for you.

Examples

Action 1: *I tell people what to do rather than ask them to do it.*

Action 2: *I don't look at people when they are talking to me. Instead I look down at the floor or off in the distance.*

Action 1: _____

What it says: _____

_____

Action 2: _____

What it says: _____

_____

Action 3: _____

What it says: _____

_____

Now decipher those actions by asking yourself what message they actually convey to your agents—despite what your intention is. You can write on the lines provided. Following are the translations for the examples.

Action 1: *I tell people what to do rather than ask them to do it.*
What it says: *I'm the boss. I'm your superior. My way is the right way and I'm not receptive to other perspectives.*

Action 2: *I don't look at people when they are talking to me. Instead I look down at the floor or off in the distance.*

What it says: *I can't give you my full attention. I have other things on my mind. I find it uncomfortable to look directly at you.*

Part 2

Next, try coming up with some messages that you do want to convey to agents and then translate them into specific actions. Note the example.

Example

What I want to convey: *I know it's often very hard to stay motivated and energetic.*
Actions that convey this message: *Smiles, words of encouragement, personal stories from my own experiences as a sales agent, reminding agents of previous successes.*

What I want to convey: _____

Actions that convey this message: _____

_____

_____

What I want to convey: _____

Actions that convey this message: _____

_____

_____

What I want to convey: _____

Actions that convey this message: _____

_____

_____

Stumped about what messages to convey through your actions? Here are a few suggestions:

- *"I trust you."*
- *"I value your contribution."*
- *"You're a professional."*

- *"I'm aware of your presence and of the work you do."*
- *"I acknowledge and appreciate your individuality and your unique strengths."*

Of course, the most important step of this exercise is the final one—putting these actions into practice in your real-time environment.

ADDITIONAL RESOURCES

Books

Brountstein, Marty. *Coaching and Mentoring for Dummies.* Hoboken, NJ: Hungry Minds Inc., 2000.

Crane, G. Thomas. *The Heart of Coaching: Using Transformational Coaching to Create a High Performance Culture.* San Diego: FTA, 2001.

Flaherty, James. *Coaching: Evoking Excellence in Others.* Stoneham, MA: Butterworth-Heinemann, 1998.

Hargrove, Robert. *Masterful Coaching: Extraordinary Results by Impacting People and the Way They Think and Work Together.* San Diego: Pfeiffer & Co., 1995.

Hargrove, Robert. *Masterful Coaching Fieldbook.* San Francisco: Jossey-Bass, 1999.

House, Henry, Whitworth, Laura, Sandahl, Phil, and Kimsey-House, Henry. *Co-Active Coaching: New Skills for Coaching People Toward Success in Work and Life.* Palo Alto, CA: Davies-Black Publishing, 1998.

Companies

Call Center Coach (dedicated to providing call center managers and leaders with a comprehensive resource package that contains the latest information affecting the customer relationship management industry). URL: www.callcentercoach.com; phone: 888-860-2622.

Impact Learning Systems (offers a training program designed specifically for coaches and supervisors). URL: www.impactlearning.com; phone: 800-545-9003.

CHAPTER 12

Make It Your Mission

Developing and Manifesting Your
Mission Statement

> "You have to stand for something; otherwise you will fall for anything."
> —Anonymous

WHAT IS A MISSION STATEMENT?

The mission statement concept has been around for a long time and has picked up increased momentum in the last 15 years. But, unlike a number of other business trends, the utility and relevance of a good mission statement have not waned. The mission statement boom has given birth to a number of spin-offs—value statements, vision statements, purpose statements—all of which can be helpful in focusing and prioritizing the actions of an organization and its members. But they all have their source in the mission statement, and that's what we'll focus on in this chapter.

Although the term *mission statement* is fairly simple and self-explanatory, there are any number of opinions about what a mission statement really is. Here's how we define it: a mission statement is a brief, terse declaration of the key purpose and associated activities of an organization, department, or individual. A mission statement answers the question, "What do we mean to be doing?" whether or not that is in fact what the organization is doing.

TIP!

If you don't already know what your company's mission statement is, find out. If your company doesn't have one, create one for your department.

A mission statement is valuable for a number of reasons, including the following:

- It helps the members of the organization to focus on a common goal.
- It allows customers to expect and receive a consistent result.
- Developing a mission statement provides a meaningful exercise in distilling what values are most important to the organization.
- It provides an organization with a signature style.
- It's inspiring.
- It's gives guidance.

Perhaps the most important value of a mission statement is its ability to be a simple fulcrum on which to weigh decisions both big and little. When deciding on a course of action or trying to prioritize activities, a manager can consult the mission statement to make sure that he or she stays on task. For example, a company that has a mission statement that includes the phrase, "serving the needs of our customers in innovative ways," will want to train and empower frontline staff people to creatively solve the customers' problems rather than restrict them to a set of rigid policies. Or, a department whose mission statement includes the phrase, "We act with integrity at all times," would train its customer service staff members to deliver bad news rather than ask them to lie about delivery dates just to keep a customer from buying from the competition.

What a Mission Statement Is Not

Although there are many views about what exactly a mission statement is, there seems to be general agreement about what it is not:

- A to-do list
- A job description
- A laundry list of goals you'd like to achieve
- A motto
- An advertising tag line
- A tactical outline

WHOSE MISSION IS THIS?

Following are excerpts from some mission statements of large, well-known organizations. Can you guess which company each mission statement belongs to? If so, good for you and good for them—that's a sign that their mission statements are being actualized by their business activities.

Once you've made your guess, take a look at the answers. No peeking!

Mission Statement 1

_____'s mission is to create software for the personal computer that empowers and enriches people in the workplace, at school and at home.

Mission Statement 2

We aspire to be the most admired and valuable company in the world. Our goal is to enrich our customers' personal lives and to make their businesses more successful by bringing to market exciting and useful communications services, building shareowner value in the process.

Mission Statement 3

The mission of _____ is dedication to the highest quality of Customer Service delivered with a sense of warmth, friendliness, individual pride, and Company Spirit.

Mission Statement 4

To market vehicles developed and manufactured in the United States that are world leaders in quality, cost and customer enthusiasm through the integration of people, technology and business systems . . .

Answers: (1) Microsoft; (2) AT&T; (3) Southwest Airlines; (4) Saturn.

MAKE IT PERSONAL

Mission statements can be personal too. If you haven't already done so, you should consider developing one for your role as a manager. One of the most difficult challenges of management, particularly in the busy, dynamic contact center environment, is the need to focus and to prioritize. A mission statement can help you to do this.

Once you've completed your personal mission statement, it becomes a tool to guide you when you're making decisions or planning a course of action. It's a constant reminder of what's important and what's not.

One thing we've discovered—and we're guessing you have too—is that there's no shortage of good ideas or intentions. There is, however, a shortage of time and resources with which to implement the infinite number of good ideas that pop into your brain or that come to you from other sources. Your mission statement can help you stay on purpose by guiding you to pursue only those activities that are relevant to your stated mission.

Managing in a contact center is a highly demanding and multifaceted job. Developing a personal mission statement will help you to prioritize your tasks and accomplish your many objectives. Many managers find that an effective mission statement provides both direction and inspiration. Most importantly, perhaps, a mission statement can prevent you from managing by default.

Following are some examples of mission statements from a diverse range of contact center managers.

Most importantly, perhaps, a mission statement can prevent you from managing by default.

My mission as a manager is to lead my customer service team to fulfill all our Service Level Agreements with customers. I gather data efficiently, maintain accurate information, and execute the contract in the most cost-effective manner possible.

I ensure that our customer contact representatives are satisfied, effective, and productive. I provide them with whatever skills, tools, and support they need to excel at their jobs. My primary goal is to make sure the representatives have a strong relationship with, and loyalty to, our company. I consider the telephone representatives to be *my* customers.

My mission is to build and sustain the loyalty of my customers and the employees who serve those customers. I do this by maintaining a high level of enthusiasm and professionalism at all times. I provide consistency, accountability, and leadership within our contact center.

My role as a contact center manager is to provide a motivating, efficient, and friendly contact center experience for my team and our customers. I strive to be a visible, approachable, and highly motivating coach/mentor. I achieve business success by caring about people.

DEVELOPING YOUR PERSONAL MISSION STATEMENT

Developing a mission statement is an iterative process. The final version will be meaningful and effective only if it's the result of considerable reflection and at least a few rounds of writing.

We suggest a four-step process for writing a mission statement:

Round 1: Chicken scratches
Round 2: Stream of consciousness
Round 3: Rough draft
Round 4: Final draft

On the pages that follow, we'll take you through this process one step at a time. (See the appendix for a reproducible version of these forms.) Here's some helpful advice:

- Allow a few hours to a few days between rounds.
- Have fun.
- Be creative.
- Think outside the proverbial box.
- Keep the mission statement focused on your role as a manager. (You can always write another one for other aspects of your life.)

DEVELOPING YOUR PERSONAL MISSION STATEMENT

Round 1: Chicken Scratches

Grab a pen, find a comfortable place to sit, and take some time to consider your responses to the following questions. You can write in the space provided in this book or you can use a separate sheet of paper.

Read each question and respond with whatever comes immediately to your mind. Don't worry about writing complete sentences; don't even edit your own thoughts. Just work through the questions one at a time and write whatever feels important to you.

1. In what ways do you contribute to the success of your team/department/center?

_____

_____

_____

_____

2. If each week you could achieve only three actions as a manager, what would they be?

_____

_____

_____

_____

3. What are the qualities, skills, and characteristics that you want your team to see in you?

_____

_____

_____

_____

4. What are the qualities, skills, and characteristics that you want your management to see in you?

_____

_____

_____

_____

5. Describe the primary responsibilities and contribution of your department to the organization.

_____

_____

_____

_____

6. Describe your primary responsibilities to your team.

_____

_____

_____

_____

Round 2: Stream of Consciousness

The next step in the development of your mission statement is to write continuously for 10 minutes about your mission as a contact center manager. Once again, there's no need to write complete sentences, edit your thoughts, or make any sense whatsoever. Just focus your mind on the task at hand, set a timer (or look at your watch), and write without stopping for 10 minutes. You can use the box provided.

Round 3: Rough Draft

OK, now on to full sentences! Before writing your draft, review what you wrote in the first two rounds. Then take some time—typically 30 to 60 minutes—to develop a rough draft of your mission statement. This time, form your thoughts into a few complete sentences and structure the statement into a logical flow.

Following are a few additional guidelines for this round of writing:

- Keep your statement in the range of 40 to 75 words.
- Write in the present tense.

  "I motivate" rather than "I will motivate."

- Use affirmative statements.

  "I do" rather than "I don't."

- Include strong, descriptive words and terms.

  "I listen attentively" rather than "I listen."

  "Empower" rather than "help."

- Make it specific.

  Vague: *"I hold my agents in the highest regard."*

  Specific: *"I treat my agents with fairness and respect."*

Round 4: Final Draft
Now for the final stretch. Read through your rough draft and make whatever revisions you feel are necessary to create a mission statement that's meaningful, relevant, motivating, descriptive, and specific. And make it concise—every word should count!

Now What?

Once you've finalized your mission statement (remember, you can always come back to revise it as needed), print out a high-quality copy or handwrite it on a piece of attractive paper. Laminate or frame the final version and find a place for it in your work area where you'll see it throughout the day.

Put it into practice for a few weeks and then ask yourself whether or not it needs to be revised. Maybe it will need revision, maybe not.

> U.S. workers want their work to make a difference, but 75% do not think their company's mission statement has become the way they do business.
>
> —Workplace 2000 Employee Insight Survey

Should You Share Your Mission Statement with Your Team?

Once you've developed your personal mission statement, is it advisable to share it with your team? That's up to you. You might decide to keep it private, or, if you want your agents to hold you accountable for carrying out your mission, you might decide to share it with them. Also, if you want your agents to develop their own mission statements, it might be a good idea to share yours as an example.

PUTTING YOUR MISSION STATEMENT INTO ACTION

Once you've developed your mission statement, you'll have a nice, noble text that looks good on your wall. But of course that isn't the objective. The most important thing about a mission statement is to put it into practice. No matter how well written, a mission statement is only as effective as it is active.

One way to translate your intentions into practice is to create action plans related to your mission statement. These action plans can be either ongoing or short-term. For example, you might create some policies or procedures—derived from or directed by your mission statement—that you're committed to continually observing. Following are a few examples:

- Hold supervisors accountable for service level agreements on a weekly basis.

- Monitor reps for compliance with new procedures.
- Follow appropriate feedback models when praising and correcting agents.
- Maintain updated hardware and software on all systems in the department.

Additionally, you can come up with some short-term action plans inspired by your mission statement:

- Meet with the employee committee once a week for the next month to discuss upgrading customer loyalty programs.
- Conduct an employee morale survey within the next 30 days.
- Update the monitoring form to include new Standards.
- Reinstate the continuing education program.

TIP!

When creating action plans, ask yourself what each aspect of your mission statement looks like in action. For example, "I inspire my employees to continually improve their customer contact skills" might be manifested through the following concrete practices:

- I give lots of praise.
- When correcting performance, I give specific tips for improvement.
- I maintain a learning climate in which questions and new ideas are encouraged.
- I remain approachable to my agents and do everything I can to remove fear and insecurity from our work environment.
- I continually remind agents of our collective mission.

Both Words Are Important

One question we often ask when we begin a new relationship with a contact center is, "What's the mission statement of your organization?" It is rare when someone can tell us with any kind of accuracy. Even more uncommon is the person who can tell us how exactly the mission statement is put into practice by the policies and activities of the organization. This is a sign that the mission statement exercise is only half-finished. Once a mission statement has been written, it must be put into action. If it's not, it's really just a statement and not a mission.

TIP!

If you're not able to recite your mission statement by memory (at least after you've been using it for a while), this is probably a sign that your statement is too long, too complex, or not personally meaningful to you. It may be time to go back to round 1!

> "Companies whose employees understand the mission and goals enjoy 29% greater return than other firms."
>
> —Watson Wyatt Work Study

DEVELOPING A MISSION STATEMENT FOR YOUR TEAM

Once you've developed your personal mission statement, you might want to go through the same exercise with your agents to develop a mission statement for your customer contact team. You can follow the same four-step process you used to develop your personal statement. The only difference is that it gets a little (and sometimes a lot) more complicated when you're trying to develop a mission statement that represents a group of diverse individuals. Nevertheless, we recommend making the effort. A departmental mission statement can do a number of good things, including:

- Focus the team on a common objective
- Educate the team about business priorities
- Inform agents about how their individual efforts contribute to big-picture goals
- Prevent agents from spending time and energy on nonrelevant tasks in the future

What's more, if you involve the entire team in developing the mission statement, the members will have a feeling of ownership—something that rarely occurs when agents are asked to embrace an organization-wide mission statement developed by senior-level executives. That's not to say that agents can't or won't embrace the ideals of the mission statement, but it's not likely they would claim it as their own creation.

A departmental mission statement should be congruent with the ideas and priorities outlined in the company's mission statement. It doesn't necessarily have to echo the company statement, but at the very least the two should not conflict with one another.

Since you'll be asking your employees to implement your mission statement, they will have more buy-in if you enlist their aid in creating it. Following is an activity you can use to create a departmental mission statement.

Mission Possible*

In a Nutshell

In this activity, team members work together to create a mission statement for the work group. This is an ideal activity for injecting enthusiasm into the department and bringing a new sense of meaning to work. The mission statement that results from this activity may or may not feel finished. If it doesn't, use this activity as the jumping-off place for a mission statement committee that can then work together to finalize the team's statement (see note at end of this activity).

Time

20 to 30 minutes

What You'll Need

- Copies of your organization's mission statement (if it has one) and/or copies of other companies' mission statements that you find inspiring
- Blank flip chart paper and colored markers

What to Do

Create a flip chart or a handout with the following information:

Defining Your Mission

- How do customers feel after dealing with us?
- What do customers tell their friends about us?
- In what ways do we help each other on our team?
- How does our team support the overall aim of our organization?

Preface the activity with a brief discussion about mission statements. Hand out your corporate mission statement or those from other companies.

Put team members into groups of three to five and give each group a piece of flip chart paper and a marker. Point out the questions on the flip chart or handout and explain to the agents that their job is to work together to come up with a brief mission statement for the team. They can begin by discussing the four questions.

*Reproduced with permission from *The Big Book of Customer Service Training Games* (Peggy Carlaw and Vasudha Kathleen Deming, McGraw-Hill, 1999).

Allow about 15 minutes for this part of the activity. If there is more than one group, ask each group to select a spokesperson to present its mission statement. Listen to the statements and discuss as needed. Be sure the mission statements do not contradict your organization's mission statement.

Note: Ask each group to appoint one member to represent the group on a committee to finalize the mission statement. Arrange for the committee members to have some time during the next few weeks to finalize the team's mission statement. When the mission statement is complete, print the final version on high-quality paper and post it in the agents' work area. You might also want to print copies for each agent to keep in his or her workstation.

KEEPING THE MISSION ALIVE

Posting a mission statement on quality paper is a good first step, but there are a few other steps to take to make sure your staff actually implements the statement. First, hold a team meeting and ask team members how they would manifest different parts of the mission statement in their jobs. For example, if the mission statement for a technical support team includes the phrase "respect the customer," the team members might state that they would implement that as follows:

- Use the customer's name
- Use proper hold techniques
- Speak or write at the customer's level of technical expertise
- Avoid jargon
- Don't lose patience
- Stay patient
- Maintain a calm tone of voice
- Acknowledge the customer's competence when demonstrated

Once team members have developed a list of behaviors they can demonstrate on the job to implement the mission statement, you need to create activities to help them remember to put the mission statement into practice. Following through with the example, you might create "Respect Our Customers Week." Here are some activities you could do during that week:

- Announce to the team that this week you will be monitoring specifically for customer respect issues. You hope to hear use of the customer's name, proper hold techniques, the rep speaking or writing at the technical level of the customer, and so on.

- Post preprinted posters around the call floor and/or hand out smaller versions for agents to post in their cubicles.

- Play Aretha Franklin's hit "Respect" to launch the initiative.

- Challenge the team to come up with a campaign in which they use RESPECT as an acronym and brainstorm words or terms for each letter.

Role-play in team meetings or one-on-one with a focus on the issues surrounding respecting customers.

ADDITIONAL RESOURCES

Books

Abrahams, Jeffery. *The Mission Statement Book: 301 Corporate Mission Statements from America's Top Companies.* Berkeley, CA: Ten Speed Press, 1999.

Jaffe, Dennis, Tobr, Glenn, and Scott, Cynthia. *Organizational Vision, Values and Mission.* Los Altos, CA: Crisp Publications, 1994.

Jones, B. Laurie. *The Path: Creating Your Mission Statement for Work and Life.* New York: Hyperion, 1998.

O'Halleron, David, and O'Halleron, Richard. *The Mission Primer: Four Steps to an Effective Mission Statement.* Pittsburgh, PA: Mission Inc., 2000.

Sobol, Mark, Solum, Robert, and Wall, Bob. *The Mission-Driven Organization: From Mission Statement to a Thriving Enterprise, Here's Your Blueprint for Building an Inspired, Cohesive, Customer-Oriented Team.* Rocklin, CA: Prima Publishing, 1999.

Appendix

Reproducible Job Aids
for Contact Center Managers

The reproducible forms in this appendix are designed to be turned into support tools for you to use in the course of your day-to-day work as a contact center manager. They are derived from material found in the chapters of this book, but in many cases are abbreviated to make it easy for you to turn them into job aids.

We suggest that you do the following:

1. Copy the forms onto colored stock.
2. Post them in your office, put them on a clipboard, or put them in a binder.
3. Refer to them as necessary in your real-time environment.

You may find that with continued practice you will assimilate many of these skills and tips and no longer need to refer to the job aids. If you need to refresh your knowledge at some future time, you can always grab this book off the shelf and make more copies!

EMPLOYEE SATISFACTION SURVEY

Please answer each question by circling the response that best describes how you feel about each aspect of your job.

1. I have the tools, support, and resources I need to   1   2   3   4   5   6   7
do my job well.

2. Management values my contributions to the   1   2   3   4   5   6   7
organization.

3. I enjoy my work.

4. I feel a sense of camaraderie with the others in   1   2   3   4   5   6   7
my work group.

5. I am rewarded when I do well.   1   2   3   4   5   6   7

6. I am taught in a helpful and constructive way how   1   2   3   4   5   6   7
I can improve at my job.

7. My manager and/or supervisor treats me with respect.   1   2   3   4   5   6   7

8. What would you change in order to improve the workplace and/or your job?

_____

_____

_____

_____

9. In what ways do you hope to grow and learn in this job?

_____

_____

_____

_____

Reproduced with permission from *Managing and Motivating Contact Center Employees* (M. Carlaw, P. Carlaw, V.K. Deming, and K. Friedmann, McGraw-Hill, 2002).

CYBER-BABBLE QUIZ

Directions: Work with your partner to translate the following emoticons and acronyms into plain English. You may have to turn your head (or the page) sideways when translating the emoticons.:)

Examples: FYI   *for your information*
FOAF   *friend of a friend*
O :-)   angel
; ^ (smirking face

ATST   _____

BTDT   _____

CUL8R   _____

FWIW   _____

IDTS   _____

IRL   _____

: 3-]   _____

P- (_____

: =)   _____

= :-)   _____

*<) : o   _____

CYBER-BABBLE QUIZ ANSWERS

ATST	at the same time
BTDT	been there, done that
CUL8R	see you later
FWIW	for what it's worth
IDTS	I don't think so
IRL	in real life
: 3-]	dog
P- (	pirate
: =)	orangutan
= : -)	punk
*<) : o)	clown

Reproduced with permission from *Managing and Motivating Contact Center Employees* (M. Carlaw, P. Carlaw, V.K. Deming, and K. Friedmann, McGraw-Hill, 2002).

TEAM QUESTIONS SHEET

Directions: Review the following questions and answer as many as you can within the next five minutes. You will be discussing them with several of your teammates.

1. If you were manager of this contact center, what is the first thing you would change?

2. What questions do you get from our customers that you can't answer?

3. What motivates you to do your best?

4. What's the best thing about working here?

5. What do you wish your supervisor would ask you?

6. What is the most stressful part of your job?

7. What could we do to have more fun at work?

8. What one thing could we do to better serve our customers?

Reproduced with permission from *Managing and Motivating Contact Center Employees* (M. Carlaw, P. Carlaw, V.K. Deming, and K. Friedmann, McGraw-Hill, 2002).

HOUSE A

Reproduced with permission from *Managing and Motivating Contact Center Employees* (M. Carlaw, P. Carlaw, V.K. Deming, and K. Friedmann, McGraw-Hill, 2002).

HOUSE B

BILL OF RIGHTS SHEET

Customers' Bill of Rights

Reproduced with permission from *Managing and Motivating Contact Center Employees* (M. Carlaw, P. Carlaw, V.K. Deming, and K. Friedmann, McGraw-Hill, 2002).

Get To Know Your Stress

Observe how you respond to the more stressful calls or situations at work. Try to catch yourself at particularly difficult moments and conduct a mental scan of your body and psyche. Notice your breathing, your body language, your thought process, and your visceral responses.

Following are some common but often unnoticed reactions to stress:

- Headache
- Stiff neck, shoulders, or back
- Tight jaw
- Furrowed brow
- Clenched teeth
- Nervous stomach
- Faster heartbeat
- Cool skin
- Cold hands or feet
- Irritability
- Fuzzy thinking
- Forgetfulness
- Emotional sensitivity
- Negative thoughts

What do you notice about your own reactions to stressful situations?

_____

_____

_____

_____

_____

_____

_____

TEN EFFECTIVE STRESS-RELIEF ACTIVITIES

① **Take a walk.**

② **Look out the window.**

③ **Stand up and stretch.**

④ **Breathe deeply.**

⑤ **Remind yourself of your wins.**

⑥ **Laugh!**

⑦ **Go within.**

⑧ **Switch mental gears.**

⑨ **Pretend you're traveling in first class (the hot towel trick).**

⑩ **Resign as general manager of the universe.**

Reproduced with permission from *Managing and Motivating Contact Center Employees* (M. Carlaw, P. Carlaw, V.K. Deming, and K. Friedmann, McGraw-Hill, 2002).

CUBICLE EXERCISES

Searching the Horizon

Close your eyes and relax for five seconds.

With your eyes closed, roll your eyes to the left and then to the right. Hold each position for three seconds.

Open your eyes. Without moving your head, move your eyes as far to the left as possible and select an object on the horizon.

Slowly move your eyes from that point on the horizon to the end of your nose.

Repeat on the right side and straight ahead.

Relax, look around the room, and blink a lot.

Repeat the complete exercise three times.

Chin Up, Chin Down

Close your eyes and drop your chin to your chest. Hold for 10 seconds.

Gently rotate your head to your left shoulder. Hold for five seconds.

Gently rotate your head and let it gently fall back. Hold for five seconds.

Gently rotate your head to your right shoulder. Hold for five seconds.

Gently let your head drop to your chest again.

Repeat the exercise in the other direction.

With your eyes closed, bring your head to the upright position. Relax in that position for five seconds. Open your eyes.

Under-the-Desk Leg Stretch

Sit upright in your chair with your feet flat on the floor.

Extend your left leg so that it is straight and your toes are pointing straight up.

Lift your foot up and touch the underside of the desk. Hold for five seconds.

Bring your foot back to the floor and relax for two seconds.

Repeat with your right leg.

Repeat the complete exercise three times.

Sit back in your chair with a straight back, feet flat on the floor, and relax.

Dancing Fingers

Hang your arms down by your side and relax.

Shake your arms and let your wrists and fingers flop around. Do this for five seconds.

Bring your hands together and press your fingers and palms together. Place a moderate amount of pressure on your fingers and hold for five seconds. Separate your hands and relax.

Make a fist with each hand and squeeze. Hold for three seconds.

Repeat the complete exercise.

Half Moon

Let your arms hang freely by your sides.

Keep your arms straight and lift them slowly over your head.

Clasp your hands and push up as high as you comfortably can.

Inhale as you bend your torso to the right. Hold for three seconds.

Exhale as you return to the center. Hold for three seconds.

Inhale as you bend your torso to the left. Hold for three seconds.

Return to the center and bring your arms down.

Repeat the exercise.

Hula Hips

Stand a few feet back from your desk with your feet slightly apart and pointed straight ahead and your knees bent.

Put your hands on your hips, extend your hips forward, and rotate to the left. Hold for three seconds.

Rotate your hips back and hold for three seconds.

Rotate your hips to the right and hold for three seconds.

Rotate your hips forward and hold for three seconds.

Repeat the exercise in the other direction.

Repeat the complete exercise twice.

Reproduced with permission from *Managing and Motivating Contact Center Employees* (M. Carlaw, P. Carlaw, V.K. Deming, and K. Friedmann, McGraw-Hill, 2002).

SIMPLE TRAINING NEEDS ASSESSMENT

Following is a short, simple version of a needs assessment to help you efficiently plan training for your team.

Step 1. Determine what agents *should be* **doing.**

Step 2. Determine what agents *are* **doing by gathering information through:**

- Monitoring forms
- Metrics
- Interviews and focus groups
- Questionnaires
- Observations
- Customer experience management (CEM)

Step 3. Determine where gaps exist between what agents are currently doing and what they should be doing.

Step 4. Determine which of these gaps can be addressed through training.

Step 5. Plan training that addresses the gaps.

Reproduced with permission from *Managing and Motivating Contact Center Employees* (M. Carlaw, P. Carlaw, V.K. Deming, and K. Friedmann, McGraw-Hill, 2002).

THE FOUR BASIC STEPS: LEARN—OBSERVE—PRACTICE—TRANSFER

Anytime you're trying to teach someone a new skill, there are four essential steps: Learn—Observe—Practice—Transfer. There are any number of training theories and practices that get much more complex than this, and most if not all of them have probably proven themselves to be effective. But, at the very least, make sure these four basics are covered anytime you're planning a training session.

Participants should:

- **Learn** a new skill.
  "Here's how you respond when a customer is angry or upset..."

- **Observe** the skill being practiced.
  Learners should see and/or hear several examples of how someone else carries out the skill.

- **Practice** the skill in the training environment.
  Learners should practice the skill (through simulations, role plays, exercises, etc.), understanding that they're still in learning mode. They should strive for success while knowing that it's safe to fail because this is only practice.

- **Transfer** the skill to the real-time environment.
  The learner must now use the skill on the job. It's at this point that coaching kicks in. In order for the learner to successfully assimilate the new skill and use it in the live environment, the manager or supervisor must reinforce use of the skill through praising and correcting. (See Chapter 9.)

Reproduced with permission from *Managing and Motivating Contact Center Employees* (M. Carlaw, P. Carlaw, V.K. Deming, and K. Friedmann, McGraw-Hill, 2002).

TEN TIPS FOR FLIPS

An effective flip chart page is legible, concise, and neat. Following are some suggestions for turning your flip chart into a powerful visual aid both inside and outside of the training classroom.

1. Use lined or graphed charts to help you write symmetrically.

2. Write in block letters and make them 1 to 1½ inches high.

3. Use a combination of colored markers, but avoid using the light-colored ones for text.

4. Before drawing with markers, use pencil marks to plot sections of the chart.

5. To highlight certain points or distinguish between items, create bullets.

6. Make your charts balanced and symmetrical (for example, don't cram all the information into the top half of the chart).

7. Make sure there's a lot of white space. It's better to go onto a second page than to force too much information onto one page.

8. When creating charts that will be filled in during the session, make light pencil marks in the margins to remind you what to do.

9. When presenting a flip chart page, make sure all participants can read it from where they're seated.

10. Don't block the chart when presenting; stand to the side and point to the chart as needed.

Reproduced with permission from *Managing and Motivating Contact Center Employees* (M. Carlaw, P. Carlaw, V.K. Deming, and K. Friedmann, McGraw-Hill, 2002).

THREE KEYS TO GETTING BUY-IN FROM PARTICIPANTS

Here's the digest version: You begin by telling participants what they'll get from the training and why it's such a good idea for them to get it. Then you end by showing them that they got it!

Here's the detailed version.

1. State the Objective of the Training Session

At the beginning of the session it's important to tell the group members what they are there to achieve. The objective should be written on a flip chart, slide, or white board (so that it can be seen by participants) and it should be verbally announced by the trainer as well (so it can be heard by participants). Keep in mind that often a training session has more than one specific objective. State them all.

To determine the objective, ask yourself, "What will the learners be able to do at the end of the training?" Then state the objective positively and concisely. Following are a few examples:

- Learn how to successfully operate the XL 22000 account management program
- Acquire skills to write e-mail messages that are clear, concise, positive, and professional
- Learn three techniques for effective cross-selling

2. Explain WIIFT

The next step is to answer the question, "What's in It for Them?" (WIIFT). Most people are motivated by answering the ever present question, "What's in it for me?" In order to get learners' buy-in and active participation in training, it's essential for you to let them know how they'll benefit by doing whatever it is that you want them to do.

There are countless possible benefits. Pick the two or three that you feel will resonate most strongly with your learners, and then point them out with enthusiasm and confidence. You can also remind the learners of these benefits throughout the course of the training. Following are some typical examples of how people can benefit from learning new skills or knowledge:

- Save time
- Reduce stress
- Handle challenging customers with ease

(Continued on next page)

Reproduced with permission from *Managing and Motivating Contact Center Employees* (M. Carlaw, P. Carlaw, V.K. Deming, and K. Friedmann, McGraw-Hill, 2002).

- Progress along a career path
- Make fewer data entry errors

3. Leave Learners with a Feeling of Accomplishment

At the end of the session, review the objective and remind learners that they've now successfully learned and practiced the new skill or knowledge. Congratulate them and encourage them to continue using what they've learned once the training is over. Although this step takes place at the end of training (at which point, hopefully, buy-in has already been achieved), it will help learners to buy into the concept of applying what they've learned. Learners will be more inspired to use what they've learned if they feel that they've worked to acquire it and succeeded in doing so.

On the next page is a concise list you can use to remind yourself of the three keys to getting buy-in from participants.

Reproduced with permission from *Managing and Motivating Contact Center Employees* (M. Carlaw, P. Carlaw, V.K. Deming, and K. Friedmann, McGraw-Hill, 2002).

THREE KEYS TO GETTING BUY-IN FROM PARTICIPANTS

1. State the objective of the training session

2. Explain WIIFT (what's in it for them)

3. Leave learners with a feeling of accomplishment

Reproduced with permission from *Managing and Motivating Contact Center Employees* (M. Carlaw, P. Carlaw, V.K. Deming, and K. Friedmann, McGraw-Hill, 2002).

TIPS ON LEADING GROUP DISCUSSIONS

One of the keys to a successful training session is strong participation from everyone in attendance. Following are some tips to help you get participants involved in group discussions.

1. **Make it safe to participate.** One way to do this is to avoid condemning anyone's response as "wrong" or otherwise making participants uncomfortable.

2. **Use open questions to solicit responses from the class.**
   What questions do you have?
   How might that happen?

3. **Use participants' names to help create an open, informal atmosphere.**
   Ronald mentioned something about that earlier.
   Tamara, what do you think?

4. **Thank participants for their input.**
   Thanks for your insight, Marvin.
   Thanks, Judy.

5. **Use participants as resources.**
   Who wants to answer Shelly's question?
   Where would you find the answer to that?

6. **When you're ready to end the discussion, use a closed question.**
   Are there any questions before we move on?

7. **When things get really tough, put the participants in small groups for a few minutes to discuss the topic; then reconvene the large group and ask each subgroup for a report.**

Reproduced with permission from *Managing and Motivating Contact Center Employees* (M. Carlaw, P. Carlaw, V.K. Deming, and K. Friedmann, McGraw-Hill, 2002).

TRAINER'S CHECKLIST FOR KEEPING SESSIONS LIVELY

Regardless of the length or the topic of a training session, participants will enjoy the learning experience more if the atmosphere is lively and refreshing. Following are some tips to keep in mind when planning a training session.

- ☑ Start with a short icebreaker activity to loosen up participants.
- ☑ Include some physical movement, even if it's just getting up to walk across the room for an activity.
- ☑ If the training session is longer than two hours, include some fun, simple energizer activities.
- ☑ Include small group activities or discussions.
- ☑ Build fun and novelty into the session where possible. For example, roll a pair of dice to determine the length of a break (one minute for every eye showing on the dice).
- ☑ Play music during breaks.

Reproduced with permission from *Managing and Motivating Contact Center Employees* (M. Carlaw, P. Carlaw, V.K. Deming, and K. Friedmann, McGraw-Hill, 2002).

SAMPLE MONITORING FORM #1
For an inbound customer service call

Supervisor _____

CSR _____ Date _____ Time _____

Customer account number _____ Name _____

Standards (X = Standard met O = Standard not met
N/A = Standard not applicable)

	Opens the Call	Comments
_____	Gives scripted greeting	
_____	Gathers account information	
_____	Acquires/spell-verifies caller information	
_____	Uses support cards if caller won't give info	
_____	Responds to caller's first statement	

Takes/Gives Accurate Information

_____	Reads help screens as appropriate
_____	Gives accurate info to answer caller question/s
_____	_____
_____	_____
_____	_____

Closes the Call

_____	Offers additional information/education to caller
_____	Gives correct scripted closing

Objectives (1 = Needs improvement 2 = Satisfactory 3 = Excellent
N/A = Not applicable)

_____	Questions to gather information
_____	Listens for key words and phrases
_____	Confirms understanding
_____	Does not ask for info already provided
_____	Handles challenges
_____	Responds professionally
_____	Builds rapport
_____	Demonstrates verbal/vocal skills

Notes

Reproduced with permission from *Managing and Motivating Contact Center Employees* (M. Carlaw, P. Carlaw, V.K. Deming, and K. Friedmann, McGraw-Hill, 2002).

SAMPLE MONITORING FORM #2
For multiple-call monitoring for outbound sales prospecting calls (can be used for up to five calls)

Sales rep _____

Date_____

Call Standards (N = No, standard was not met   Y = Yes, standard was met)

Confirms prospect	N Y	N Y	N Y	N Y	N Y
Uses prospect name	N Y	N Y	N Y	N Y	N Y
Uses intro script	N Y	N Y	N Y	N Y	N Y
Responds to first statement	N Y	N Y	N Y	N Y	N Y
Questions for info	N Y	N Y	N Y	N Y	N Y
Tells what to expect	N Y	N Y	N Y	N Y	N Y
Thanks prospect	N Y	N Y	N Y	N Y	N Y
Closes appropriately	N Y	N Y	N Y	N Y	N Y

Professional Demeanor (1 = Needs improvement   2 = Satisfactory
3 = Excellent)

Attitude	1 2 3	1 2 3	1 2 3	1 2 3	1 2 3
Tone of voice	1 2 3	1 2 3	1 2 3	1 2 3	1 2 3
Use of language	1 2 3	1 2 3	1 2 3	1 2 3	1 2 3
Builds rapport	1 2 3	1 2 3	1 2 3	1 2 3	1 2 3

Comments

Reproduced with permission from *Managing and Motivating Contact Center Employees* (M. Carlaw, P. Carlaw, V.K. Deming, and K. Friedmann, McGraw-Hill, 2002).

SAMPLE MONITORING FORM #3
For an inbound technical support call

Technician _____ Date

Supervisor _____ Time of call start

Time of call end _____

Tech Support Standards   Comments
(X = Completed   O = Not completed   N/A = Not applicable)

_____ Uses scripted greeting

_____ Echoes caller's problem statement

_____ Reassures caller

_____ Questions to diagnose problem

_____ Takes notes

_____ Accurately diagnoses problem/s

_____

_____

_____

_____ Solves problem or calls for supervisor

_____ Confirms caller's understanding

_____ Confirms caller's satisfaction

_____ Offers additional assistance

_____ Uses scripted closing

Tech Support Objectives   Comments
(1 = Below average   2 = Average   3 = Above average   N/A = Not applicable)

_____ Listens to caller

_____ Empathizes with caller

_____ Walks caller through problem solving

_____ Explains tech terms in plain English

_____ Educates caller

_____ Exhibits CFE (courtesy, friendliness, enthusiasm)

_____ Handles challenges

Overall Rating

_____ Poor   _____ Fair   _____ Good   _____ Excellent

Reproduced with permission from *Managing and Motivating Contact Center Employees* (M. Carlaw, P. Carlaw, V.K. Deming, and K. Friedmann, McGraw-Hill, 2002).

SAMPLE CONTACT QUALITY GUIDE

Standards

Gives scripted greeting	Uses greeting on screen, captures media code
Gathers account information	Asks for account number and explains why
Acquires/spell-verifies info	Key-spells caller info and asks caller to confirm
Uses support cards if necessary	Uses appropriate statements if caller won't give info
Responds to first statement	Leads into call by taking care of caller's question first
Reads help screens as appropriate	Does not read too much or too little info; checks in with caller
Gives accurate info	Gives full and correct answer to caller's specific question
Offers additional info/education	Gives whatever additional info is appropriate to call
Gives correct scripted closing	Follows correct closing screens; logs call correctly

Objectives

Questions to gather information	Uses open/closed questions appropriately
Listens for key words and phrases	Shows by response that agent understands caller
Confirms understanding	Asks for confirmation that understanding is correct
Does not ask for info provided	Does not ask caller to repeat what he/she said earlier
Handles challenges	Uses appropriate skill model to handle challenges
Responds professionally	Is positive, polite, and skilled at all stages of call
Builds rapport	Uses caller's name, shows appreciation, responds to caller
Demonstrates verbal/vocal skills	Uses right tone, pace, grammar; avoids slang/jargon

Reproduced with permission from *Managing and Motivating Contact Center Employees* (M. Carlaw, P. Carlaw, V.K. Deming, and K. Friedmann, McGraw-Hill, 2002).

TIPS FOR WRITING COMMENTS ON MONITORING FORMS

- If you want to point out something the rep said during the call, write the exact comment and put it in quotation marks.

- Draw an arrow or a line to tie your comment to the Standard or Objective it relates to.

- Put a + or a − in front of comments to indicate whether the comment relates to something you want to praise or something you want to correct.

- Never write comments that you wouldn't want someone else to read.

Reproduced with permission from *Managing and Motivating Contact Center Employees* (M. Carlaw, P. Carlaw, V.K. Deming, and K. Friedmann, McGraw-Hill, 2002).

THE SEVEN FUNDAMENTALS OF FEEDBACK

① **Be specific.**

② **Focus on performance, not personality.**

③ **Focus on behavior that can be changed.**

④ **Keep it simple—and sincere.**

⑤ **Give feedback as soon as possible.**

⑥ **Pay attention to your body language.**

⑦ **Avoid the ambush approach.**

Reproduced with permission from *Managing and Motivating Contact Center Employees* (M. Carlaw, P. Carlaw, V.K. Deming, and K. Friedmann, McGraw-Hill, 2002).

PRAISING

B   **Behavior**

E   **Effect**

T   **Thanks**

CORRECTING

B   **Behavior**

E   **Effect**

E   **Expectation**

S   **Secure commitment**

Alternatively, you can use:

B   **Behavior**

E   **Effect**

S   **Solicit suggestions**

S   **Secure commitment**

TEN TIPS FOR COMMUNICATING WITH PROBLEM EMPLOYEES

① **Deal with the issue right away.**

② **Discuss the issue privately.**

③ **Stay calm and poised.**

④ **Allow the agent to vent.**

⑤ **Empathize.**

⑥ **Focus on the issue, not the person.**

⑦ **Find common ground.**

⑧ **Point out alternative ways for the agent to express himself or herself.**

⑨ **Always give the agent an out.**

⑩ **Focus on a solution.**

Reproduced with permission from *Managing and Motivating Contact Center Employees* (M. Carlaw, P. Carlaw, V.K. Deming, and K. Friedmann, McGraw-Hill, 2002).

TWO-WAY COACHING

Troubleshooting

Step 1: Describe the behavior

Step 2: Explain the effect of the behavior

Step 3: Ask for an explanation of the behavior

Step 4: Suggest/solicit solutions and show support

Step 5: Develop an action plan for correcting the behavior

Negotiating

Step 1: State both sides of the issue

Step 2: Ask for suggestions

Step 3: Accept solutions or offer alternatives

Step 4: Reach agreement

Warning

Step 1: State the issue

Step 2: Ask for an explanation

Step 3: Describe the consequences of noncompliance

Step 4: Secure commitment

Reproduced with permission from *Managing and Motivating Contact Center Employees* (M. Carlaw, P. Carlaw, V.K. Deming, and K. Friedmann, McGraw-Hill, 2002).

TEN KEY PRACTICES OF SUCCESSFUL CONTACT CENTER MANAGERS

① **Set effective and realistic goals**

② **Create action plans**

③ **Use positive language**

④ **Listen**

⑤ **Maintain a sense of humor**

⑥ **Praise**

⑦ **Observe your environment**

⑧ **Interact with agents on a daily basis**

⑨ **Solicit feedback from agents**

⑩ **Empower your agents**

Reproduced with permission from *Managing and Motivating Contact Center Employees* (M. Carlaw, P. Carlaw, V.K. Deming, and K. Friedmann, McGraw-Hill, 2002).

EFFECTIVE AND REALISTIC GOALS ARE:

- **Specific and measurable**
- **Positive**
- **Results-oriented**
- **Obtainable**

Reproduced with permission from *Managing and Motivating Contact Center Employees* (M. Carlaw, P. Carlaw, V.K. Deming, and K. Friedmann, McGraw-Hill, 2002).

ACTION PLAN

Goal:

_____

_____

_____

_____

Action Plan:

_____

_____

_____

_____

_____

_____

_____

_____

_____

_____

_____

_____

TIPS FOR EFFECTIVE LISTENING

- Focus.
- Listen for key information and key feelings.
- Let the other person finish speaking.
- Pause before you respond.
- Show your support.
- Confirm your understanding.

Reproduced with permission from *Managing and Motivating Contact Center Employees* (M. Carlaw, P. Carlaw, V.K. Deming, and K. Friedmann, McGraw-Hill, 2002).

MANAGING WITH POISE

Praise

Observe your environment

Interact with agents on a daily basis

Solicit feedback from agents

Empower your agents

Reproduced with permission from *Managing and Motivating Contact Center Employees* (M. Carlaw, P. Carlaw, V.K. Deming, and K. Friedmann, McGraw-Hill, 2002).

DEVELOPING YOUR PERSONAL MISSION STATEMENT

Round 1: Chicken Scratches

Grab a pen, find a comfortable place to sit, and take some time to consider your responses to the following questions. You can write in the space provided in this book or you can use a separate sheet of paper.

Read each question and respond with whatever comes immediately to your mind. Don't worry about writing complete sentences; don't even edit your own thoughts. Just work through the questions one at a time and write whatever feels important to you.

1. In what ways do you contribute to the success of your team/department/center?

_____

_____

_____

_____

2. If each week you could achieve only three actions as a manager, what would they be?

_____

_____

_____

_____

3. What are the qualities, skills, and characteristics that you want your team to see in you?

_____

_____

_____

_____

(Continued on next page)

*Reproduced with permission from *Managing and Motivating Contact Center Employees* (M. Carlaw, P. Carlaw, V.K. Deming, and K. Friedmann, McGraw-Hill, 2002).

4. What are the qualities, skills, and characteristics that you want your management to see in you?

_____

_____

_____

_____

5. Describe the primary responsibilities and contribution of your department to the organization.

_____

_____

_____

_____

6. Describe your primary responsibilities to your team.

_____

_____

_____

_____

(Continued on next page)

*Reproduced with permission from _Managing and Motivating Contact Center Employees_ (M. Carlaw, P. Carlaw, V.K. Deming, and K. Friedmann, McGraw-Hill, 2002).

Round 2: Stream of Consciousness

The next step in the development of your mission statement is to write continuously for 10 minutes about your mission as a contact center manager. Once again, there's no need to write complete sentences, edit your thoughts, or make any sense whatsoever. Just focus your mind on the task at hand, set a timer (or look at your watch), and write without stopping for 10 minutes. You can use the box provided.

(Continued on next page)

Round 3: Rough Draft

OK, now on to full sentences! Before writing your draft, review what you wrote in the first two rounds. Then take some time—typically 30 to 60 minutes—to develop a rough draft of your mission statement. This time, form your thoughts into a few complete sentences and structure the statement into a logical flow.

Following are a few additional guidelines for this round of writing:

- Keep your statement in the range of 40 to 75 words.
- Write in the present tense.

  "I motivate" rather than "I will motivate."

- Use affirmative statements.

  "I do" rather than "I don't."

- Include strong, descriptive words and terms.

  "I listen attentively" rather than "I listen."

  "Empower" rather than "help."

- Make it specific.

  Vague: *"I hold my agents in the highest regard."*

  Specific: *"I treat my agents with fairness and respect."*

(Continued on next page)

Round 4: Final Draft

Now for the final stretch. Read through your rough draft and make whatever revisions you feel are necessary to create a mission statement that's meaningful, relevant, motivating, descriptive, and specific. And make it concise—every word should count!

Reproduced with permission from *Managing and Motivating Contact Center Employees* (M. Carlaw, P. Carlaw, V.K. Deming, and K. Friedmann, McGraw-Hill, 2002).

Index

About the Authors

Malcolm Carlaw is president, **Peggy Carlaw** is vice president, **Vasudha K. Deming** is an instructional designer, and **Kurt Friedmann** is director of business development at Impact Learning Systems, a training and consulting firm specializing in customer service, sales, and technical support. For more information about the programs and services offered by Impact Learning Systems, please visit www.impactlearning.com or call 800-545-9003.